BUSINESS CYCLES

BUSINESS CYCLES

The Nature and Causes of Economic Fluctuations

Thomas E. Hall

PRAEGER

New York
Westport, Connecticut
London

Library of Congress Cataloging-in-Publication Data

Hall, Thomas E. (Thomas Emerson), 1954–
    Business cycles : the nature and causes of economic fluctuations /
Thomas E. Hall.
        p. cm.
    Includes bibliographical references.
    ISBN 0-275-93085-8 (alk. paper)
    1. Business cycles.   2. Macroeconomics.   I. Title.
    HB3711.H265   1990
    338.5′42—dc20   89-70955

Library of Congress Catalog Card Number: 89-70955
ISBN: 0-275-93085-8

First published in 1990

Praeger Publishers, One Madison Avenue, New York, NY 10010
An imprint of Greenwood Publishing Group, Inc.

Printed in the United States of America

The paper used in this book complies with the Permanent
Paper Standard issued by the National Information Standards
Organization (Z39.48—1984).

10 9 8 7 6 5 4 3 2 1

to my parents, Robert and Jean

Contents

Figures

Tables

Preface

This book is a discussion of the nature and causes of aggregate economic fluctuations that addresses the following issue: Why do economies grow at variable rates over time? This issue, one of the oldest in economics, used to be the subject of courses in economic fluctuations that were offered at many colleges and universities around the country. Interest in the subject waned, however, following the great expansion in economic activity during the 1960s. The subject is now making a comeback, largely because of the unstable macroeconomic conditions during the 1970s and early 1980s.

The coverage begins with a general overview of economic cycles and economic indicators followed by a discussion of several theoretical models that attempt to explain the cyclical behavior of economic aggregates. Some older models are covered because several of them are the foundation for more modern theories. Modern cycle theories are discussed next, consisting of the monetarist, rational expectations, new-Keynesian, and real business cycle models. Each is discussed in detail, and empirical evidence is presented with respect to each model. The book then goes on to describe the nature and causes of several business cycles during the twentieth century which allows the reader to see how the alternative models of cycles explain actual phenomena over time. Next, some interesting modern puzzles in the study of cycles are introduced. The book concludes with comments on macroeconomic forecasting methods and performance.

This book is designed for individuals interested in the topic of macroeconomic cycles, or it could also be used as a textbook for a college course on economic fluctuations. The reader should already be familiar with macroeconomic concepts. Necessary background might include courses in principles of microeconomics and macroeconomics, plus an intermediate-level macroeconomics course such as money and banking or, preferably, intermediate-level macroeconomic theory and policy.

After reading this book, anyone who wishes to pursue the topics further or monitor current economic conditions is urged to make use of the publications and data from the various regional Federal Reserve Banks available at no cost to subscribers. All twelve regional banks publish a periodic economic review that contains up-to-date research on various issues in economics, and many of the articles directly relate to business cycles. Some of these banks also provide macroeconomic data. Among the publications I find especially useful in this regard are *Monetary Trends* and *National Economic Trends* published by the Federal Reserve Bank of St. Louis, and *Economic Trends* published by the Federal Reserve Bank of Cleveland. Addresses of the regional Federal Reserve Banks can be found at the back of any issue of the *Federal Reserve Bulletin* which is published by the Federal Reserve Board of Governors and available in virtually every university library (and many public libraries) in the United States. Other valuable resources, also available at most libraries, include the U.S. Commerce Department publications *Business Conditions Digest* and *Survey of Current Business*.

I decided to write this book while teaching an upper division course on business cycles at Miami University. I was unable to find a book that stressed the topics I consider important, so I developed my own set of classroom notes. The student feedback was so positive that I decided to use the notes as the basis for a book. The book was written while I was teaching at Miami University and during the time I was employed as a visiting economist at the United States Department of State. I thank the State Department for giving me permission to spend some time on this project while I was employed there. The views expressed in this book are mine and do not necessarily reflect those of the State Department or the federal government.

Several individuals provided valuable input into this book. I thank students enrolled in my business cycles course at Miami University who made several valuable comments on the material presented in class. I also thank several individuals who read various chapter drafts, made numerous comments and suggestions, and pointed out flaws along the way. These individuals are my co-workers at Miami University: George K. Davis, John David Ferguson, and T. Windsor Fields; and at the State Department: Richard S. Grossman and Randall Jones (now with OECD in Paris). This book also benefited from my ongoing conversations with William G. Dewald at the State Department on a variety of projects I was involved with there.

Finally, my parents, Robert J. Hall and Jean A. Hall, read several chapters and provided comments, as did my wife, Christine, who has lovingly supported my work on this project at every step along the way. Any errors that still remain are my responsibility.

BUSINESS CYCLES

1 | Introduction

The standard measure of economic activity is Gross National Product (GNP) which measures a nation's output of final goods and services produced during a particular time period. GNP is important because it provides a measure of economic standards of living, and by studying the growth of GNP, we determine how living standards change over time. For example, GNP adjusted for price changes, real GNP (at 1972 prices), was about $98.2 billion in 1875, rising to $3,676.5 billion by 1986. This rise tells us that the United States was producing approximately thirty-seven times as many goods and services in 1986 compared to 1875.

Although real GNP increased thirty-seven-fold, the average American's living standard did not rise by that same amount over the period because the U.S. population rose. There were approximately 46 million Americans in 1875 compared to about 241 million in 1986. To adjust for this population increase, we use a measure called real GNP per capita, which is total real GNP divided by the population. We find that real GNP per capita in 1875 was about $2,134 and by 1986 had grown to $15,255, representing more than a sevenfold increase in living standards for the average American.

How is this increased standard of living manifested? In many ways we enjoy a much more pleasant life than our ancestors did (Bettmann 1974). For example, we are healthier thanks to enormous improvements in medicine. We can travel much faster in our jets and automobiles than people could in 1875 on railroads and horses. Communication today is virtually instantaneous. Electricity and indoor plumbing were not universal features of American homes in 1875 as they are today. We average significantly fewer hours of work per week, allowing us much greater leisure time for enjoying various recreational activities.

Unfortunately, the road to increased economic well-being has not been smooth. Rather than growing steadily year after year, the U.S. economy has experienced cycles in economic activity. Recurring periods of economic expansion followed by periods of recession have occurred for as long as records have been kept. These economic ups and downs are problematic because each time an economy enters a period of declining output, people suffer increased hardship in the form of lost jobs, declining incomes, reduced consumption of goods and services, and the concurrent physical and mental stresses that accompany these losses. And while economic growth is certainly desirable, often the economy grows more rapidly than is sustainable, bringing rapid price increases that lead to arbitrary wealth transfers and distortions in the economy.

The ideal, of course, is an economy that grows steadily at a rate consistent with reasonable gains in living standards and without the inflation and unemployment problems that accompany the boom/bust cycle. Since we do not observe this ideal, but instead observe virtually every world economy growing at erratic and sometimes negative rates, we are interested in the study of business cycles. It is, therefore, our task to study the nature and causes of economic fluctuations. Only by understanding the causes will society ever be able to eliminate the cycles and achieve a minimum of macroeconomic distortions and public hardship which are currently associated with economic fluctuations. We begin our investigation by covering some basic concepts that lay the groundwork for topics addressed in later chapters.

CYCLES

The Temperature Cycle

To introduce the concept of a cycle, let us begin with something familiar to all of us: the temperature cycle. Figure 1.1 shows average monthly temperatures in Chicago. Although this cycle does not look exactly the same each year, it does recur year after year because of the natural tendency of the earth north of the equator to angle toward the sun in the summer and away from the sun in the winter.

Cycles are described by several terms. The peak is the largest observation, 73 degrees, which occurs in July. The trough is the smallest observation, 21 degrees, in January. The cycle amplitude, which measures the variability of the series, is the difference between the maximum and minimum temperatures over the cycle, 52 degrees. The periodicity of the cycle is the time from the trough to the next trough or peak to the next peak of the cycle, one year. A cycle is said to be periodic if it has constant periodicity which is, in general, the case for the temperature cycle in a particular area.

Different cycles can possess different characteristics. Figure 1.2 shows the temperature cycle in Los Angeles. While the temperature cycles in Chicago and Los Angeles both have constant periodicity of one year, Los Angeles has higher peak and trough values than Chicago. Furthermore, the temperature variability is much lower in Los Angeles than in Chicago because the amplitude in Los

Figure 1.1
Average Monthly Temperature in Chicago, 1951–1980

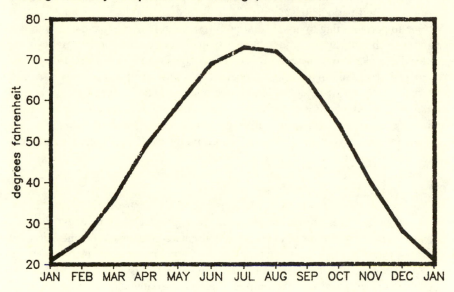

Figure 1.2
Average Monthly Temperature in Los Angeles, 1951–1980

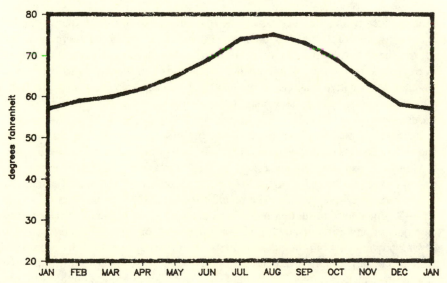

Angeles is only 17 degrees compared to Chicago's 52 degrees. Therefore, cycles can have the same periodicity but different amplitudes. It is also possible for cycles to have the same amplitude but different periodicities, or to have different amplitudes and periodicities.

One important thing to note is that both temperature cycles have a zero trend. A trend is the rate at which the average value rises or falls over several cycles. Since the cycles shown here are based on averages over many years, the overall average is constant. If we plotted average monthly temperatures over several years as the earth was entering a new ice age, we would observe a cycle with a negative trend—each year the average monthly temperatures would be incrementally lower, and the overall average would be declining. Conversely, the temperature cycle would have a positive trend if the earth were entering a tropical age.

The Business Cycle

We now apply our terminology to the business cycle. A business cycle is identified by the behavior of aggregate economic activity which is measured by a wide variety of series including output, sales, employment, and income (Moore 1983). The output measure we consider here is the most widely aggregated one of all, real GNP, which is the output of all final goods and services produced each quarter (three months) of the year, the shortest frequency of reported GNP. While the peaks and troughs of real GNP do not always precisely correspond to the peaks and troughs in the business cycle, real GNP is an acceptable measure to study and provides a reasonable gauge of the magnitude of cyclical changes in economic activity.

Figure 1.3 plots the pattern of real GNP from 1975.I to 1982.IV, a period that includes two entire business cycles from trough to trough. Expansions and recessions are defined as sustained movements in aggregate economic activity as measured by a variety of economic series. A useful rule of thumb that is correct most of the time is to consider expansions and recessions as being two or more consecutive quarterly movements of real GNP in the same direction. This rule can be broken (as we see later), but it works in the vast majority of cases.

A trough in real GNP occurred during the first quarter of 1975 (in March), the end of a recession that began in late 1973. Following that trough, an economic expansion began that continued until the peak in January 1980. The expansion lasted a total of fifty-eight months, longer than the post–World War II expansion average of forty-five months. The small dip in real GNP in the fourth quarter of 1977 does not constitute a recession because the output decline lasted only one quarter and did not show up in other measures of economic activity.

The movement from the peak in 1980.I to the trough in 1980.III represents a short, but surprisingly severe, recession. This recession indicates how the "two consecutive quarter movement in real GNP" rule doesn't always hold as Figure

Figure 1.3
Business Cycles, 1975–1982

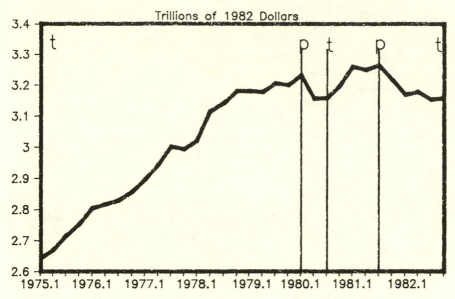

1.3 shows only a one quarter decline. A problem with quarterly data is that it effectively averages away monthly information, allowing monthly output movements in one direction to be cancelled out by monthly movements in the opposite direction.

The National Bureau of Economic Research's Business Cycle Dating Committee uses monthly data such as retail sales, the unemployment rate, employment, and industrial production to determine in which months peaks and troughs in economic activity really occur. In the case of the 1980 recession, the committee determined that the peak was in January and the trough in July. Quarterly GNP data only show a decline in 1980.II because during 1980.I the expansion during January was larger than the decline in February and March, and during 1980.III the decline in July was exceeded by the gains during August and September. Thus, the first and third quarters show a rise in real GNP. Using monthly data, the committee determined that the period from February to July was a recession because the duration of declining economic activity was six months long (two quarters); furthermore, real GNP later peaked at levels greater than those achieved in 1980.I.

Economic activity started to expand again in August 1980 and continued rising until the peak in July 1981, a short twelve-month expansion. The next recession started in August, a lengthy and serious decline that lasted until the trough in November 1982. The problem with quarterly data is illustrated again in this situation. GNP data show an increase in 1982.IV even though the trough occurred during that quarter.

It is important to note several differences between the temperature cycles in figures 1.1 and 1.2 and the business cycle in Figure 1.3. First, while the temperature cycle has very little trend over time, the business cycle is a trended cycle. While our economy experiences recessions and expansions, real GNP rises over long periods of time. This long-run growth rate of real GNP is called trend growth, and depending on precisely which time period you consider, it averages around 3 percent annually. The study of the long-run growth rate is called economic growth theory and is not our primary concern here because we are more interested in shorter-term movements in output.

Second, although the temperature cycle is periodic, the business cycle is not. The time between economic peaks and troughs can vary considerably; for example, since 1921, business cycles, measured by the number of months from trough to trough range from a low of twenty-eight months (1980–1982) to a high of 117 months (1961–1970). This variability in cycle lengths results from considerable differences in the duration of both recessions and expansions.

Finally, while temperature cycles exhibit very stable amplitude from year to year, business cycle amplitudes vary a great deal. When comparing changes in real GNP across different time periods, rather than considering simple dollar changes, it is more meaningful to compute percentage changes because the growth of real GNP over time means that a $5 billion change in 1875 is a greater relative change than a $5 billion change in 1987. So we calculate percentage declines during recessions and percentage increases during expansions. These numbers, along with the dates of business cycle peaks and troughs since 1921, are shown in Table 1.1. We see that since 1921 the amplitude of real GNP during expansions ranges from a high of over 100 percent from 1938 to 1945, to a low of 2 percent from 1945 to 1948. Recessions range from the Great Contraction, 1929–1933, when real GNP fell by a little over one-third to relatively minor declines in 1948–1949 and 1960–1961 when real GNP fell by only 1 percent.

Table 1.1 also shows that the length of expansions and recessions has varied greatly. The expansion of 1980–1981 is the shortest in our sample, twelve months; the longest, an amazing 106 months during the 1960s. Recessions vary from the short six months in 1980 to the Great Contraction's forty-three months. Table 1.2 summarizes the cycle duration data by presenting average lengths and corresponding standard deviations of expansions and recessions.

Table 1.2 also shows the average length of expansions when 1938–1945 and 1961–1969 are excluded. Both of these expansions were very long and prosperous which can be partly explained by the highly expansionary policies carried out during World War II and the Vietnam War. For this reason, both can be viewed in some sense as unusual; when these two episodes are ignored, the average expansion length is 33.72 months, with a corresponding standard deviation of

Table 1.1
Business Cycles, 1921–1982

REFERENCE DATES (P=peak,T=trough)		TYPE	LENGTH (months)	TOTAL PERCENT CHANGE IN REAL GNP	CYCLE LENGTH (months)
7/21(T)	5/23(P)	EXP	22	+27.0	
5/23(P)	7/24(T)	REC	14	-3.1	36
7/24(T)	10/26(P)	EXP	27	+18.7	
10/26(P)	11/27(T)	REC	13	-3.2	40
11/27(T)	8/29(P)	EXP	21	+12.7	
8/29(P)	3/33(T)	REC	43	-36.2	64
3/33(T)	5/37(P)	EXP	50	+54.3	
5/37(P)	6/38(T)	REC	13	-10.0	63
6/38(T)	2/45(P)	EXP	80	+107.8	
2/45(P)	10/45(T)	REC	8	-14.5	88
10/45(T)	11/48(P)	EXP	37	+2.0	
11/48(P)	10/49(T)	REC	11	-1.4	48
10/49(T)	7/53(P)	EXP	45	+28.0	
7/53(P)	5/54(T)	REC	10	-3.2	55
5/54(T)	8/57(P)	EXP	39	+13.2	
8/57(P)	4/58(T)	REC	8	-2.7	47
4/58(T)	4/60(P)	EXP	24	+10.2	
4/60(P)	2/61(T)	REC	10	-1.0	34
2/61(T)	12/69(P)	EXP	106	+47.2	
12/69(P)	11/70(T)	REC	11	-1.0	117
11/70(T)	11/73(P)	EXP	36	+16.7	
11/73(P)	3/75(T)	REC	16	-4.9	52
3/75(T)	1/80(P)	EXP	58	+24.3	
1/80(P)	7/80(T)	REC	6	-2.3	64
7/80(T)	7/81(P)	EXP	12	+3.9	
7/81(P)	11/82(T)	REC	16	-2.8	28

*   Reference dates are taken from U.S. Department of Commerce Business Conditions Digest. Type: EXP=expansion, REC=recession. Percent changes in real GNP are computed from the quarterly real GNP data in Nathan S. Balke and Robert J. Gordon, "Appendix B: Historical Data." In The American Business Cycle: Continuity and Change, edited by Robert J. Gordon (Chicago: University of Chicago Press, 1986).

Table 1.2
Average Duration of Business Cycles, 1921–1982

```
              EXPANSIONS (Number of Months)

     Average Length, All Expansions..... 42.85
     Standard Deviaton.................. 26.19

     Average Length, Excluding WWII
     and Vietnam Expansions............. 33.72
     Standard Deviation................. 13.91


              RECESSIONS (Number of Months)

     Average Length, All Recessions..... 13.77
     Standard Deviation.................. 9.29

     Average Length, Excluding
     Great Contraction.................. 11.33
     Standard Deviation.................. 3.17

  CYCLES - TROUGH TO TROUGH (Number of Months)

     Average Length, All Cycles......... 56.61
     Standard Deviation................. 24.16

     Average Length, Excluding WWII        *
     and Vietnam Cycles................. 48.27*
     Standard Deviation................. 12.67
```

---

*
Excluding the business cycles from 1938-1945 and 1961-1970.

13.91 months which still indicates a high degree of variability of expansion length.

It is also interesting to note the extreme severity of the Great Contraction from 1929 to 1933. This Great Contraction was the start of the Great Depression (1929–1941) and by far the longest and most severe recession in this century, perhaps in all of U.S. history. The incredible hardships endured by millions of Americans are indicated by the unemployment rate peak of 25 percent in March 1933. Since automatic stabilizers such as unemployment compensation did not exist during the early 1930s, many Americans were literally out on the street. It is not surprising that this episode is still discussed by economists. When the 1929–1933 recession is excluded from the calculations in Table 1.2, recessions have been relatively short, averaging 11.33 months, and the standard deviation of 3.17 months implies relatively small variation around the mean.

Business Cycles versus Growth Cycles

The previous discussion indicates that an acceptable way to define business cycles is in terms of changes in the level of real GNP over time. An alternative approach, popularized during the 1960s when many industrialized economies experienced several years of positive growth without a recession, describes economic cycles in terms of economic growth rates. These growth cycles are defined in terms of the growth of real GNP relative to long-term trend growth. For example, if an economy's long-term growth rate is 3 percent, then a growth expansion occurs when GNP grows faster than 3 percent, and a growth recession occurs when GNP grows slower than 3 percent but stays positive. During expansions it is not unusual for the growth rate of real GNP to fluctuate above and below the trend rate; thus, growth expansions and growth recessions are much more common than business cycle expansions and recessions.

The main emphasis of this book is the study of cycles in the level of output. Growth cycles are also discussed because the forces that cause cycles in the level of output also cause growth cycles. Also, since it is conceivable that macroeconomists may someday possess the knowledge and tools to eliminate recessions, the study of business cycles may evolve into the study of growth cycles. But since economies still experience recessions, our main focus is on cycles in the level of economic activity.

ENDOGENOUS VERSUS EXOGENOUS THEORIES

A model is composed of a set of structural equations which specify relationships between the exogenous and endogenous variables. A variable is said to be endogenous if its value is determined by and determines the values of other variables in the model. An exogenous variable only determines the values of the endogenous variables in the system. For example, the temperature cycle is determined by exogenous forces—the angle of the earth to the sun (the exogenous variable) determines the average monthly temperature (the endogenous variable); whereas the average monthly temperature does not determine the angle of the earth to the sun.

Business cycle models are generally categorized as endogenous or exogenous—that is, the behavior of output, the endogenous variable, is usually modeled as being determined by endogenous or exogenous forces. For example, Jevons' sunspot theory (discussed in chapter 3) contends that business cycles are caused by exogenous forces: enormous explosions on the surface of the sun alter the weather on earth and, therefore, agricultural yields. An example of an endogenous theory would be Hawtrey's model of bank credit fluctuations under a gold standard. During an economic expansion a nation's imports rise relative to exports, causing a balance of trade deficit. This trade deficit results in a gold outflow which contracts the money supply under a gold standard and causes an economic contraction. This recession reduces imports which moves the trade balance into surplus and causes a gold inflow which expands the money supply and stimulates the economy. The process is assumed to repeat itself continuously. In this case, the money supply is causing output, and output is causing the money supply via the balance of trade and the gold standard.

When considering different business cycle theories, it is important to keep this endogenous/exogenous distinction in mind because they imply very different behavior for an economy. On the one hand, someone who believes that business cycles are primarily caused by exogenous factors tends to view economies as being inherently stable but shocked by outside forces such as sunspots, erratic central bank policy, and wars. On the other hand, endogenous theorists generally consider economies as being inherently unstable and subject to self-generating cycles. This distinction in macroeconomics is very old and exists today between the monetarists (primarily exogenous) and Keynesians (primarily endogenous).

OVERVIEW

The purpose of this book is to provide an understanding of the nature and causes of business cycles. Chapter 2 begins the investigation by documenting the behavior of several economic variables over the cycle. We consider the cyclical pattern of key variables such as GNP, interest rates, prices, and unemployment to help us understand typical patterns over the business cycle.

A valid theory of the cycle must be able to explain these variables' behavior, and several theories are covered in chapters 3 through 8. Chapter 3 discusses early theories of the cycle. Some of these models are obsolete or discredited, but several are valid and provide the basis for modern theories.

Chapter 4 provides an account of Keynes' theory which focuses on the investment function. While this theory is over fifty years old, it still attracts considerable interest because investment is by far the most unstable component of aggregate demand. We also discuss the old-Keynesian model, the variant of Keynes' model that dominated macroeconomics from the end of World War II to the early 1970s.

Chapter 5 presents the monetarist theory of the cycle. Based on the work of several economists, monetarists view changes in monetary growth as a major source of economic instability. Therefore, they place most of the blame for business cycles during the past several decades at the feet of the Federal Reserve. The monetarist view was widely accepted during the 1970s, but in recent years it has come under increasing attack.

Chapter 6 discusses the rational expectations model of economic fluctuations. This model is relatively new and provides useful insights into the behavior of economic agents. It also derives the controversial policy neutrality result which states that discretionary monetary and fiscal policies may be unable to alter aggregate output. This theory was very popular during the late 1970s but was discredited somewhat by the 1981–1982 recession.

Chapter 7 presents the new-Keynesian model. While a number of economists were becoming disenchanted with the monetarist and rational expectations models, Keynesian economists provided several modifications to the old-Keynesian model in an attempt to correct the problems that originally led to its decline. Currently, many consider the new-Keynesian model to be the dominant theory.

Chapter 8 presents the newest model, the real business cycle theory. This model represents a significant break from the others by contending that external shocks to aggregate supply are the dominant cause of business cycles. Currently, macroeconomists are busy empirically testing the model's predictions, and the jury is still out.

Chapter 9 compares and contrasts the modern models discussed in chapters 4 through 8. We consider some unsettled issues in macroeconomic models and discuss how each model addresses those issues.

Chapters 10 and 11 describe the actual pattern of American business cycles during the past several decades. We discuss in some detail the forces that economists believe were responsible for specific expansions and recessions. This discussion also helps the reader understand the evolution of macroeconomic thought during this century.

Chapter 12 delves into some of the modern puzzles in macroeconomics. While there is a great deal that we have learned about macroeconomics during this century, there is plenty we don't know, and answers to five interesting questions are presented.

Finally, chapter 13 discusses the major methods of forecasting future values of macroeconomic variables. A discussion of the accuracy of macroeconomic forecasting suggests that the performance has been quite good, but there have been a few major errors.

Before continuing, consider a few words of caution. The reader should not look for one specific factor that causes economic fluctuations. The fact is that macroeconomic models suggest that a wide variety of factors are responsible. Unfortunately, macroeconomists are often perceived as belonging to "tribes" where each tribe is identified with a particular cause of economic fluctuations. To cite just one example, monetarists are sometimes associated with the statement "*only* money matters," which is a gross distortion of monetarism. In point of fact, monetarists consider many factors responsible for the business cycle with changes in monetary growth being the most important. Similarly for the other "tribes" as well, each group focuses on a particular cause of cycles, often considering one factor to be most important, but not to the exclusion of others. Finally, this book contains nothing that is new. Instead, it brings together a large quantity of work in the field of business cycles, a subject as old as macroeconomics. Economic fluctuations was the original problem that the people now called macroeconomists worked on. We can be fairly certain that economists will be working on this topic for many more years.

2 | Economic Behavior over the Cycle

This chapter documents the behavior of some important economic variables over the business cycle. Theories of economic fluctuations should be able to explain this behavior. For example, market interest rates are procyclical: they tend to rise during economic expansions and fall during recessions. This pattern has been confirmed as standard behavior over several business cycles, and any theory that purports to explain macroeconomic fluctuations must explain why interest rates are procyclical. So the essential question addressed here is the following: What is the typical behavior of economic variables during business cycles? We answer this question by first describing the cyclical pattern of the components of aggregate demand, then discussing several other economic indicators.

GNP COMPONENTS OVER THE CYCLE

The income-expenditure approach to measuring aggregate demand is the familiar method which states that aggregate demand (AD) is the sum of expenditures on consumption (C), investment (I), government purchases (G), and net exports (X–M), or

$$AD = C + I + G + (X - M)$$

where all values are expressed in real terms. The equilibrium condition imposes the result that aggregate demand in real terms equals real GNP (Y), so

$$Y = C + I + G + (X - M)$$

which tells us that real GNP is the sum of the four components of aggregate demand.

There is considerable difference among the magnitudes of the four components of aggregate demand. Here are the proportions of real GNP accounted for by consumption, investment, government purchases, and net exports averaged from 1919 to 1982:[1]

Real Consumption	65%
Real Investment	14%
Real Government Purchases	20%
Real Net Exports	1%
Total	100%

When studying percentage changes in the four components, and how these changes relate to changes in real GNP, we must adjust for these relative shares. For example, suppose that over a given period consumption rose by 1 percent. The dollar magnitude of this change would be equivalent to a 65 percent change in net exports because the dollar value of consumption is sixty-five times larger than net exports' dollar value. The situation is similar for investment and government purchases; while both components are much larger than net exports, they are clearly dominated by consumption spending.

According to the expenditure approach, observed changes in real GNP equal the changes in the components of aggregate demand. Table 2.1 presents the annualized percentage changes in real GNP, consumption, investment, government purchases, and net exports during the expansions and recessions that occurred from 1919 to 1982. The other variables in the table—GNP deflator inflation, the unemployment rate, and commercial paper rate—are discussed later in this chapter. The sum of the growth rates of the four components of aggregate demand do not add up to the growth rate of GNP because of the differences in dollar magnitudes explained earlier. In other words, if the percentage changes in each aggregate demand component were weighted by their relative shares of GNP, the sums would approximately add up to the percentage change in GNP.

A common method used to characterize the behavior of economic variables is in terms of their cyclical nature during business cycles. A variable is said to be procyclical if it typically moves in the same direction as aggregate economic activity. A countercyclical variable usually moves in the opposite direction of aggregate economic activity. A variable can also be acyclical—showing no consistent pattern in terms of its movement over business cycles.

Keeping these distinctions in mind, note in Table 2.1 that not all components of aggregate demand are procyclical. For example, during the first expansion, March 1919 to January 1920, both government purchases and net exports fell. But since these two components were offset by rising expenditures on consumption and investment, real GNP rose during the period. Close inspection of Table 2.1 indicates that the only component that is consistently procyclical is investment. We now briefly discuss the four components of aggregate demand.

Table 2.1

Changes in Key Economic Variables during Expansions and Recessions, 1919–1982

NOTE: Entries are estimates based on quarterly data. All changes except those for the unemployment rate and commercial paper rate are expressed in terms of annualized growth rates over the duration of the expansions and recessions. Changes in the unemployment rate and commercial paper rate are total changes in those variables over the periods.

Percent change in:	3/19–1/20 expansion	1/20–7/21 recession	7/21–5/23 expansion
Real GNP	+0.3	-7.7	+14.0
Real Consumption	+4.1	+2.9	+6.1
Real Investment	+109.8	-65.4	+86.9
Real Government Purchases	-44.2	+3.9	-2.5
Real Net Exports	-16.5	-12.5	-87.3
GNP Deflator	+22.0	-13.6	-0.7
Unemployment Rate	+3.8	+6.5	-9.3
Commercial Paper Rate	+1.1	-0.3	-1.0

Percent change in:	5/23–7/24 recession	7/24–10/26 expansion	10/26–11/27 recession
Real GNP	-2.4	+7.7	-3.2
Real Consumption	+3.0	+2.5	-.9
Real Investment	-21.8	+23.5	-14.0
Real Government Purchases	+5.8	+1.4	+6.9
Real Net Exports	+98.3	+8.7	+16.7
GNP Deflator	-2.3	+0.3	-1.0
Unemployment Rate	+2.6	-3.2	+1.5
Commercial Paper Rate	-1.8	+1.1	-0.3

Percent change in:	11/27–8/29 expansion	8/29–3/33 recession	3/33–5/37 expansion
Real GNP	+6.9	-12.6	+10.3
Real Consumption	+3.9	-8.2	+6.7
Real Investment	+13.0	**	**
Real Government Purchases	+4.2	+0.8	+6.2
Real Net Exports	-20.8	-33.7	**
GNP Deflator	+0.5	-8.8	+4.7
Unemployment Rate	-0.1	+22.0	-10.9
Commercial Paper Rate	+2.1	-4.2	-0.9

Table 2.1 (continued)

Percent change in:	5/37-6/38 recession	6/38-2/45 expansion	2/45-10/45 recession
Real GNP	-10.4	+11.0	-20.3
Real Consumption	-6.5	NA	NA
Real Investment	-77.0	NA	NA
Real Government Purchases	+9.1	NA	NA
Real Net Exports	**	NA	NA
GNP Deflator	-2.8	+3.8	+6.8
Unemployment Rate	+4.8	-17.2	NA
Commercial Paper Rate	-0.1	-0.1	0.0

Percent change in:	10/45-11/48 expansion	11/48-10/49 recession	10/49-7/53 expansion
Real GNP	+0.7	-1.4	+7.6
Real Consumption	NA	+2.2	+3.8
Real Investment	NA	-25.2	+10.9
Real Government Purchases	NA	+6.8	+17.4
Real Net Exports	NA	-26.7	-15.6
GNP Deflator	+10.6	-2.0	+3.6
Unemployment Rate	+1.9	+3.2	-4.4
Commercial Paper Rate	+0.8	-0.2	+1.3

Percent change in:	7/53-5/54 recession	5/54-8/57 expansion	8/57-4/58 recession
Real GNP	-3.3	+3.8	-3.6
Real Consumption	+0.4	+3.9	0.0
Real Investment	-11.1	+7.0	-27.2
Real Government Purchases	-8.8	+1.1	+6.0
Real Net Exports	+49.0	+18.6	-85.5
GNP Deflator	+1.3	+2.8	+1.0
Unemployment Rate	+3.2	-1.6	+3.2
Commercial Paper Rate	-1.0	+2.3	-2.2

Percent change in:	4/58-4/60 expansion	4/60-2/61 recession	2/61-12/69 expansion
Real GNP	+4.9	-1.7	+4.4
Real Consumption	+4.5	-0.7	+4.3
Real Investment	+13.4	-22.3	+6.5
Real Government Purchases	+1.0	+4.1	+4.0
Real Net Exports	+10.2	+73.3	-19.8
GNP Deflator	+2.1	+0.6	+2.9
Unemployment Rate	-2.2	+1.6	-3.2
Commercial Paper Rate	+2.3	-1.1	+5.6

Table 2.1 (continued)

Percent change in:	12/69/11/70 recession	11/70-11/73 expansion	11/73-3/75 recession
Real GNP	-0.7	+5.2	-4.0
Real Consumption	+1.5	+4.4	-0.3
Real Investment	-5.4	+11.8	-32.1
Real Government Purchases	-1.6	+0.7	+2.4
Real Net Exports	+77.0	+63.6	+34.5
GNP Deflator	+4.9	+5.2	+9.9
Unemployment Rate	+2.2	-1.0	+3.4
Commercial Paper Rate	-2.3	+2.7	-2.4

Percent change in:	3/75-1/80 expansion	1/80-7/80 recession	7/80-7/81 expansion
Real GNP	+4.4	-2.3	+3.3
Real Consumption	+4.1	-2.0	+3.1
Real Investment	+8.7	-9.8	+13.4
Real Government Purchases	+1.4	+1.0	+0.2
Real Net Exports	+8.9	+5.4	-20.1
GNP Deflator	+6.8	+9.5	+7.5
Unemployment Rate	-1.9	+1.3	-0.2
Commercial Paper Rate	+7.7	-4.6	+6.6

Percent change in:	7/81-11/82 recession	average all expansions	average all recessions
Real GNP	-2.3	+6.0	-5.4
Real Consumption	+1.7	+4.3	-0.5
Real Investment	-22.8	+27.7	-27.8
Real Government Purchases	+3.6	+3.2(*)	+3.3
Real Net Exports	-39.6	-6.4	+17.5
GNP Deflator	+5.0	+5.1	+0.6
Unemployment Rate	+3.2	-3.5	+4.5
Commercial Paper Rate	-7.5	+2.3	-2.0

Notes: NA = not available. * = this average excludes the 1919-1920 expansion because the period includes demilitarization from WWI and if included heavily skews the average. ** = unable to calculate since the series went from positive to negative (or vice versa) values; for example gross investment (1972$) went from 8/29 to 3/33 went from $59.4 billion to -$.5 billion where the negative value resulted from inventory disinvestment exceeding purchases of equipment and structures. Changes in the unemployment rate prior to World War II are based on annual data. Data source: Nathan S. Balke and Robert J. Gordon, "Historical Data," in The American Business Cycle, Continuity and Change, Robert J. Gordon, Editor. (Chicago: The University of Chicago Press, 1986.)

Consumption Spending

Consumption spending measures households' purchases of goods and services and is the largest component of aggregate demand, accounting for almost two-thirds of GNP. Goods are tangible products such as automobiles, appliances, or bottles of soda purchased at the grocery store. A service is a purchase that usually does not involve the actual exchange of a physical substance. Examples include haircuts, airplane travel, and brain operations. Table 2.1 shows that consumption spending is acyclical, always rising during expansions and often continuing to rise during recessions, although at reduced rates. This acyclical behavior is explained in chapter 4 in the context of the permanent income hypothesis of consumption spending.

Investment Spending

The national income accounts break investment spending into four components: firms' spending on new business equipment, firms' spending on new business structures, new residential construction, and changes in business inventories. Table 2.1 shows that investment is the only consistently procyclical component of aggregate demand. It is also the most unstable component as percentage changes in investment are often greater than changes in any of the other components of aggregate demand, with the possible exception of net exports. The dollar amount of investment spending, however, is fifteen times that of net exports. Thus, the instability of investment spending and its consistently procyclical behavior suggest that it is potentially a major source of economic instability—the basis of the Keynesian business cycle model discussed in chapter 4. The last two sets of entries in Table 2.1 contain percentage changes in the components of aggregate demand averaged over expansions and recessions. Investment spending exhibits the greatest variability and, even adjusting for the smaller dollar magnitude of investment compared to consumption, investment accounts for the greatest procyclical spending variability over business cycles.

Government Purchases

The third component of aggregate demand, purchases of goods and services by all levels of government (federal, state, and local) has averaged 20 percent of GNP. It is interesting to note the difference between the ideal behavior of government purchases and reality. At the introductory level of macroeconomics, students are taught that discretionary changes in government purchases are a component of the fiscal policy "tool kit." That is, during recessions the government should increase spending to offset declining consumption and investment in order to help bring about an expansion. During an inflationary expansion, spending should be cut to "cool off" the economy. Thus, the textbook story about government spending is that it should be countercyclical during peacetime.

Table 2.1 shows that, in general, this suggested countercyclical pattern held only before World War II. In fact, since World War II government purchases have been largely procyclical during expansions and on a few occasions during recessions as well. This pattern suggests that government purchases during the post–World War II period may have been a source of economic instability, not stability. Indeed, Moore (1983) reports that during the post–World War II period federal employment was procyclical.

Net Exports

Net exports are foreign purchases of domestically produced goods and services (exports) minus domestic purchases of foreign produced goods and services (imports). Table 2.1 indicates that net exports are acyclical—as likely to rise or fall during recessions or expansions—and at the same time subject to a large degree of variability. The net export component accounts for only about 1 percent of GNP during the sample period.

OTHER IMPORTANT ECONOMIC VARIABLES

Besides being procyclical, countercyclical, or acyclical, economic variables can also be characterized in terms of whether they lead, lag, or are coincident with aggregate economic activity. Two early pioneers in empirical business cycle research, Arthur Burns and Wesley Mitchell (1946) developed a method to plot the average behavior of series over business cycles, allowing them to identify when peaks and troughs in different series occurred relative to the peaks and troughs in aggregate economic activity.

Using their plots, they categorized a series as coincident if its peaks and troughs normally occurred at the same time as overall economic peaks and troughs. A series that peaks and troughs just prior to peaks and troughs in the overall economy is a leading indicator. A series that peaks and troughs after the peaks and troughs in the overall economy is called a lagging indicator. Remember that these classifications are based on average behavior. There can be instances where an indicator that is classified as leading might be coincident with or lag particular economic peaks and troughs. But, on average, the leading indicator will lead. We now discuss several economic indicators in terms of their cyclical behavior.

The Unemployment Rate

The unemployment rate measures the proportion of the civilian labor force that wants to work but is not actually working. To be counted as unemployed, an individual must have actively sought work during the past four weeks, or be on temporary layoff awaiting recall. While there are problems with the measure in that it ignores underemployment and discouraged workers, it is the most commonly cited indicator of labor market conditions.

Not surprising, the unemployment rate is countercyclical, and this is shown in table 2.1 which shows the total change in the unemployment rate during expansions and recessions. During recessions, the unemployment rate rises as layoffs increase and new entrants into the labor force take longer to find jobs. During expansions, the aggregate unemployment rate falls because layoffs decline and new entrants into the labor force find jobs more quickly.

While the unemployment rate is countercyclical, it is not coincident with overall economic activity; instead it leads economic peaks and lags economic troughs. In other words, the unemployment rate troughs prior to peaks in overall economic activity, and peaks after economic troughs. It leads economic peaks because near the end of economic expansions output typically grows more slowly and firms reduce their hiring rate. At the same time, individuals continue to enter the labor force, and the unemployment rate begins to rise before the economy peaks. Peaks in unemployment lag economic troughs because, when recessions end and output begins to rise, firms initially add hours to existing employees as opposed to hiring new employees. After time passes and firms believe that the expansion will continue, they begin to increase their hiring rate. Hence, some time after the economic trough the unemployment rate falls.

The Capacity Utilization Rate

The capacity utilization rate measures the percentage of the total capital stock that is actually being used, thus it can be viewed as the employment rate of the capital stock. This measure is procyclical: during economic expansions, firms utilize larger proportions of their capital as they produce more output. During recessions capacity utilization falls as firms cut production but continue to hold durable capital in expectation of better days ahead.

Like the labor unemployment rate, the capacity utilization rate leads economic peaks and lags economic troughs. As the economy nears its peak, output grows more slowly. Meanwhile, large quantities of new capital are coming on line that were ordered earlier in the economic expansion. As a result, the capacity utilization rate begins to decline before the economy peaks. Following economic troughs, output begins to rise, but the capacity utilization rate continues to fall for a brief time as firms fill some of their new orders out of inventories before significantly raising output. Once the inventories are down to desired levels, firms increase output and the capacity utilization rate rises.

The Inflation Rate

The inflation rate is defined as the rate of change of a price index, usually the growth rate of the Consumer Price Index (CPI) or GNP deflator. In the case of the CPI, inflation measures the rate of change of prices of an ''average basket'' of goods and services that a household buys. For the GNP deflator, inflation measures how rapidly prices of all final goods and services are changing.

Inflation is typically procyclical, but the lead-lag relationship depends on the particular price index used. Inflation's procyclical nature comes about because rising demand for goods and services during economic expansions causes sellers to raise prices as they incur rising marginal costs. As long as demand continues to grow, sellers can raise prices without suffering significant losses of sales. As the expansion ages, sellers incur costs that rise at increasing rates as input suppliers are faced with capacity constraints. The sellers of goods and services continue to pass these cost increases on to buyers in the form of higher prices, and the inflation rate rises. During recessions when demand for goods and services falls, firms find that they can't raise prices without significant losses in sales. Furthermore, input costs are not rising as rapidly as before and may even be falling. The combination of falling demand and downward pressure on costs causes the inflation rate to decline.

In terms of the lead-lag relationship, CPI inflation generally leads economic peaks and is roughly coincident with economic troughs. The GNP deflator inflation rate lags economic peaks and troughs. As the economic growth rate slows prior to the peak in economic activity, demand for goods and services rises less rapidly. This causes the CPI to grow more slowly since an important component of consumption expenditures is food, and food prices are very responsive to supply and demand conditions. GNP deflator inflation lags economic peaks because prices firms pay for investment goods and what the government pays for goods and services are much slower to respond to changes in supply and demand conditions than are consumer prices (Moore 1983). The CPI inflation rate is roughly coincident with economic troughs because food prices bottom out at the economic trough and then rise with the expansion. The GNP deflator inflation rate lags the economic trough for the same reason it lags economic peaks, because prices of investment goods and government purchases are relatively slow to respond to changes in supply and demand.

There is apparently a relationship between the inflation rate and the rates of unemployment and capacity utilization. During the late stages of many expansions, usually the unemployment rate is low and the capacity utilization rate high. A low unemployment rate is consistent with a tight labor market with rapidly rising wages. A high-capacity utilization rate implies that firms have brought less productive equipment into use. In this situation with an economy with capacity constraints, firms incur rapidly rising costs which they try to pass on to buyers in the form of higher prices. Figure 2.1 plots the three measures: the change in the CPI inflation rate, the capacity utilization rate in manufacturing, and the inverted unemployment rate (to make it procyclical) from 1949 to 1982. To make all three magnitudes comparable, each is standardized by subtracting out its average value and dividing by its standard deviation. During periods when the unemployment rate is low and capacity utilization is high, costs are rising rapidly and the inflation rate should be rising. We would expect the converse to

Figure 2.1
Capacity Constraints and Changing Inflation, 1949–1982

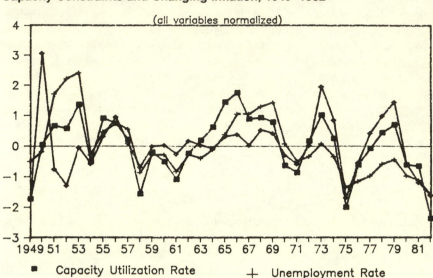

be true as well. Figure 2.1 shows a definite positive correlation between the three measures.[2]

Inventories

Inventories are often considered a buffer against unexpected changes in sales. A firm does not want to get caught unable to fill demand because it may lose business to a competitor. As a result, the optimal amount of inventories for most businesses that sell goods is something greater than zero.[3]

Several economists, including Keynes (1936), emphasize inventories' role in business cycles. In Keynes' view, inventories serve as a signal for firms to change output—if they suddenly observe inventories building up because of an unexpected decline in sales, then they cut output and sell off the unwanted inventories. Conversely, if firms find their inventories being drawn down because of an unexpected rise in sales, then this signals firms to increase output.

It is important to distinguish between level of inventories and change in inventories. The level of inventories is the stock of goods that firms hold as a buffer against sales, while the change in inventories is a flow that enters the National Income Accounts as inventory investment. The level of inventories is procyclical. In other words, during expansions expected sales rise and firms increase their inventories to provide a larger buffer against larger possible sales changes, and during recessions firms run down inventories because they desire a smaller buffer against smaller expected sales changes.

Peaks and troughs in the level of inventories lag peaks and troughs in the aggregate economy through the signaling process described by Keynes. Around the economic peak, sales begin to decline. Firms don't expect this decline, and inventories continue to rise. Once they realize that the sales decline will persist, firms cut output and fill orders partly out of inventories. When the economy reaches its trough and sales begin to rise, firms meet the increased demand out of existing inventories, depleting them further. When firms realize the increase in sales will persist, they increase output to meet the new demand and add inventories to provide the buffer against higher expected future sales.

With respect to inventory investment, or the change in inventories, this measure is procyclical with a lead. Inventory models postulate that the change in inventories depends on the change in sales: the faster sales are rising, the more rapidly firms add to their inventories, and when sales growth falls, firms add to inventories more slowly. In the early stage of economic expansions, output and sales typically rise quite rapidly. As a result, firms add to inventories at an increasing rate and the change in inventories is rising. However, as the expansion ages and nears its peak, output continues to grow, but more slowly. Since output grows more slowly, firms add to inventories at a slower pace, and the change in inventories declines. Thus, the peak in inventory investment leads the peak in output.

During recessions, output falls rapidly at first. Firms actually reduce their inventories so the change in inventories is negative. As the recession progresses and nears its trough, output typically drops more slowly, and firms run down their inventories at a slower pace. Therefore, the change in inventories, while still negative, rises, and the trough in the change in inventories leads the trough in overall economic activity.

Corporate Profits

Both real and nominal after-tax corporate profits are procyclical with a lead. Rising sales during expansions bring profits up, but as the expansion ages, costs eventually begin to rise rapidly when capacity constraints become problematic. While output prices are rising, costs rise even faster, and the profit margin begins to fall. Furthermore, prior to economic peaks sales growth declines which, combined with the narrowing of the profit margin, causes profits to fall before the peak in overall economic activity. Profits decline during the ensuing recession along with sales, but as the recession ages, input costs eventually fall rapidly, and sales begin to fall more slowly. Prior to the trough in overall economic activity, the profit margin widens while sales growth falls more slowly, hence, corporate profits rise.[4]

Nominal Wage Growth

While nominal wages have been rising virtually continuously since the end of World War II and are, therefore, acyclical, the growth rate of nominal wages is procyclical with a lag. Wages rise at an increasing rate during economic expansions because of both rising labor demand and related rising cost of living adjustments which are a result of procyclical inflation. During recessions, the converse is true. There is some disagreement as to why peaks and troughs in wage growth lag peaks and troughs in overall economic activity. One explanation contends that wages are relatively rigid for some period of time. Perhaps individuals work under contracts that state the nominal wage for a one-year period, or possibly they work for firms that annually reviews workers' performances and typically do not grant wage increases except at review time.

Whatever the source of the rigidity, nominal wage growth lags overall economic activity. Labor costs rise at increasing rates during expansions, and when the economy peaks, wage growth continues to rise as hours are cut instead of wages. Once the downturn in economic activity has persisted for some time, downward pressure is put on wage growth, and it eventually declines. During the recession, wage growth continues to fall, but once the economy turns up again, inertia causes wage growth to continue declining until the expansion has persisted for some time.

The precise explanation of wage behavior is not settled. Disagreements exist over the source of rigidities in wages and the behavior of both real and nominal wages over the business cycle. This issue is discussed in much greater detail in chapters 4 and 12.

The Money Supply

Whether the money supply is defined as M1 or M2, measured in terms of nominal growth rates or real levels, it is procyclical with a lead. In fact, the Commerce Department uses the level of real M2 as a component of its index of leading indicators. There are basically two explanations for this procyclical leading behavior: the first holds that changes in money cause changes in economic output with a lag—the basis of the monetarist theory discussed in chapter 5. The second explanation claims that changes in economic output alter the demand for money, which in turns causes the quantity of money to change. This latter view is part of the old Keynesian model discussed in chapter 4 and the real business cycle model addressed in chapter 8. Money's role in the business cycle is discussed at length in later chapters of this book.

Interest Rates

Both long- and short-term interest rates are procyclical with a lag. (The behavior of the short-term commercial paper rate is shown in Table 2.1.) The procyclical lagging nature exists because during expansions rising income increases the demand for business credit. Furthermore, since inflation is procyclical, transactors expect inflation to rise which is an inducement to borrow to buy assets whose value rises along with inflation, such as real estate, precious metals, and consumer durables. As a result, demand for credit rises faster than supply, and interest rates rise. After the economy peaks, interest rates continue to rise, perhaps because expected inflation continues to increase. Shortly after the recession begins, falling income and declining inflationary expectations reduce loan demand, and interest rates decline. They continue to decline after the expansion begins, perhaps because near-term expectations of inflation continue to fall.

Stock Prices

Stock prices (another component of the index of leading indicators) are procyclical with a lead. Stock prices are the present value of the future expected dividends on stocks. The stock price formula is

$$P_s = D1/(1+r) + D2/(1+r)^2 + \ldots + DN/(1+r)^n$$

where P_s is the price of the stock, Di is the expected dividend in period i, N is the last period dividends are expected to be received, and r is the discount rate.

This formula shows that two factors affect stock prices: changes in expected future dividends and interest rates. Expected dividends are in the numerator and have a positive effect on stock prices. Expected interest rates are in the demoninator and have a negative effect on stock prices since higher interest rates reduce the present value of future dividends.

The procyclical behavior of stock prices suggests that the dividend effect dominates the interest rate effect over the business cycle. This notion is consistent with Keynes' (1936) theory (discussed in chapter 4) of the relationship between stock prices and output. During economic expansions expected dividends rise enough to offset expected rising interest rates which drives stock prices up. During recessions, expected dividends fall enough to offset the effect of expected declines in interest rates, and stock prices decline.

Why do stock prices lead economic activity? Remember that corporate profits are a leading indicator. Apparently late in the economic expansion people expect corporate profits to fall, which reduces expected dividends. At the same time, interest rates are rising rapidly, and the joint effects cause stock prices to decline. During a recession, as the economy approaches the trough, expected dividends rise. Near-term interest rates are expected to continue falling, hence, stock prices are driven up.

CONCLUSION

Table 2.2 summarizes the behavior of the indicators discussed in the previous section. Readers seeking a more comprehensive list and their average lead and

Table 2.2
Summary of Economic Indicators' Behavior

Variable	Behavior	At Peaks	At Troughs
unemployment rate	countercyclical	leads	lags
capacity utilization rate	procyclical	leads	lags
CPI inflation	procyclical	leads	coincident
GNP deflator inflation	procyclical	lags	lags
level of inventories	procyclical	lags	lags
change in inventories	procyclical	leads	leads
corporate profits	procyclical	leads	leads
nominal wage growth	procyclical	lags	lags
growth of nominal M1	procyclical	leads	leads
level of real M2	procyclical	leads	leads
long term interest rates	procyclical	lags	lags
short term interest rates	procyclical	lags	lags
stock prices	procyclical	leads	leads

Notes: These results are based on data covering the period 1947 to 1982. Source: U.S. Department of Commerce *Handbook of Cyclical Indicators*, 1984.

lag times are referred to the monthly Commerce Department publication *Business Conditions Digest*. We now turn to theories of the business cycle, beginning with the early (pre-Keynes) models.

NOTES

1. The sample period excludes 1942.I to 1946.IV because quarterly national income account data on consumption, investment, government purchases, and net exports are not available over that period.

2. See Gittings (1989) for a detailed discussion of the relationship between capacity utilization and inflation.

3. There are industries where goods producers do not hold inventories. These tend

to consist of firms that produce specialized goods for order, such as large shipbuilders and aircraft manufacturers.

4. The behavior of corporate profits is discussed further (in chapter 3) in the context of Mitchell's cost-price margin theory.

3 | Early Theories of the Cycle

In this chapter we review some early theories of the business cycle. The discussion is designed to provide the reader not only with a historical background to cycle theory, but to lay foundations for more modern theories discussed later. While some older theories have been discredited, aspects of others endure as components of modern models.

The theories are categorized according to the endogenous/exogenous distinction discussed in chapter 1. Remember that endogenous theories are self-generating: the cycle naturally recurs over and over as endogenous forces determine and are determined by aggregate economic activity. Exogenous theories are models where output is determined by factors outside of the model, so cycles of this sort are not expected to naturally recur. Some of the theories discussed in this chapter are not solely endogenous or exogenous—for example, an endogenous theory may require an exogenous shock to set the self-generating cycle in motion. Since some of these theories contain both endogenous and exogenous elements, they are categorized according to whether they are predominantly one or the other.

ENDOGENOUS THEORIES

Early Monetary Theory under the Gold Standard

A gold standard describes a monetary system where a country's quantity of money is based on its gold holdings. This system can take the form of a metallic standard where all legal tender consists of gold and the value of each monetary unit's content equals the unit's face value. Or it could take the form of specie conversion where a central authority promises to redeem currency for gold at a fixed rate. In the case of the metallic standard, obviously a nation's quantity of money outstanding depends on its gold holdings. Under specie conversion, if the agency supplying currency has promised conversion, the authority must make certain that the face value of the currency does not exceed their gold holdings at the fixed price of gold. Under both the metallic standard and specie conversion, more money can be created only when a country's gold holdings rise. Conversely, currency must be taken out of circulation when the gold stock falls.

The gold standard allows nations to fix rates of exchange with other countries' currencies. For example, if the United States set the price of gold at $20 per ounce, and England set the price of gold at 4 British pounds per ounce, then the exchange rate between the dollar and the pound is equal to $20/4 pounds, or $5 per pound. In this way, the gold standard is combined with a system of stable exchange rates.

The monetary theory of the business cycle under a gold standard was suggested by Hawtrey (1913), among others. Hawtrey suggested a transmission mechanism where increases in the quantity of money raise the availability of credit. This in turn causes lenders to charge lower interest rates in order to induce more borrowing. The increased borrowing would be by businesses to purchase investment goods for expansion, but mostly by merchants to increase their stocks of inventories. Merchants are the key players here. According to Hawtrey, the value of merchants' inventories typically exceeds the value of their capital. A small reduction in interest rates causes a large decline in merchants' costs of carrying inventories. Thus, when interest rates fall, merchants increase their purchases. As they place more orders with suppliers, output rises, inducing additional consumption spending and bringing about an economic expansion. The expansion continues because rising demand puts upward pressure on prices which works to raise output via two channels. First, as prices begin to rise, merchants expect prices to rise further and place still more orders from suppliers. Second, rising prices reduce the real value of idle money balances, providing an incentive for households to spend these balances on goods and services.

Since Hawtrey assumes a gold standard, the expansion must eventually end. The rise in domestic income induces more consumption spending on both domestic and foreign goods. Assuming that domestic output expands faster than foreign output, the nation experiencing the boom will run a trade deficit, thereby importing more than it exports. The trade deficit, combined with fixed exchange rates, means that the deficit country will undergo a gold outflow to settle its balance-of-payments deficit. Since the nation is on a gold standard, the gold outflow causes the quantity of money to decline, thus initiating the whole process in reverse.

The decline in the money supply puts upward pressure on interest rates. Here again, the merchants play an important role as they cut orders from suppliers because of rising inventory carrying costs. Suppliers cut production, which lowers income and consumption and puts downward pressure on prices. Once prices begin to decline, merchants expect them to fall further; in response, merchants cut orders still further and output continues to fall. The fall in prices also raises the real value of money balances, inducing households to hold larger idle money balances. Thus, the demand for goods and services declines, and the economy moves into a recession.

The recession ends because the nation's trade account moves into surplus. Falling income and consumption lower the demand for foreign goods, and, assuming that domestic demand for foreign goods falls faster than foreign demand for domestic goods, the country incurs a trade surplus, exporting more than it imports. The trade surplus causes a gold inflow which results in a rising money supply, starting another expansion.

The gold standard and fixed exchange rates make this model of the business cycle self-generating, as the natural tendency of the money supply to change with the balance of trade causes economic activity to cycle up and down. Hawtrey recognized that the self-generating feature would disappear if the country left the gold standard and moved to a fiat monetary standard (money not backed by precious metals or debt), where the supply of money (or its growth rate) could be fixed. In fact, he considered it possible that an economy with a fiat monetary system could be immune to a perpetual business cycle.

Hawtrey's theory does not apply to modern economies because the industrialized world left the gold standard in the 1930s, although it is possible countries may return to it some day. Nevertheless, Hawtrey's theory is important in that it posits a relationship between the supply of money and economic activity by describing a transmission mechanism for money to influence output. Elements of this relationship are contained in the modern monetary theory described in chapter 5.

The Underconsumption Theory

The underconsumptionist school of thought has a long history. Dating back to the early 1800s, Malthus and Sismondi attacked Say's Law ("supply creates its own demand") by claiming that aggregate consumption could be too low to absorb all of the goods and services being produced. This overproduction of consumption goods would cause unsold output to pile up, and a recession would ensue as firms cut output in an attempt to reduce unwanted inventories.

The underconsumption theory described here is along the lines suggested by Sismondi and, later, Hobson (1909, 1922).[1] The theory has modern adherents and has been a basis for economic policy decisions—in particular, policies to redistribute income as a means to reduce the amplitude of the business cycle. In its original form, it was not a theory of a recurring business cycle, but instead was designed to explain how an economy could enter a long economic downturn.

The Sismondi/Hobson theory revolves around the distinction between the rich and the poor. The well-off in society are assumed to receive much of their income from returns on financial assets and real property. These households are also assumed to have relatively high average propensities to save—that is, they save relatively large proportions and consume relatively small proportions of their incomes. The less-well-off receive most of their income in the form of wages from labor and tend to have lower average propensities to save, thus spending larger proportions of their incomes on consumption than do the well-off. The model also assumes that during expansions wage income grows less rapidly than income from financial assets and real property, thereby improving wealthy households' position relative to poor households.

As a result, during economic expansions the aggregate average propensity to save rises, and the aggregate average propensity to consume falls. Increased growth of savings is converted into increased investment growth, but the increased investment spending does not immediately lead to increased output of consumer goods because, the underconsumptionists argue, a time lag exists from spending on new capital goods to the installation of those goods. Therefore, during the early stages of expansions when the average propensity to consume is falling and the increased spending on new capital goods has not yet resulted in increased production of new consumption goods, the demand for consumption goods grows at roughly the same rate as the supply of consumption goods.

Once the new capital goods are installed, new consumption goods are produced in greater quantities. However, since society's average propensity to consume continues to fall, the supply of consumption goods rises more rapidly than the demand for these goods. This is when underconsumption occurs. The increased supply of consumption goods causes their prices to fall until eventually they are sold at unprofitable prices. When output becomes unprofitable, firms reduce production and a recession results.

The fact that income is distributed unequally causes society to underconsume and brings about a recession. While this view that expansions are doomed to reverse into recessions is not widely accepted, the suggested behavior of the average propensities to save and consume is consistent with observed phenomena. Underconsumptionists argue that the behavior of the average propensities to save and consume would be altered by total equality of income distribution. That is, if income were equally distributed, then the average propensities of consumption and saving would not exhibit such wide variation with changes in output. Therefore, economic expansions would no longer be doomed to end in recessions. This argument has been used by underconsumptionists to justify income redistribution schemes in an attempt to reduce the amplitude of business cycles.

Investment-based Theories

In the early 1900s economists began addressing the empirical fact that the production of capital goods varies more in percentage terms than total output of all final goods and services. Research on this issue led to the development of investment-based theories of the business cycle. Here we discuss two theories: the overinvestment model and the accelerator.

The overinvestment theory of the business cycle proceeds along two lines, the monetary and nonmonetary versions. Both are based on the notion of natural versus money interest rates developed by Knut Wicksell (1936).[2] Wicksell defines the natural interest rate as the rate which equates the demand for loanable funds with the supply of savings, or the equilibrium rate in the loanable funds market. The money rate is the rate banks charge on loans and is determined by monetary forces as opposed to saving-investment decisions. Both the monetary and non-monetary theories assume that the supply of bank credit, or money created by banks, is quite interest-rate elastic (i.e., for a given level of bank reserves, as long as excess reserves exist, banks are quite willing to issue new loans without significantly raising rates).

The monetary overinvestment model holds that monetary forces are the source of the cycle. In this respect the theory is similar to Hawtrey's but does not rely on international considerations to generate changes in the money supply.[3] According to the monetary version, reduced demand for bank credit during a recession drives the money interest rate below the natural rate. As firms are able to borrow at rates below the expected rate of return on investment projects, more investment projects become profitable, and expenditure on new capital goods rises. Investment exceeds saving by the amount of newly created bank credit, and an economic expansion begins. The increase in investment raises income, induces more consumption expenditures, and prices begin to rise as consumers are bidding against the capital goods industry for scarce resources.

The expansion eventually ends because banks stop creating new money. Once the banks are fully loaned out (i.e., they have loaned out all of their excess reserves), they are unable to create more bank deposits. Because the demand for bank credit continues to grow, money rates rise above the natural rate, and the number of profitable investment opportunities declines. Society has over-invested in the sense that available saving is too small to finance desired investment. The decline in investment reduces output and consumption, and the economy moves from expansion to recession. Eventually the recession ends because falling demand for bank credit drives down the money rate, reestablishing more profitable investment opportunities.

The nonmonetary overinvestment model focuses on spurts of investment brought about by innovations.[4] This theory assumes that economies are subjected to investment cycles. A new innovation or the opening of a new market brings about profitable new investment opportunities and stimulates investment in the economy. The process is accompanied by expanding bank credit that causes interest rates to decline, but this is not the main focus here. As in the monetary version, the expansion stops when investment becomes greater than saving; society overinvests in the sense that there is not enough saving to maintain the level of desired investment. The end of the investment boom moves the economy into a recession, but eventually another set of innovations or the opening of new markets will start another expansion.

Another investment-based theory is J. M. Clark's (1917) accelerator model. This theory differs from the overinvestment model by hypothesizing a different causal relationship. Whereas the overinvestment model postulates that changes in investment cause changes in output, Clark's accelerator contends that changes in output cause investment. The accelerator model is important because it derives investment cycles that we observe and has empirical support.

Clark models the demand for capital goods as a function of the change in output of the final product being produced. Using data on railroad freight cars (the capital goods) and freight and passenger miles (output), he demonstrates that freight cars in use and orders for new cars closely follow the change in freight and passenger miles. In this way he shows that cycles in the production of capital goods occur as a result of acceleration in the output of final products.

Clark's accelerator can be illustrated in the following way: I^g is gross investment, the total spending on new plant and durable equipment. Gross investment is defined to be the sum of net investment (I^n), which is the addition to the capital stock, plus replacement investment (I^r) which is spending on capital goods to replace the ones that wear out. Algebraically,

$$I^g = I^n + I^r$$

The expression for the net investment accelerator is

$$I^n = f(\Delta \text{ output})$$

which shows that net investment is a function of the acceleration in output. The equations can be combined to give an expression for the gross investment accelerator:

$$I^g = f(\Delta \text{ output}) + I^r$$

According to Clark's accelerator, as long as output is constant (its change is zero), net investment is zero, and gross investment equals replacement investment. Once output begins to rise (the change becomes positive), firms demand more capital goods and net investment becomes positive. Once output stops growing, and firms' capital stocks are large enough to produce the new higher level of output, net investment returns to zero. Gross investment is now higher because firms are replacing a fixed proportion of a larger capital stock.

Chenery (1952) criticized Clark's model for assuming that firms could acquire all of the desired new capital goods in the current period. Since many types of capital goods, such as buildings, factories, and highly specialized equipment, take time to build, investment may respond gradually to changes in output. To incorporate a more gradual adjustment pattern of investment spending, Chenery developed the flexible accelerator which assumes that firms acquire a portion of the desired capital in the current period, then more in later periods. For example, if an increase of $20 billion of new capital goods occurs this period, perhaps $5 billion is acquired this period, $10 billion next period, and $5 billion two periods away, so that it takes three periods to get the entire $20 billion. Chenery's prediction of a smooth lagged response of investment to changes in the demand for capital is more consistent with observed phenomena than Clark's version.

The accelerator model does not actually explain how business cycles get started, but does explain some of the cycle's amplitude. The model requires some exogenous force to initiate the increase in demand for final products, then net investment first rises as firms build up capital to new desired levels and then falls once the capital stock has reached the new desired level. This behavior of investment, a component of aggregate demand, amplifies the rise in total output during expansions when output is growing at increasing rates. If the demand for final products declines, then net investment becomes negative if firms stop buying capital goods and wait for some proportion of the capital stock to wear out to achieve a smaller desired stock of capital. The decline in investment amplifies the output decline.

The accelerator is a generally accepted proposition. It has been tested several times and does seem to explain some of the behavior of investment.[5] However, its role in explaining business cycles is limited because it doesn't explain why the demand for products initially changes. Yet the accelerator endures as an integral part of the Keynesian model of economic instability (discussed in chapter 4).

Cost-Price Theory

The cost-price theory of business cycles was developed by Wesley Mitchell (1941). This model focuses on the cyclical behavior of the cost-price margin, or profit margin, defined as the average price received per unit of output minus the average cost of production. Mitchell's research on this measure led to its inclusion as a component in the index of leading indicators.

According to Mitchell, during the early stages of an expansion, the profit margin rises. Output prices are relatively stable because firms have excess capacity and are quite willing to sell off inventories and increase output without raising prices. At the same time, three forces are at work to lower the average costs of production. First, as the economy comes out of a recession, inventories are large. A buyers' market exists, and input suppliers are willing to sell off their excess inventories without raising prices. Second, recessions tend to break up cartel arrangements among input suppliers. Competition is stronger during periods of economic slack which tends to hold down input prices. Third, average costs fall for the familiar reason that as firms producing well below capacity raise output, they incur falling average fixed costs. While the first two of these factors works to hold average costs constant, the third causes average costs to decline. Since average costs are falling and prices received are stable, the profit margin rises in the early stages of an expansion.

This rise in the profit margin feeds the economic expansion. Mitchell assumes that the expected profit margin held by decision makers is based on the actual profit margin. As firms observe the rising profit margin, they become more optimistic about future opportunities. They increase investment spending because they believe the expansion will continue, and their action causes output to keep rising.

As the expansion progresses, upward pressure is put on average costs. When the economy approaches full capacity, costs rise because firms are bringing older, less productive capital into use, paying overtime to workers, incurring higher freight charges, and paying higher interest rates for loans. Furthermore, as inventories are driven down, input markets become sellers' markets, and cartel arrangements are formed. Wages paid to labor rise, but slowly since wages tend to lag changes in economic activity. However, this slow wage growth is countered by the fact that labor quality is diminishing; fatigue from overtime takes its toll, and as employment increases, the last workers hired tend to be less productive. All of these factors work to drive up average costs.

Firms attempt to pass on these cost increases to consumers and purchasers of capital goods in the form of higher prices. If they could pass these price increases on fully, the profit margin would remain constant. According to Mitchell, however, prices do not rise as fast as average costs for a variety of reasons. First, a combination of public regulation and contracts works to hold down price increases. Mitchell cites several industries where price increases are held back by institutional factors: public transportation, public utilities, and other heavily regulated industries. Second, increased capacity is coming on line as a result of the increased investment spending earlier in the expansion. This larger capacity allows firms to continue raising production of goods and services, thus holding down price increases. Third, as interest rates rise with output, the cost of holding inventories increases. This provides an incentive for firms to sell off inventories at a more rapid rate, further holding down price increases. Finally, in an argument similar to that of the underconsumptionists, the average propensity to save rises along with output, dampening consumption growth.

Ultimately, the profit margin begins to fall as the expansion ages. Since expectations of future profits depend on this margin, firms become more pessimistic and reduce their demand for new capital goods. The resulting spending reduction initiates a decline in output, lowering household income and inducing less consumption spending. Inventories pile up and provide a signal for firms to cut production. The economy moves from expansion to recession.

The recession does not continue indefinitely because the profit margin has a natural tendency to rise again. During the recession both prices and average costs fall, but costs fall more rapidly than prices. Costs fall because cartels break up, input suppliers' inventories rise, and firms become more efficient as the less productive capital and labor are disemployed. Prices fall, but slowly, because the institutional factors that held prices down during the boom work to hold prices up during the recession. Furthermore, lower interest rates make firms more willing to hold inventories, so some products are withheld from the market. Consumption lags behind income, implying a falling average propensity to save that holds up consumption demand somewhat. As a result of these factors, costs fall more rapidly than prices, and the profit margin rises. Once the profit margin rises, the information is incorporated into firms' expectations of future profits. Investment demand rises, causing output to rise, and the economy is back on the road to recovery.

Mitchell's theory is interesting because it provides an explanation for the behavior of the profit margin over the business cycle. Furthermore, the emphasis on changes in expectations of future profits as a primary force in causing recessions and expansions is very much in line with Keynesian views of the business cycle.

Long Wave Theories

Russian economist Nikolai Kondratieff (1935) observed long waves of economic activity. He studied commodity prices, interest rates, wages, industry production, and consumption figures covering the period from the late 1700s to the early 1900s for Britain, France, and the United States.[6] While Kondratieff notes that these series exhibit cyclical ups and downs over periods of a few years, he claims they are dominated by long-term expansions and contractions lasting several decades. No explanation is postulated as to why these long waves occurred.

He classifies the period from the late 1700s to early 1900s into three long waves:

1st wave:	rises from late 1780s to 1810–1817
	falls from 1810–1817 to 1844–1851
2nd wave:	rises from 1844–1851 to 1870–1875
	falls from 1870–1875 to 1890–1896
3rd wave:	rises from 1890–1896 to 1914–1920
	falls from 1914–1920 to ?

He is unable to precisely date turning points, but claims that they fall within a range of around seven years. He also states that the long waves (peak to peak or trough to trough) average between forty-eight and sixty years.

Kondratieff notes that his findings are based on only a few observed long cycles. While he does not provide an explanation for their existence, he does assert that certain events seem to occur over cycles; events during upturns include wars, revolutions, increased gold production, increased application of new technology, and the assimilation of new countries into the world economy. He argues that such events are not causes, but are the effects of waves of prosperity and recession.

Joseph Schumpeter (1939) provides an explanation for Kondratieff's observed long waves. He postulates that long cycles are caused by waves of new technological innovations. He attributes the first long wave from the late 1700s to the mid-1800s to the Industrial Revolution which was characterized by great advancements in textile and iron production. He calls the second wave, from the middle to late 1800s the "age of steam and steel," and the third wave starting in the late 1800s is described as the "age of automobiles, electric power, and chemicals."

Schumpeter theorizes on the source of these waves of technological innovations. He claims that people with the ability necessary to develop and market new technologies and products are rare. When conditions are right, a relatively small number of highly talented, innovative people bring forth great advancements that spawn entire new sets of products and production methods. Furthermore, these new products and technologies set off a whole new set of ancillary industries that provide inputs for the new products, or apply the new products to other uses.

According to Schumpeter, these waves of prosperity end because new products eventually displace products based on older technologies. Industries unable to adapt to this change ultimately fail. This process takes several years as the new products infiltrate the market. In time, the failing industries are unable to obtain additional financing and go out of business. This is the period of depression as displaced industries no longer need workers and stop producing, and fewer new products are introduced because market conditions are not conducive to their appearance. When the adjustment to the previous wave of innovations is completed, the long depression ends. Once some degree of stability has been achieved, a new group of individuals comes forth with a new set of technologies and products. As these technologies and products appear in the marketplace, yet another long expansion is set off which will eventually end when the next period of readjustment occurs.

Kondratieff and Schumpeter's long wave theory has received considerable attention in recent years. Modern long wave adherents identify 1937 as the trough of the last long wave and argue that the upturn continued until 1973. This would put us in the early stages of a long wave decline that will turn into a major depression around 1990, ending around 2000–2010.[7]

EXOGENOUS THEORIES

Agricultural-based Theories

In earlier times, the agricultural sector accounted for a much larger proportion of aggregate output than it does today. As recently as 1850, 85 percent of the American population lived on farms. Today, less than 3 percent do. Clearly, agriculture used to be a far more important industry. So it should come as no surprise that some early business cycle theories focused on agricultural cycles.

One such theory was developed in the 1800s by W. S. Jevons (1884) who hypothesized that sunspots were a major cause of business cycles. Sunspots are enormous explosions that occur on the surface of the sun and influence earth's weather. Periods of high sunspot activity seem to be associated with favorable growing conditions, and periods of low sunspot activity are considered unfavorable for agriculture.

Jevons considers agricultural output data and reports that cycles average 10.43 years in length. In Jevons' day, sunspot cycles were believed to average 10.45 years in length. Thus Jevons believed he had discovered a cause for agricultural and, therefore, economic cycles. Unfortunately for Jevons' theory, sunspot cycles were later found to average just over eleven years in length—different enough from the agricultural cycle's average length to render his theory invalid.

Another theory of agricultural cycles, the cobweb theory, is designed to explain why prices and output of certain products rise and fall from year to year.[8] The model applies to goods that cannot be stored, thus it explains agricultural markets because fresh fruits and vegetables must be supplied to the market quickly once they are harvested. Farmers have to accept the going price; if they withhold the goods from the market, the goods will rot and become worthless.

The cobweb assumes that the current demand for a commodity is based on its current price, while the current supply is based on its price in the previous period. In the spring farmers decide which crops to plant, but they do not know precisely what price they will receive when the crop is harvested in the fall. They are assumed to base their spring planting decisions on what they expect the price to be in the coming autumn which depends on the price that prevailed the previous autumn.

The cobweb is illustrated in Figure 3.1. Assume that the demand (D) is stable from period to period, and the supply schedule under normal growing conditions is S. Now suppose that a one-time exogenous event occurs that shifts the supply schedule to the left to S', for example a one-year drought that does not recur in the following years. The supply schedule shifts to S' during the drought year and afterwards returns to S and remains there during future periods.

The drought raises the price to P(2) and lowers the quantity to Q(2). The next year, the farmers plant the crop based on the previous year's price, P(2), which raises the quantity supplied to Q(3) when the crop is harvested in the fall. For the farmers to sell all of this increased quantity, the price must fall to P(3) on the demand schedule. The next year, the farmers are pessimistic about the price they will receive because the prior year's price was low. They reduce their planting to the point where P(3) meets the supply schedule S. In the fall, they supply Q(4), and since this reduced quantity corresponds to a point up the demand schedule, the price is driven up to P(4). The next spring, the farmers are more optimistic, so they raise their plantings of the crop to the point where P(4) intersects the supply schedule and harvest Q(5) in the fall. The price falls to where Q(5) meets the demand schedule. The process continues in this manner and the adjustment path forms a cobweb shape. After several periods, the market moves to a stationary equilibrium where S and D intersect. The path of the crop's output is plotted at the bottom of Figure 3.1. The cyclical nature is

Figure 3.1
The Cobweb Model

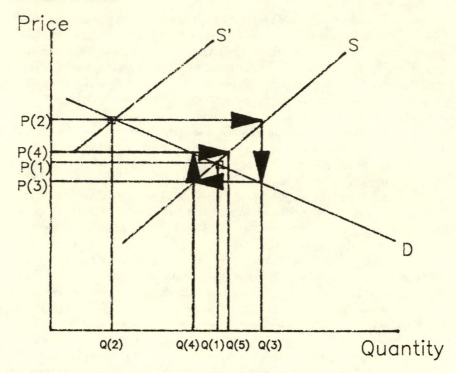

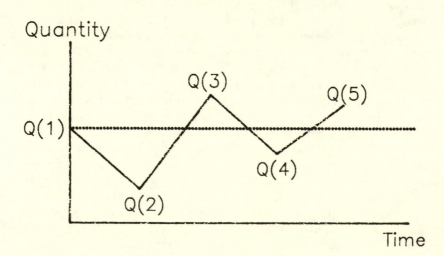

observed as output alternatively rises and falls from year to year with falling amplitude. Output eventually stabilizes after several periods have elapsed.

In our example, the adjustment path moves toward a final stationary equilibrium in what is called a convergent cycle. It converges because we are assuming that the supply schedule is steeper than the demand schedule (in absolute value). If the supply and demand schedules have different relative slopes, two other possible adjustment paths are possible: if the supply schedule is flatter than the demand schedule, the adjustment path moves farther and farther from a stationary equilibrium in what is called an explosive model. The other possibility is that the supply and demand schedules have the same slope. If so, the market never achieves a stationary equilibrium nor does it explode away from equilibrium. This case is called a cycle of constant amplitude.

Theories of agricultural cycles may help explain economic fluctuations of earlier times. As the American economy has industrialized, however, agriculture has taken a smaller and smaller relative role. Although the industry is still enormous in absolute terms, as a proportion of GNP it has declined to where it accounted for only 2.4 percent of U.S. GNP in 1984. Consequently, these theories may help explain agricultural cycles, but their contribution to explaining aggregate economic cycles is limited.

The Classical Model

The classical model, whose proponents included Adam Smith, David Ricardo, and John Stuart Mill, is especially important because it dominated macroeconomics from the late 1700s to the 1930s. As we will learn in the next chapter, the model was discredited during the Keynesian revolution in the 1930s. Nevertheless, this theory provides a foundation for several modern theories of the business cycle, especially the monetarist and real business cycle models discussed in chapters 5 and 8, respectively.

The classical model makes four assumptions. First, quantities and prices are determined in markets by an auctioneer with recontracting ability. The notion of the auctioneer was developed by Walras (1954) (the "Walrasian Auctioneer") and is an imaginary individual who calls out a set of prices to transactors in the economy. Recontracting, emphasized by Edgeworth (1881) refers to the fact that the auctioneer keeps track of the quantities supplied and demanded at different prices and allows trading to take place only when the market is in equilibrium. The process works something like this: all transactors in the economy gather at the market and the auctioneer calls out a randomly selected price. The auctioneer then records how much of the product is demanded and supplied at that price. If the price is too high, the quantity supplied will exceed the quantity demanded, and a lower price is in order. If the price is too low, quantity demanded exceeds quantity supplied, and a higher price is required. The auctioneer continues to call out prices and record the quantities supplied and demanded until an equilibrium price is reached. Only then is trading allowed to take place. If the market is knocked out of equilibrium by some exogenous force, the transactors must return to the market where the auctioneer calls out a new set of prices until a new equilibrium is reached. In this way, the Walrasian Auctioneer combined with Edgeworth's recontracting ability ensures that all prices are perfectly flexible and trading takes place in equilibrium.

Second, the classical model assumes that transactors do not suffer from money illusion. This assumption means that real decisions such as labor supply and demand are based on real values of economic variables. These real decisions are independent of changes in any nominal values—for example, if the real wage rate stays the same because both the nominal wage and the price level rise by the same proportion, the quantity of labor supplied and demanded remains the same.

Third, the classical model assumes that price expectations are unit elastic. This simply means that if prices rise by, say, 1 percent, then transactors incorporate the 1 percent increase into their expectations. So if the price level rises from 100 to 101, then transactors expect the price level to be 101 in the future.

Finally, the classical model assumes that no distribution effects occur. In other words, as the economy moves from one equilibrium to another, the distribution of income and wealth remains the same. Or, equivalently for our purposes, if a redistribution of income or wealth does occur, it does not affect the supply and demand schedules.

Output is determined by the production function. Output (Y) is a function of labor (L) and capital (K) where the specific function (f) depends on the state of technology:

$$Y = f(L, \bar{K})$$

The bar over the capital stock denotes that it is assumed to be fixed.[9] Since capital is assumed constant, two factors can change the level of output: the quantity of labor employed and technology (which changes the functional form).

The quantity of labor is determined in the labor market. The demand for labor is a function of the real wage rate (W/P), the fixed capital stock ($\bar{K}$), and the state of technology (f). The supply of labor depends on the real wage rate and demographic factors affecting the labor force, such as immigration and emigration rates. The labor market is shown in Figure 3.2 where the equilibrium real wage rate and quantity of employment are determined at the intersection of the labor supply (S) and demand (D) schedules. An important aspect of this equilibrium is that no involuntary unemployment exists; everyone who wants to work at the existing wage is working.

The quantity of labor employed will change if either the supply or demand for labor changes. For example, in the top diagram the appearance of immigrants into the labor force would cause the supply of labor to shift to the right to S'. This change would knock the labor market out of equilibrium with the quantity supplied exceeding the quantity demanded at the existing real wage. Labor

Figure 3.2
The Labor Market in the Classical Model

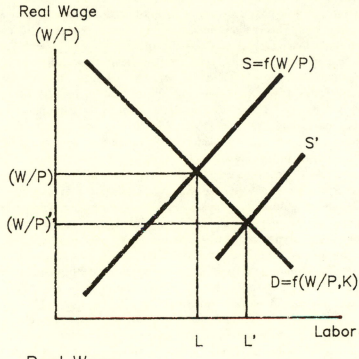

Real Wage
(W/P)

S=f(W/P)

S'

(W/P)

(W/P)'

D=f(W/P,K)

L   L'   Labor

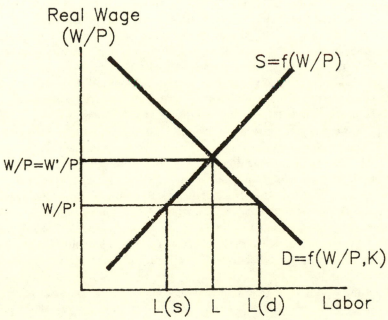

Real Wage
(W/P)

S=f(W/P)

W/P=W'/P

W/P'

D=f(W/P,K)

L(s) L L(d)   Labor

transactors would have to call in the auctioneer to find a new equilibrium with a lower real wage (W/P)′ and higher level of employment, L′. At this new equilibrium there is again no involuntary unemployment.

One factor that does not change the quantity of labor employed is a change in the price level. This is shown in the bottom diagram of Figure 3.2 in an initial equilibrium with a real wage of W/P and employment L. Suppose that as a result of an increase in aggregate demand, the price level rises from P to P′. At the existing nominal wage, W, the higher price level lowers the real wage rate to W/P′ and at this new real wage the quantity of labor demanded, L(d), exceeds the quantity supplied, L(s). Even though the nominal wage has not changed, the real wage has, which influences the quantity supplied and demanded because of the assumption of no money illusion. The labor market is out of equilibrium so it's time to bring the auctioneer back.

The excess demand for labor puts upward pressure on the nominal wage. The auctioneer will find a new nominal wage rate that along with the new price level will reestablish equilibrium in the market. Since a change in the price level does not shift either the supply or demand for labor, the labor market must return to the original equilibrium point, which means that the new equilibrium real wage, W′/P′, must equal the original real wage, W/P. If, for example, the increase in the price level from P to P′ is 10 percent, then to reestablish equilibrium in the labor market the increase in the nominal wage from W to W′ must also be 10 percent. Once equilibrium is reestablished, trading resumes.

This analysis illustrates a fundamental result of the classical model: the quantity of labor employed is independent of the price level. The assumptions of perfectly flexible prices (including wages), no money illusion, and unit elastic price expectations ensure that when the price level changes, the quantity of labor employed remains the same. Furthermore, since the quantity of labor employed is a determinant of output through the production function, then it must be true that the level of output is also independent of the price level. This result of independence between output and the price level makes the aggregate supply vertical as shown in Figure 3.3. Regardless of the price level, output is at Y(*), a level consistent with full employment in the labor market.

The classical aggregate supply schedule shifts (but is always vertical when plotted against the price level) when exogenous events occur that alter technology and/or change the equilibrium quantity of labor employed. These changes must be real effects such as demographic factors that shift the labor supply schedule or changes in technology and the capital stock that shift the production function and labor demand schedule. Advancements in technology and/or forces that increase the quantity of labor employed increase output and shift the aggregate supply schedule to the right. Backward movements in technology and/or forces that reduce the quantity of labor employed shift the aggregate supply schedule to the left.

In its pure form, when the four assumptions hold, the classical model is a total supply-side model which is also shown in Figure 3.3. If the aggregate

Figure 3.3
Aggregate Supply and Demand in the Classical Model

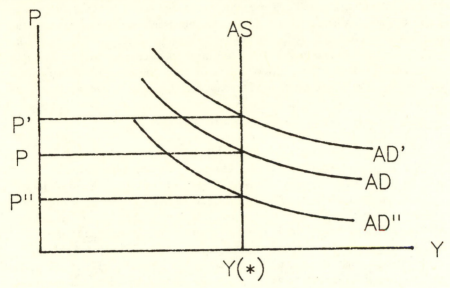

demand schedule (AD) increases, output and employment remain the same, and the price level simply rises from P to P'. Similarly, if aggregate demand declines, the price level falls to P'' with no change in employment. Aggregate demand has no influence over output in the pure classical model; instead only changes in aggregate supply can change real GNP. Factors that change the quantity of labor employed and/or change the production function change output and shift the vertical aggregate supply schedule.

The classical economists themselves recognized that the auctioneer with re-contracting did not actually exist and, therefore, that prices are not perfectly flexible. But they did believe that prices are very flexible, thus changes in aggregate demand could change output, but the high degree of price flexibility would quickly return the economy to full employment. Thus, the classical economists played down demand-side effects and instead focused on supply-side effects in the economy. Negative shocks such as declines in technology or reductions in labor supply that reduce employment result in falling output. Favorable shocks to the production function or the labor market are consistent with rising output. The classical model, therefore, views positive shocks causing expansions and negative shocks causing recessions.

The main shortcomings of the classical model are the results that aggregate demand has no lasting influence on output and the associated lack of emphasis on involuntary unemployment. The Great Depression that began in 1929 was the classical model's undoing; it was difficult to blame almost four years of declining output on exogenous shocks to the production function or the labor market. In contrast, declining aggregate demand seemed to be a very important cause of the depression. In short, the depression was viewed as simply inconsistent with the classical model. This inconsistency led Keynes (1936) to formulate his demand-side model (discussed in the next chapter) that represents a major break from the classical model and provides the foundation for modern demand-side theories of economic fluctuations.

CONCLUSION

Although you may be hard pressed to find many strict adherents of any of the models described, certain elements of those theories are contained in the more modern views discussed in the following chapters. In particular, Keynes' model, described in the next chapter, is an investment-based model similar to Mitchell's cost-price theory and also contains the accelerator. The monetarist model described in chapter 5 is similar in some ways to Hawtrey's and also assumes that the classical model describes long-run economic relationships. The real business cycle model discussed in chapter 8 is a modern throwback to the classical model that assumes that real exogenous shocks to the production function are the main source of business cycles.

NOTES

1. Sismondi's work is in French. Sismondi and Hobson's models are discussed in Haberler (1958). The underconsumption theory also proceeded along other lines: see Haberler (1958, chap 5).
2. Wicksell's book was originally published in 1898 in German.
3. The monetary version is often associated with Hayek (1933, 1935a, 1935b).
4. The nonmonetary version is associated with Wicksell (1936), Spietholf, whose work is in German but discussed in Haberler (1958), and Cassel (1924). Sources of innovations are discussed later in this chapter.
5. See, for example, Eisner and Nadiri (1968).
6. Kondratieff's work was originally published in 1926 in German.
7. "Storm Warnings from the Wave Theorists," *The Economist*, April 1987.
8. The cobweb model is reviewed by Ezekial (1938).
9. Holding the capital stock fixed is a simplifying assumption.

4 | Keynesian Theories

KEYNES

John Maynard Keynes (1883–1946) was a brilliant economist. He was the major economic scholar of his day, leaving an abundance of writing on probability, economic policy, and monetary theory. Among other things, he made important contributions to the consumption function, the theory of money demand, the multiplier, and investment. Perhaps Keynes' greatest contribution to economics is the quasi-general equilibrium analysis he used to describe the economy. Set forth in his magnum opus, *The General Theory of Employment, Interest and Money* (1936), Keynes developed quasi-general equilibrium analysis by applying general equilibrium analysis to aggregated markets. In doing so, he provided an entirely new way to study economic activity.

General equilibrium analysis, developed by Leon Walras, studies the interaction of all markets. For example, if we discovered that eating red meat was unhealthy, general equilibrium analysis would study the effects of this change on all markets. The demand for white meats like chicken and fish would rise, driving up prices and quantities in those markets, and the demand for beef would fall, causing prices and quantities in that industry to decline. The effects would move through the entire economy—employment and wages in different meat-producing industries would change, and different regions of the nation would be affected. The economies of beef states like Texas, Nebraska, and Colorado would be adversely affected while the economies of the fish- and chicken-producing areas of the eastern seaboard, the Southeast, and the Pacific Northwest would benefit.

The macroeconomy includes such an enormous number of markets that applying general equilibrium analysis to all of the different markets is effectively impossible. Keynes' idea was to aggregate the markets in the economy into a small number and then apply general equilibrium analysis. For example, he combined all households and identified their collective labor-leisure decision as the supply of labor. All firms were combined to yield the aggregate demand for labor. When firms' labor demand and households' labor supply are combined, the resulting "labor market" determines the aggregate level of employment and average real wage. Keynes aggregated the entire economy into four distinct markets: goods, labor, money, and bonds, and then applied general equilibrium analysis to them. The result is called quasi-general equilibrium analysis and is the framework we use to study macroeconomics. In this way, Keynes invented modern macroeconomics. Because of this achievement, any list of great economists must include John Maynard Keynes.[1]

Keynes' Attack on the Classicals

We learned in chapter 3 that the classical economists could not explain the existence of involuntary unemployment because their model assumes the existence of a Walrasian Auctioneer with Edgeworth recontracting. This results in perfectly flexible wages and prices which predicts that the economy is always at full employment. In *The General Theory* Keynes points out that something is truly wrong with a theory that can't explain the severe unemployment of the 1930s.

Keynes attacked the classicals' assumption of perfect wage and price flexibility.[2] When a market price is perfectly flexible and supply and demand schedules have their normal upward and downward slopes, a shift in either the supply or demand schedule results in both price and quantity adjustments. In the classical case discussed in chapter 3 where the aggregate supply schedule is vertical when plotted against the price level, a shift in the aggregate demand schedule involves only price adjustments. There is no resulting change in quantity. This is shown in Figure 4.1. When the aggregate demand schedule shifts from AD to AD', the economy moves from point E to E'. While the classical economists recognized that prices are not perfectly flexible, they considered them flexible enough that any movements away from full employment output would be reversed quickly.

Suppose instead that prices are temporarily rigid. The Walrasian Auctioneer who recontracts does not exist, so prices are not determined in a centralized auction market. When the demand for goods and services changes, for whatever reason, the price does not immediately fall to P'. In this case quantity adjustments will occur. The resulting point where the economy will end up is somewhere in the range from points X to E' depending on just how much prices do fall. In the extreme case of complete price inflexibility (a fixed price level), there would be a total quantity adjustment to Y'. The economy ends up at point X because the fall in demand causes firms' inventories to build up, and since firms do not cut prices to increase sales, output declines instead. For reasons discussed later, Keynes believed that prices and wages were less than perfectly flexible—in fact, inflexible enough to cause persistent involuntary unemployment. Consequently,

Figure 4.1
The Role of Price Adjustment

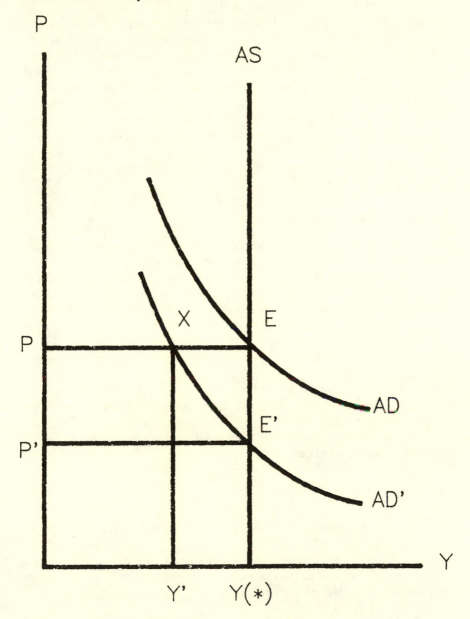

reductions in aggregate demand result in falling output and increased unemployment. Increases in demand stimulate output and employment when the economy is below full employment.[3]

The important point of this discussion is the relative roles of aggregate supply and demand with different degrees of price flexibility. In the pure classical model with perfectly flexible prices and the resulting vertical supply schedule, a shift in the supply schedule moves the economy along the given demand schedule. This implies that the pure classical model is a total supply-side model—only changes in aggregate supply change output. Changes in aggregate demand have no influence on aggregate economic activity. If instead we agree with Keynes that prices are less than perfectly flexible, then aggregate demand does influence output as shown in Figure 4.1. Therefore, Keynes' postulates a model where changes in output largely depend on changes in aggregate demand. Aggregate demand is the driving force in the economy—instability of aggregate demand combined with less than perfectly flexible prices is how Keynes generates his business cycle.

Keynes' Theory of Investment

Keynes' theory of the business cycle places the investment function at center stage which is entirely consistent with the observed fact that investment is the most unstable component of aggregate demand. The investment component of GNP is composed of fixed business investment (spending on new plant and equipment), new residential construction (new houses and apartments), and changes in business inventories. Keynes' model of investment is a model of fixed business investment only. In *The General Theory* he does not discuss residential construction and he views inventory changes resulting from unexpected changes in sales.

Keynes' model of fixed business investment views a firm as having a series of expected dollar returns associated with a particular capital asset. These yields are denoted *Q(1), Q(2), Q(3), . . . ,Q(n)*, where *Q(i)* represents the expected return *i* periods into the future, and we assume the asset is expected to last for *n* periods. Since the firm is making the investment decision today, it is interested in the present discounted value of these expected yields,

$$Q(1)/(1+r) + Q(2)/(1+r)^2 + \ldots + Q(n)/(1+r)^n$$

where *r* is the discount rate. Firms also consider the supply price of capital, P_k, which Keynes defines (1936, p. 135) as "the price which would just induce a manufacturer newly to produce an additional unit of such assets, i.e., what is sometimes called its *replacement cost*." Keynes equates the supply price with the present value of the expected returns as

$$P_k = Q(1)/(1+r) + Q(2)/(1+r)^2 + \ldots + Q(n)/(1+r)^n$$

and defines the marginal efficiency of capital (MEC) as the discount rate, r, which equates the supply price of capital with the present value of the expected returns.

Firms consider an entire schedule of potential capital projects. At the top of the list are projects that have high marginal efficiencies of capital, such as investments in profitable new technologies and office buildings in rapidly growing cities. At the bottom of the list are projects that have low or even negative MECs, such as investments in declining industries or something ridiculous like a tourist hotel in Siberia.

Firms compare the market interest rate on borrowed funds to the MECs of the different capital projects to determine how many new capital goods they will demand. As long as the interest rate is less than or equal to the MEC, the capital project is expected to be profitable and the firm will wish to purchase it because the expected returns exceed the cost of borrowing. How many new capital goods are actually forthcoming and, therefore, the level of gross investment is determined by the capital goods-producing firms. The capital goods-producing firms produce investment goods up to the point that the marginal cost of producing an additional unit equals the supply price of capital. The quantity of new capital goods produced is the level of gross investment.[4]

In this theory, there are three major determinants of aggregate investment: the market interest rate, the supply price of capital, and expectations of prospective yields. Investment is inversely related to the interest rate because as the interest rate rises, it exceeds the MEC of more investment projects and makes a smaller number profitable. Investment is inversely related to the supply price of capital because when the supply price rises, it lowers the MEC of all capital projects. Finally, investment is positively related to the prospective yields on capital projects because an increase in these yields raises the MEC. It is this determinant, prospective yields, that Keynes considers the main source of investment instability.

Keynes argues that prospective yields have become increasingly unstable over time because of the evolution of the institutional arrangement in which they are formed. In the distant past, it was common for the owner of a firm to manage and also make the investment decisions. Keynes (1936, p. 150) considers this situation advantageous because "decisions to invest in private business of the old-fashioned type were . . . largely irrevocable, not only for the community as a whole, but also for the individual." As a result, a commitment to business expansion through investment was a long-term commitment which could not be easily reversed because the individual who made the decision was the owner who had to live with it over the long term.

In more modern times it is common for firm ownership to be separate from management. The corporation owners, the shareholders, have little say in short-run business decisions of management. Furthermore, according to Keynes, these owners are often more interested in short-term profits in the form of capital gains on their stocks than longer-run income in the form of dividends. The problem then, Keynes argues, is that we have a system where speculators seeking short-term gains cause erratic movements in stock prices which leads to unstable investment. Stock prices, which are partly based on the prospective yields on capital, are determined by "a large number of ignorant individuals" and "liable to change violently as the result of a sudden fluctuation of opinion due to factors which do not really make much difference to the prospective yield" (Keynes 1936, p. 154). Keynes contends that these speculators can be seized by fits of optimism or pessimism he terms their "animal spirits" which cause the fluctuations in share prices. This is consistent with the "greater fool" theory of stock prices which states that individuals will buy stocks at perhaps greatly inflated prices as long as they believe that greater fools exist who will pay even more for the stocks. During downturns stock prices collapse because there are no fools left to buy shares. Indeed, this behavior characterizes several of the famous speculative bubbles that have occurred throughout history, such as the 1720s South Sea bubble and the 1920s Florida land bubble.

If we accept Keynes' story about the instability of stock prices, it remains to explain why it causes investment volatility. The reason is that a firm wishing to expand can do so in one of two ways. The first method is to buy new factories and equipment at prices charged by the capital goods producers. This method increases the investment component of aggregate demand and raises the productive capacity of the economy. The second method is to buy existing capital by purchasing a large proportion of another firm's equity. This does not increase aggregate demand but may increase economic growth if significant economies of scale exist.[5] Which method is chosen depends on which route is less expensive. If existing capital, as the stock exchange values it, is less expensive than new capital goods, then it is clearly preferable to acquire existing capital. However, if share prices are overvalued, then it is cheaper to buy new capital goods than to buy existing firms' capital.[6] So when share prices are "low," investment in our economy will be "low," and when share prices are "high," investment will be "high."

This discussion explains why volatile share prices cause the instability of investment. Since shareholders have "animal spirits" about the outlook for share prices, these prices can fluctuate enormously which alters the method firms use to expand. Therefore, the instability of stock prices causes investment to swing between very high and low levels.[7]

Keynes' Business Cycle

Investment volatility sets off Keynes' business cycle. During an economic expansion two factors eventually work to put downward pressure on investment. First, increased demand for capital goods drives prices up as producers incur rising marginal costs, and the marginal efficiency of capital falls. Second, as income rises, the demand for money increases which raises interest rates and makes some potential projects unprofitable. As downward pressure is placed on investment demand, Keynes considers it quite likely that doubt could set in about the prospective yield on capital goods. When this pessimism sets in, stock prices will tumble which does two things: first, it cuts investment even more, and second, it reduces household wealth. Since Keynes considers wealth to be a determinant of consumption, the decline in stock prices drives down autonomous consumption spending. The resulting reduction in aggregate demand causes firms' inventories to build up which is their signal to cut production.

Once the decline in output occurs, the multiplier begins to work. Since Keynes views current consumption as also depending on current income, falling induced consumption causes further reductions in aggregate demand and GNP. At some point, households get nervous about the future, and their precautionary demand for money rises which drives up interest rates and cuts investment spending even further. The multiplier continues to drive output down as inventories are still piling up. At this point, the economy is in real trouble.

It is important to recognize that in this model wages and prices are not flexible enough to reestablish full employment. As mentioned, Keynes views wages and prices as being less than perfectly flexible in contrast to the classical model where wage and price flexibility ensures continuous full employment. In Keynes' world, wages and prices are "sticky" downward—meaning that when demand falls, wages and prices will fall, but not by enough to return the economy to full employment.

Keynes considers wages and prices to be sticky because he assumes both money illusion in the labor market and that workers are concerned about their wages relative to the wages received by others in the economy. Money illusion in the labor market occurs if suppliers of labor base their labor-leisure decisions on nominal as opposed to real wages. If involuntary unemployment puts downward pressure on nominal wages, labor suppliers consider this decline in wages to be a reduction in the opportunity cost of leisure which causes them to supply less labor. This is true even if real wages are rising because prices are falling faster than nominal wages.

Keynes' notion that labor views the wages received by other workers as a relevant piece of information in their work decisions means that labor is reluctant to take nominal wage cuts unless they observe other workers taking cuts too. Also, employed workers may have no particular incentive to accept wage cuts for the simple reason that they are already employed. This view does not imply that nominal wages are fixed but instead that they fall slowly during periods of involuntary unemployment. In fact, due to this wage stickiness in the labor market, prices may fall faster than nominal wages. In this case, the real wage rises which is Keynes' source of unemployment following a reduction in aggregate demand—rising real wages reduce firms' demand for labor. Firms reduce employment while labor suppliers do not realize that their real wages are rising. Since wages are sticky downward and labor is a major cost of production, firms' costs and, therefore, prices may not fall by as much as the decline in aggregate demand.

Since wage and price flexibility does not bring about an end to the recession, an expansion of aggregate demand is required to do the job. In the absence of expansionary monetary or fiscal policies, Keynes feels that the marginal efficiency of capital must rebound to stimulate the economy. A rising MEC requires that the excess capital either wear out or become technologically obsolete before profitable new investment opportunities arise. A long period of time is necessary for capital to depreciate because most capital goods possess the twin features of durability and irreversibility. Durability simply means that capital goods last a long time, and irreversibility means that they often cannot be used for purposes besides those for which they were originally intended.

To illustrate durability and irreversibility, consider the capital stock used in the air travel industry. If a large decline in air travel occurred, what would society do with vacant airports and unused airplanes? An airport is a unique structure that probably has no alternative uses. Furthermore, since the cost of tearing down buildings is not trivial, the airport may sit vacant for many years while the owner continues to incur the costs of ownership, which includes property taxes and security, while hoping for a reversal of fortune. The airplanes? Maybe we could sell them at low prices to entrepreneurs who would tow them onto fields and rent them to students to live in. Much of the complementary equipment such as luggage conveyers, the vehicles that load the food containers onto the jets, and the tractors that push the jets away from the terminal are highly specialized for one thing: air travel. It is difficult to envision them being used for any other purpose. If you are not convinced, consider the number of "white elephant" passenger railroad stations in the United States that no one has the heart to tear down. In many cases they are beautiful, grand buildings.

Because of this durability and irreversibility, during a recession a great deal of idle capital exists—unused factories, office buildings, and machinery. For the marginal efficiency to rise, profitable investment opportunities must exist, but this is unlikely with so much idle capital generating losses. Over time as depreciation and obsolescence occur, capital will eventually become relatively scarce which will drive up the MEC and cause a higher level of investment. The resulting rise in output will work through the multiplier, increasing consumption to drive up aggregate demand. The general shift from pessimism to optimism will drive stock prices up as the economy comes out of the slump. These forces will stimulate the consumption and investment components of aggregate demand, and the economy is back on the road to prosperity.

Keynes' business cycle is self-generating. The economy will undergo a long expansion, but eventually the forces that caused the previous contraction will reappear. Profitable investment opportunities will begin to run out, and the decline in aggregate demand will initiate a fall in output in the manner just described.

KEYNESIANS

The General Theory is a difficult book to read. Keynes uses different terms interchangeably, some sections appear to be disjointed, and parts of the book are simply confusing. Because the book is so difficult to understand, several economists attempted to interpret Keynes for others. It was out of this attempt that IS-LM analysis and the Keynesians were born.

IS-LM analysis was developed by Sir John Hicks (1937). He took the analysis of *The General Theory* and invented a graphic device we use to this day to analyze the effects of exogenous shocks in Keynes' quasi-general equilibrium framework. This familiar model with the LM schedule representing money market equilibrium and the IS curve representing the goods market equilibrium became the tool for the Keynesians to battle the monetarists over the effects of monetary versus fiscal policies.[8]

The American version of Keynesian economics was developed largely from the attempt of two economists, Lawrence R. Klein (1947) and Alvin H. Hansen (1954), to explain Keynes to everyone else. As it turns out, Klein and Hansen misinterpreted Keynes on some crucial points. What they presented as Keynes' ideas, which we call Keynesian economics, is in some ways very different from Keynes' economics. In particular, the Keynesians interpreted Keynes to mean that monetary policy is ineffective and fiscal policy effective for changing GNP. This monetary/fiscal debate was the basis of the argument between the monetarists and Keynesians from the 1940s to the 1960s. In fact, Keynes does not agree with the Keynesians on this point. He prefers fiscal policy to monetary policy, not because monetary policy is ineffective, but because he didn't trust the central bank authorities in England and the United States because of their role in prolonging the depression. Interestingly, the difference between Keynes' economics and Keynesian economics wasn't explained until the late 1960s in the significant work of Axel Leijonhufvud (1968).

The major similarity between Keynes and the Keynesians is that both view output fluctuations as being caused by changes in aggregate demand. While Keynes views prices and wages being sticky, the Keynesians view wages and prices as fixed. Referring back to Figure 4.1, the Keynesian case is when the reduction in aggregate demand from AD to AD' causes no price adjustment, only output adjustment. In fact, the Keynesian model is a total demand-side model—output changes by the full amount of the change in aggregate demand.

The Role of Consumption

The difference between Keynes' and the Keynesians' view of the business cycle is not as striking as on other issues. Essentially, the difference revolves around the role of consumption expenditures. Keynes, as we have seen, considers the investment component of aggregate demand to be the major cause of economic cycles. Consumption expenditures play a passive role; as income and wealth change over the cycle, consumption expenditures fluctuate in a predictable manner amplifying the cycle. Changes in autonomous consumption expenditures do not initiate the cycle. The Keynesians accept Keynes' views on the role of investment but also believe that autonomous consumption expenditures help cause business cycles. The important point, according to the Keynesians, is to disaggregate consumption into its different components.

Consumption can be divided into three categories: services, nondurables, and durables. Services were described in chapter 2 as purchases that do not involve an actual exchange of a physical substance. Durables and nondurables have physical substance; the distinction between the two depends on their economic life. By arbitrary definition a nondurable has an economic life of less than three years, while a durable provides services for three years or more. For example, a major nondurable expenditure is food. Most forms of food are used up fairly quickly after they are purchased—a meal in a restaurant is consumed in an hour or so, a box of strawberries should be eaten within a week, and so on. Other major nondurables include gasoline, heating oil, tobacco products, and clothing. The major durable goods are automobiles and parts, furniture, and household appliances which together account for over 80 percent of spending in this category.

This distinction is important because household purchases of services and nondurables follow a very different pattern from their purchases of durables. Services and nondurables are similar in that consumers buy them in a stable manner over time, based in large part on habits. If you consider your own purchases of food, gasoline, electricity, housing, and personal hygiene sundries, it is likely that these expenditures are quite stable from month to month. One glaring exception might be your spending on the services and nondurables associated with traveling while on vacations. In contrast, your expenditures on durable goods probably varies considerably from period to period. How often do you buy a new piece of furniture, a new appliance, or an automobile? Yet you consume these goods on an ongoing basis much like you consume services and nondurables.

It is important to distinguish between consumption and expenditure on consumption goods. Consumption is the actual services derived from consumer goods. In the case of a major nondurable, food, your consumption and expenditure take place at roughly the same times. Many families go to the supermarket once a week, consume the food over the week, and then return to the store for more. Thus, they purchase seven days' worth of food and consume about one-seventh of it each day until the next trip. In the case of durable goods, the expenditures on, and consumption of, are very different than for services and nondurables. For example, suppose a family purchases a new bed. They incur a one-time expenditure of several hundred dollars, and then someone sleeps on the bed every night for several years. Similar patterns exist for other types of furniture as well as for autos and appliances. These goods are purchased very rarely yet consumed on a daily basis just as food is. Therefore, while the consumption of durable goods is relatively stable over time, expenditures on these goods need not be.

Economists have spent a great deal of time and energy attempting to model consumption expenditures. Two widely accepted theories of consumption, the permanent income and life cycle hypotheses, postulate that a household's consumption is a function of their long-run, expected income which is the component of their after-tax income they expect to prevail over their lifetime.[9] Given an individual's education and wage history, expected income over that person's lifetime should be stable barring unexpected events like an accident that causes permanent disability or being discovered by a television producer to star in a soap opera. The implication of the permanent income and life cycle hypotheses is that consumption and consumption expenditures should be stable since long-run expected income is stable.

Outcomes of aggregate tests of the permanent income and life cycle hypotheses depend on which type of consumption expenditures are being explained. These hypotheses do a good job of explaining spending on services and nondurables but a poor job of explaining spending on durables. As predicted by the consumption models, expenditures on services and nondurables are quite stable over the business cycle, in fact often continuing to rise even during recessions. Spending on these items is fairly stable over time because these purchases are often based on habit. Furthermore, they are purchased on a regular basis because storage costs are significant, or in the case of some nondurables like electricity, certain types of food, and virtually all services, they cannot be stored for any length of time. The stability of services and nondurables from 1952.I to 1986.IV is illustrated in Figure 4.2. During this entire period the series declined during only ten quarters compared to a total of thirty-three quarterly declines in real GNP.

Expenditures on durable goods follow a different pattern because of two features that distinguish consumer durables from services and nondurables. First, durable goods tend to be big ticket items. Their cost often represents a significant portion of an individual's monthly income and large enough that people often borrow to buy new refrigerators or autos. Second, these purchases can often be postponed. Since products like autos, beds, stoves, and refrigerators provide service for years, if a household wanted to replace the aging family car, they may wait until they feel flush to do so. So if a working member of a family believed that a temporary layoff from work was highly probable, the family may postpone the new car purchase and instead keep the old one running for another year. Alternatively, if a bonus check was received from work, they may decide to use it as a down payment on a new car.

Both the permanent income and life cycle theories of consumption can explain the behavior of expenditures on durables. A household's income can be viewed as having both a permanent and transitory component. Permanent income is expected to recur period after period—for example, wage income from a stable job or interest income on your savings. Transitory income is not expected to continue period after period, and examples include prize winnings, an inheritance, income from a seasonal extra job, or a bonus check from work. Households

Figure 4.2
Expenditures on Consumer Services and Nondurables

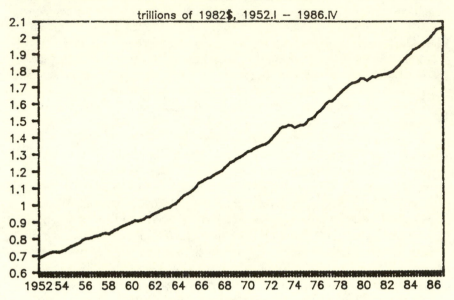

trillions of 1982$, 1952.I — 1986.IV

spend a fairly stable proportion of their permanent income on services and nondurables. The question becomes: What do they do with their transitory income?

Households are likely to save or spend their transitory income on durables. If you received $10,000 from winning a TV game show, would you save it, spend it on durables, or stock up on food, beverages, gasoline, movie tickets and the like? You would probably save it or buy a new durable because in each case you have acquired something that will provide you with utility for several years.[10] Furthermore, storage is not a big issue here. Savings can be kept at the bank and have the added advantage that the interest income may be viewed as permanent. In the case of durables, typically these aren't stored for later use; usually households replace existing kitchen appliances and autos or buy additional ones. It is unlikely you would spend the $10,000 on nondurables and services. In the case of nondurables, where are you going to store the vast amount of food, tobacco, clothing, and gasoline that $10,000 can buy? As far as services, most of these must be consumed on the spot and only provide utility for a short period of time.

This distinction between permanent and transitory income explains why consumption of durables is unstable. During a recession, households suffer income losses, but they are not usually viewed as permanent losses. In other words, few people on layoff expect to be unemployed for the rest of their lives. When these households cut back on their consumption, they do so largely by reducing their purchases of durables because this spending can be postponed to a later date. On the other hand, their consumption of services and nondurables is not as affected because in most cases these are recurring expenditures which are based on habits or cannot be postponed. During an economic expansion, just the opposite occurs: households view the rising income as partly transitory from overtime work, raises, or bonuses. This income is largely saved or used to buy durables.

There are, of course, other factors that influence spending on consumer durables. The first is interest rates. Since many durables are bought with borrowed money or by taking funds out of savings, the interest rate is important. All else being equal, during periods of high interest rates, we would expect fewer durables to be sold, and when interest rates are low, more spending on durables. A second factor is households' optimism or pessimism about the future. Since a household may make payments on a new car for the next few years, household expectations of future income are very important. If individuals considered the probability of layoff to be high in the near future, they would be less likely to tie themselves up with monthly auto payments. If they considered their employment to be very stable with certain raises at work, they would be more likely to buy a car. This explains why forecasters pay so much attention to consumer sentiment studies that attempt to measure households' perceptions of the economic future.

Keynesian Business Cycle

Keynesian models of the business cycle stress the contribution of investment spending and consumer durables. The cycle can be initiated by a change in fixed business investment, residential construction, or autonomous consumption of durables. These components of aggregate demand possess the common feature that they represent commitments to the future: plant and equipment come on line long after the original decision to buy them and have useful economic lives of several years; new homes and apartments take time to build and stand for decades; and consumer durables provide services for years and are sometimes purchased with borrowed funds. Because of this commonality, purchasers of these goods must in some way be basing their decisions on expectations of the future. Firms that desire to expand must feel that the new plant and equipment they acquire will be profitable. The construction industry must feel that new subdivisions of homes and apartments they build will be sold and rented out upon completion. Consumers of durable goods must be fairly certain that their future incomes will be able to support monthly payments on new cars, furniture, and appliances.

The Keynesian business cycle is ultimately generated by changes in the expectations that alter investment and durable consumption expenditures in combination with the multiplier and investment accelerator. In the early stages of an expansion, interest rates are low; consumers and firms are optimistic about future opportunities; and households view part of their rising income as transitory. Spending on investment and consumer durables rises rapidly, and the multiplier works to generate additional consumption and income. As income rises, the investment accelerator induces more investment in structures and equipment, further increasing aggregate demand and output. The reason the expansion eventually ends has to do with the lags involved in the building and acquisition of capital goods and residential construction.

The acquisition of new capital goods takes time. Unlike consumer goods which are acquired rather quickly once you decide to purchase them, new plant and equipment must be planned, financing acquired, and then built. This is not true of all capital goods. If a firm demands a new typewriter or truck, these capital goods can be purchased very quickly. In contrast, new electric generating plants, auto assembly plants, commercial jets, or supertankers take a long time to build. A widely cited study by Meyer (1960) reports that the average time from the decision to acquire capital goods until the peak response of investment is seven quarters. In other words, as expansions progress, firms demand new capital, but much of it does not come on line for almost two years.

This time to build characteristic of capital goods is why the expansion eventually ends. As the expansion progresses, great quantities of new capital goods come on line that were planned some time in the past. The marginal efficiency of capital declines as a result of this abundance. Office buildings are "overbuilt" in the sense that developers have difficulty renting the available space. Subdivisions of houses and apartments lack buyers and renters. Because these investment projects are now less profitable, firms' demand for investment goods declines and the multiplier and accelerator work in reverse. Consumer and business expectations about the future become more pessimistic, putting downward pressure on consumer durables and investment demand. This overall decline in aggregate demand drives business inventories above their desired levels and causes firms to cut production.

Eventually the economy will move into expansion, but before this happens consumers must become more optimistic, and the idle capital must be utilized to drive up the marginal efficiency of capital. There's no reason to build new office buildings until the available ones have been rented. The inventories of unsold autos must be reduced before the assembly lines operate again. During this time workers in the industries that build consumer durables and investment goods are on layoff. They experience declining income, partly viewed as a transitory loss, which lowers their spending on consumer durables.

Eventually, the economy does expand. As the capacity utilization rate rises, capital goods become more scarce and the marginal efficiency of capital rebounds. Investment demand rises, inventories are run down, and firms increase production. The multiplier induces additional consumption expenditures, and households and businesses become more optimistic which causes further increases in investment and consumption.

SOME EVIDENCE

Fixed Business Investment

Keynes' theory of the business cycle emphasizes the role of stock prices on fixed business investment. The "animal spirits" of shareholders influence stock prices which in turn alters fixed business investment and initiates recessions and expansions. Recessions are started by pessimistic stockholders driving down stock prices which causes firms to cut back on their investment spending. This in turn reduces aggregate demand, inventories build up, and firms cut production. Expansions are initiated by rising share prices causing investment demand to rise.

If Keynes' theory is correct, it must be true that stock prices and fixed business investment decisions are leading indicators of real GNP. Stock prices most certainly do lead economic activity as the Commerce Department uses the Standard and Poor's index of 500 common stocks' prices in their index of leading indicators.

It is more difficult to establish that fixed business investment is a leading indicator. The problem here is how the national income accounts measure investment; new capital goods are not measured as investment until they are brought on line. For example, a developer planning a new office building identifies a site, acquires the real estate, designs the building, and hires a contractor to start building the structure. The contractor then hires workers, purchases materials, and starts construction. It may take at least a year, and in the case of a very large building several years before the building is completed. It is at this point, when it becomes an economically productive asset, that it shows up in the national income accounts as investment. Therefore, an increase in the capital stock shows up in the national income accounts as investment long after production of the capital goods actually begins.

Figure 4.3 plots the behavior of business fixed investment from 1954.I to 1986.IV along with peaks (p) and troughs (t) in aggregate economic activity. Investment spending on plant and equipment as currently defined is not a leading indicator. In fact it more often is coincident or lags by one or two quarters. This evidence does not contradict Keynes because the data are from the national income accounts. The Meyer (1960) study claims that the average lag time from the decision to invest to the time the projects come on line is seven quarters. So if measured investment is a coincident or slightly lagging indicator, then decisions to invest must be a leading indicator as Keynes suggests.

The evidence on stock prices and business fixed investment is, therefore, consistent with Keynes. Since share prices and decisions to invest are leading real GNP, it may be true that investment does, in fact, initiate the business cycle.

Figure 4.3
Expenditures on Business Equipment and Structures

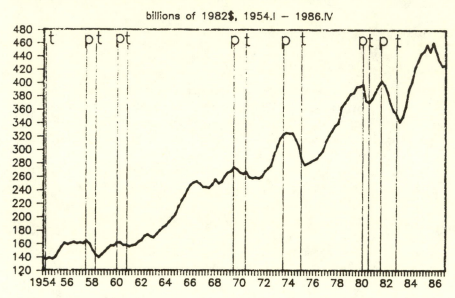

billions of 1982$, 1954.I − 1986.IV

This evidence, however, does not necessarily imply that alternative theories of business cycles are incorrect.

Durable Consumption Goods

The Keynesians also consider the behavior of consumer durables to be an important determinant of the business cycle. If the Keynesians are correct, consumption of these goods should lead changes in real GNP. Investigating this proposition is relatively straightforward because there is little, if any, lag time involved from the time households decide to buy durables until they actually acquire the goods. In most cases, if you decide to buy a new appliance, auto, or piece of furniture, you go to the store and buy it. While you may wait a few days for delivery, this lag is irrelevant since we are considering quarterly data.

Figure 4.4 shows the behavior of consumer durable expenditure from 1952.I to 1986.IV. We see that consumer durables usually lead output. While there are instances where they are coincident with real GNP such as the recession in 1960, in general durables possess the leading indicator characteristic Keynesians stress. Moreover, there are few false signals where durables fall or rise for more than one quarter without an ensuing recession or expansion.

Keynesians claim consumers' optimism or pessimism is the driving force behind durables. Figure 4.5 plots an index of consumer sentiment that is designed

Figure 4.4
Expenditures on Consumer Durables

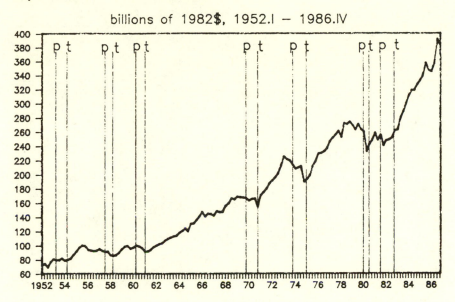

billions of 1982$, 1952.I – 1986.IV

to measure households' optimism or pessimism about the future.[11] The behavior of consumer sentiment is consistent with the Keynesian model of consumer durables; in most cases it declines prior to recessions and rises prior to expansions. At worst, it is a coincident indicator on some occasions.

The evidence presented here does not contradict Keynes' and the Keynesians' interpretation of the business cycle. Stock prices, fixed business investment, and expenditures on consumer durables follow the patterns suggested by Keynes and the Keynesians. Keep in mind, however, that this evidence does not necessarily invalidate the alternative business cycle theories discussed in the following chapters.

CONCLUSION

Keynes and the Keynesians set forth macroeconomic ideas that continue to be a major force in the study of business cycles (see chapter 7). In particular, their emphasis on wage and price inflexibility leads them to emphasize aggregate demand's role in causing changes in economic activity. What sets the theories of Keynes and the Keynesians apart from other demand-side theories—in particular the monetarists discussed in the next chapter—is the source of the changes in aggregate demand.

Figure 4.5
Index of Consumer Sentiment

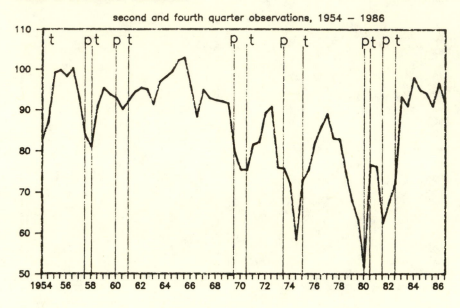

NOTES

1. Keynes is not without his critics. There are several mistakes and inconsistencies in his work. For a discussion, see Leijonhufvud (1968).

2. In *The General Theory* Keynes attacks the classicals on several other points as well. For our purposes, the most important issue is price and wage flexibility.

3. Keynes (1936) does not focus on the effects of rising aggregate demand when output is at full employment, presumably because he was trying to explain the depression.

4. Keynes' theory of investment is truly unique because all other theories (e.g., accelerator, neoclassical) are models of investment demand that do not incorporate supplies of capital goods forthcoming. Keynes' theory, by explaining the actual output of capital goods, is a theory of actual investment.

5. Whether mergers are economically efficient because firms gain economies of scale by being larger, or inefficient because they gain market power, is a major issue in the recurring debate over corporate mergers. The pro-merger arguments are advanced by Bork (1978) and the anti-merger position is described by Adams and Brock (1986).

6. This notion is the basis of the q theory of investment demand developed by Tobin and Brainard (1968).

7. To illustrate the degree of variability Keynes refers to, the Dow Jones Industrial Average of daily closing prices went from 311.24 in 1929 to 64.57 by 1932. Source: U.S. Department of Commerce (1989).

8. The old debate between the monetarists and the Keynesians was about the slope of the IS and LM schedules. Monetarists considered the IS schedule to be flat and the

LM schedule to be steep. In this case, monetary policy is potent for changing output, but fiscal policy is not. Keynesians considered the IS schedule to be steep and the LM schedule flat. Here, fiscal policy is potent, but monetary policy is not.

9. The permanent income hypothesis was developed by Milton Friedman (1957), and the life cycle hypothesis by Franco Modigliani and R. E. Brumberg (1954).

10. You may also spend transitory income on services and nondurables while on a vacation. Notice, for example, the noncash prizes (transitory income for the winners) awarded on TV game shows. They tend to be durable goods and vacation packages.

11. Data are from U.S. Department of Commerce, *Business Conditions Digest*. The index is based on a survey that asks households five equally weighted questions, four of which are about their expectation of future economic conditions. See Strumpel, Cowan, Juster, and Schmiedeskamp (1975).

5 | The Monetarist Model

One of the oldest issues in economics is money's role in determining economic activity. From at least the mid-1700s, economists such as David Hume understood that changes in the quantity of money could lead to changes in output. However, the early economists did not emphasize this point and instead stressed the neutrality of money—the idea that changes in the quantity of money do not change any real values including output but instead change only nominal values. While this view of money emphasizes its long-run relationship to economic aggregates, it became the dominant macroeconomic theory throughout the 1800s and into the early 1900s, although models focusing on the short-run relationship between money and output did exist (see chapter 3). What became known as classical economics held that changes in aggregate demand caused by changes in money were not a major cause of changes in output. Instead, changes in aggregate supply were the major cause of changes in real GNP.

The Great Depression that started in 1929 turned the economics profession on its ear. The widespread belief during the depression was that the conventional theory, the classical model, was wrong because it could not explain the existence of widespread involuntary unemployment. This opened the door for a new view of the economy, and Keynes was the one who provided it with his emphasis on aggregate demand as an important determinant of output. An important aspect of this Keynesian revolution was the belief discussed in the previous chapter that changes in the money supply have only a weak effect on aggregate demand. Therefore, an integral part of this Keynesian revolution was a virtual denial that money had an influence on real GNP.

The Keynesian view dominated economics from the 1930s through the 1960s. The Keynesians' belief that unstable autonomous expenditures on investment goods and consumer durables were the major source of business cycles led economists to place their emphasis on controlling aggregate demand. The idea was to offset fluctuations in aggregate demand by using countercyclical demand management policy—primarily discretionary fiscal policy and automatic fiscal stabilizers—in an effort to maintain economic stability. Stabilization policy was supposed to work something like this: if an autonomous decline in aggregate demand occurred, the government would step in and stimulate demand by increasing government spending on goods and services or by cutting taxes. Conversely, if aggregate demand rose rapidly, government spending could be cut or taxes raised to cool off the economy. Ideally, policies such as these taken at the proper times would stabilize aggregate demand growth, maintain full employment, and eliminate the business cycle.

The belief that the business cycle had been conquered reached its pinnacle during the 1960s. The Kennedy and Johnson administrations were staffed with economic policymakers of the Keynesian persuasion and pursued activist fiscal stabilization policies throughout that decade. The combination of Keynesian economic policies and the fact that the U.S. economy was in an expansion that eventually lasted almost nine years led a number of economists to really believe that business cycles were a thing of the past.

Not all economists converted to Keynesian economics. A number of them were unwilling to abandon the classical model, recognizing that the classical result of monetary neutrality is a long-run relationship. They argued that in the short run (which can be quite long) changes in aggregate demand can and do change real values. These economists argued with the Keynesians about the source of fluctuations in aggregate demand. Rather than autonomous consumption and investment being the primary cause of aggregate demand instability as the Keynesians claimed, this other group, called monetarists, argued that autonomous spending components are actually quite stable. Changes in the supply of money are a major cause of economic instability, they said.

The monetarists also attacked the Keynesian model for its assumption of fixed prices by noting that the fixed price model implies that expansionary aggregate demand policies can permanently raise the level of output. Furthermore, even when the Keynesians allowed the price level to fluctuate as in the Phillips curve model, they still believed that the inverse relationship between inflation and unemployment was a long-run relationship. Monetarists argued that the economy tends to return to the full employment level of output which they call the natural rate of output. Therefore, if demand policies are carried out that cause output to deviate from the natural rate, price flexibility works to return output back to the natural rate. Hence, demand management policies can not change output in the long run, and many business cycles are deviations of output around the natural rate.

Numbered among these monetarists are Milton Friedman and Anna Schwartz who are perhaps most responsible for moving monetarism to the forefront of economic thinking.[1] They published a series of books and articles during the 1960s, 1970s, and 1980s that claim to show a systematic relationship among changes in the quantity of money, economic activity, and prices over several decades.[2] The implication of their work is that the economy is an inherently stable system that tends to move toward full employment with much of the observed economic instability being caused by the monetary authorities. Their evidence, combined with the realization in the late 1960s and early 1970s that several years of Keynesian demand stimulus had helped cause accelerating inflation, and that the business cycle was alive and well, brought monetarism many converts. Monetarism went on to replace Keynesian economics as the dominant model during the 1970s and into the early 1980s, although it has slipped during the mid-1980s.

In terms of explaining observed business cycles, the monetarists and Keynesians aren't that far apart. Their most important point of agreement is that aggregate demand instability is the major source of business cycles. Their argument is essentially over the source of the instability: monetarists claim that it is largely a function of monetary instability while the Keynesians believe that autonomous consumption and investment are the culprits. Furthermore, both believe that since aggregate demand is unstable, the fact that prices are slow to adjust leads to changes in real output. Yet here they argue about the source of sluggish price adjustment. Monetarists feel that changes in aggregate demand are usually unexpected, and expectations are slow to adjust. Therefore, the public takes time to adjust their money balances and spending patterns to achieve a new equilibrium while firms and workers are fooled about price increases for some time. Modern Keynesians tend to blame slow price adjustment on institutional rigidities such as wage contracts and firms with some degree of market power.

THE NATURAL RATE HYPOTHESIS

Fundamental to the monetarist model is the notion that while aggregate demand can influence output and unemployment in the short run, the long-run rates of output and unemployment are independent of aggregate demand. While this long-run result is completely consistent with the classical model, the short run result contrasts with the classical model by allowing changes in aggregate demand to change output. Thus, in the short run the natural rate hypothesis incorporates the Keynesian view that aggregate demand influences output, but in the long run incorporates the classical result that output is independent of aggregate demand.

This natural rate hypothesis was developed independently by Milton Friedman (1968) and Edmund Phelps and his colleagues (1970), and while now one of the most widely accepted propositions in macroeconomics, at the time of its development it was a real break from conventional (Keynesian) thought. The natural rate hypothesis argues that the long-run rate of output is determined by real factors including technological growth, the growth of the labor supply, the rate of investment, and institutional arrangements. In the short run, changes in aggregate demand can and do influence output, not because prices are rigid (monetarists assume they are flexible), but instead because economic transactors can be mistaken about their expectations of prices.

Monetarists view the short-run relationship between prices and output as follows. Assume initially that prices are rising at some rate and are expected to continue doing so. Real wages (net of productivity growth) are constant because nominal wages are rising at the same rate as prices. Now assume that an unexpected increase in aggregate demand growth occurs. Firms experience an increase in sales so they sell more of their product and raise prices at a faster rate.

In the labor market, the model assumes that workers base their labor supply decision on the expected real wage which is composed of their nominal wage rate and expected inflation rate. The relevant variable is what workers think they will earn in real terms in the future, not what they are actually earning in the present. Monetarists assume this expectation of inflation is formed adaptively—that is, it depends on past actual inflation rates—which is an important point because it suggests that workers expect inflation to rise only after they actually observe it doing so. Therefore, while workers' nominal wages are rising faster, they do not initially expect inflation to rise, thus they are "fooled" into thinking that their real wages are going up. But, in fact, firms move down the labor demand schedule because real wages are falling (i.e., nominal wages are rising but not as rapidly as prices are). Hence, there is a peculiar asymmetry in this model. Firms know what the inflation rate is and base their hiring decisions on the actual real wage, while workers base their labor supply decisions on the expected real wage which is based in part on adaptive expectations of the inflation rate.

In the long run, however, economic transactors are assumed to have correct expectations of the inflation rate. In response to rising inflation caused by increases in aggregate demand growth, workers revise their expectation of inflation upward. They demand higher nominal wage growth to compensate for the expected rate of price increases. Wage rigidities do not exist in this model, so firms are willing to pay higher nominal wages. If they do not, workers will be unwilling to supply the quantity of labor firms wish to employ. As nominal wages rise, so do real wages, and firms move back up the labor demand schedule where they employ fewer workers. This process continues until workers' expectation of the inflation rate equals the actual inflation rate at which time nominal wages and prices are growing at the same rate as they were before the original increase in aggregate demand growth. Once the real wage has returned to its original level (net of productivity growth), the labor market is back in long-run equilibrium producing the natural rate of output, and the unemployment rate equals the long-run natural rate.

THE QUANTITY THEORY OF MONEY

The monetarists' theory of the business cycle is based on the familiar quantity theory of money which is the framework developed in the 1700s to explain the relationship between money and prices. We start with the Cambridge cash-balances approach that emphasizes the demand for money for transactions purposes which is postulated to be largely a function of nominal income. This version takes the form

$$M^d = kPY$$

where M^d is the demand for nominal money balances and k is the proportion of nominal income households and firms desire to hold in the form of money, P is the average price level, Y is real output, and thus PY is nominal income. This version imposes the condition that the supply of money equals the demand for money,

$$M^s = M^d = M$$

which yields

$$M = kPY$$

showing that the equilibrium quantity of money is a constant proportion of nominal income.

An alternative approach to the relationship between money and output is Irving Fisher's equation of exchange,

$$MV = PY$$

where M is the stock of money, V is the velocity of money, P is the average price level, and Y is real GNP. The left side of the equation represents nominal aggregate demand: the stock of money is the number of dollars in the hands of the public at a point in time, and velocity measures the average number of times per period that the typical dollar is used to purchase final goods and services. Multiplying the number of dollars in circulation times the number of times each one is used on average to buy final goods and services provides us with the volume of total expenditure per period on final goods and services, or aggregate demand in nominal terms.

The right side of the equation represents nominal GNP. P is the GNP deflator which is the average price of final goods and services, and Y is real GNP or, conceptually, the physical output of final goods and services. GNP at current prices, or nominal GNP, can be viewed as aggregate supply in nominal terms. Setting the left side equal to the right side imposes the equilibrium condition that aggregate demand equals aggregate supply.

The cash-balances version is numerically equal to the equation of exchange when $k = 1/V$. The difference between the two versions is that in the equation of exchange V is measured velocity while in the cash balances version k is the reciprocal of desired velocity. Both versions show us that there are two ways that aggregate demand can change: through a change in the nominal supply of money (M in both versions) or the demand for money (V in the equation of exchange, k in the cash-balances version). Note also that an increase in the demand for money at any given level of nominal income raises k in the cash balances version and lowers V in Fisher's equation.

THE SUPPLY OF AND DEMAND FOR MONEY

The Supply of Money

According to Friedman and Schwartz (1963a), in a fiat monetary system like the one that exists in the United States, the supply of money is largely determined by three factors: (1) the monetary base, or high powered money, (2) the proportion of deposits banks hold in the form of reserves, and (3) the ratio of bank deposits to currency holdings.

The monetary base is composed of currency in the hands of the public plus reserves in the banking system. In the United States this magnitude is very tightly controlled by the Federal Reserve through their open market operations. For example, when the Federal Reserve buys bonds on the open market, they issue new money to buy them by simply writing a check drawn on the Federal Reserve System. When bond sellers receive the checks and deposit them in their bank accounts, the reserves of the banking system rise by the amount of the checks. Conversely, when the Federal Reserve sells bonds, the monetary base goes down.[3]

The reserve ratio is the proportion of deposits that banks hold on reserve. This ratio is composed of both the amount the banks must hold on reserve (required-reserves) plus the reserves banks choose to hold in excess of the required amount (excess-reserves). The Federal Reserve has a great deal of influence over this reserve ratio through their legal authority to set the required-reserve ratio. However, the Federal Reserve does not enjoy total control over the reserve ratio because banks determine the excess-reserve ratio based on factors including interest rates, probability of deposit withdrawals, and demand for loans.

The Federal Reserve has virtually no control over the deposit-currency ratio. This variable represents how the public chooses to hold their money—the amount held in bank deposits divided by the amount held in currency. This ratio is determined by factors including interest rates on deposits, accepted methods of payment for goods and services, and confidence in the banking system.

The monetarists' main point about the supply of money is simply this: the Federal Reserve has ultimate control over the nominal quantity. Even though the banking system and the public help determine the money supply through the reserve ratio and the deposit-currency ratio, the Federal Reserve through open market operations can offset any changes in the money supply caused by the behavior of the banks and the public. If, for example, the banking system chooses to reduce their lending by increasing the excess-reserve ratio and thereby putting downward pressure on the money supply, the Federal Reserve can offset this by increasing their open market purchases of bonds to increase the base and drive up the money supply. Therefore, to the monetarists observed changes in the nominal money supply are a result of Federal Reserve actions or inactions.

Demand for Money and the Role of Velocity

If the Federal Reserve prints new money through open market operations, what does the public do with this new money? For example, if we stuff all of this new money in our mattresses, no change in spending occurs because we have simply chosen to hold the new money. On the other hand, if we spend the new money on final goods and services, then obviously prices and/or output will be affected.

This question of what we do with our money depends on our demand for money which is reflected in the velocity of money. The demand for money refers to how many dollars we desire to hold, not spend. One measure of the demand for money is V, the velocity of money. Velocity is calculated by writing Fisher's equation of exchange in terms of V,

$$V = (PY)/M$$

which shows that velocity is the number of times each dollar is used to purchase final goods and services. For example, if the stock of money is $500 billion and nominal GNP is $4,000 billion per year, then velocity is 8, or the typical dollar is being spent eight times per year on final goods and services. One can also think of velocity as determining the level of total spending that a stock of money supports. In our example, when the stock of money is $500 billion and each dollar is being spent eight times a year, then total spending, or nominal GNP, must equal $4,000 billion per year.

Another way to think of the demand for money is to invert the equation that determines velocity

$$1/V = M/(PY) = \$500B/\$4000B/yr. = 12.5\%/yr.$$

which tells us that the public's money holdings are 12.5 percent of their annual nominal income (about six weeks of income) at any point in time. For example, if an individual earns income of $100 per week, his or her money holdings of currency and bank deposits would average $600.

Suppose that, for whatever reason, the public suddenly decides to reduce their demand for money. Instead of holding six weeks' worth of income in the form of money, they decide to hold only four. To see what happens to velocity and total spending, substitute this new value into the equation. Four weeks is 8.33 percent of a year, so

$$1/V = M/(PY) = .0833/\text{yr}.$$
$$\text{or, } V = 12/\text{yr}.$$

and since velocity is 12, the money stock of $500 billion now supports $6,000 billion (= 12 x $500 billion) of nominal GNP per year.

Since the public is now holding smaller money balances as a proportion of income, the dollars must be turning over more frequently. Because these dollars are being spent on final goods and services more times per year than before, a given stock of money supports a higher level of total spending in the economy.

This example illustrates the relationship among the demand for money, velocity, and total spending. The result is as follows: if, for a given level of income, the demand for money goes down, then velocity rises and a given stock of money supports a higher level of nominal GNP. Conversely, an increase in the demand for money for a given level of income lowers velocity and reduces total spending for a given stock of money. An understanding of this relationship is important for understanding monetarism because of the question posed earlier: if the Federal Reserve prints new money, what does the public do with it? Spend it or hold it? Referring back to Fisher's equation, MV is the level of nominal aggregate demand. If M rises because the Federal Reserve prints new money, total spending will rise if V rises, is constant, or falls by less than M rises. It is also possible that nominal aggregate demand could remain constant if V falls by the same proportion that M rises, or, conceivably, spending could fall if V fell by more than M rose.[4] To determine the factors influencing the velocity of money (V), we now investigate the demand for money function.

Friedman's Theory of Money Demand

Monetarists view households holding their wealth in a variety of forms: money, corporate equities, bonds, physical assets like houses and autos, and human wealth which is an individual's investment in education, skills, and training. The important point is that money is just one way to store your wealth. Because there are alternatives to money, individuals consider rates of return on these alternative assets when determining their money holdings.

Based on this notion, Friedman (1956) suggests the following money demand function:

$$(M/P)^d = f(W, r_m, r_e, r_b, p^e, u)$$

where $(M/P)^d$ is the demand for real money balances (the real purchasing power the money holdings represent) and is influenced by the following:

1. Real wealth or real permanent income (W). Since this theory is about allocating the portfolio of wealth, an increase in wealth will result in larger holdings of all of the alternative forms to hold wealth, including money. The notion of wealth here includes

both human and nonhuman wealth. Permanent income can be substituted for wealth because an individual's permanent income can be viewed as the discounted return on human and nonhuman wealth.[5]

2. The expected rate of return on money (r_m). The rate of return on money positively influences the demand for money because it changes money's own return relative to returns on alternative assets in the wealth portfolio. Therefore, an increase in the expected return on money would cause transactors to hold more money and less alternative assets for a given amount of wealth. During much of the twentieth century in the United States, the return on M1 (currency and checking accounts) was zero; however, the advent of NOW (Negotiable Order of Withdrawal) accounts in the 1980s has made the interest rate on M1 positive. If we define "money" to be M2 (M1 plus savings deposits, small time deposits, and money market mutual fund and deposit accounts), then the rate of return also includes the expected yields on these other deposits.

3. The expected rate of return on corporate equities (r_e). The expected return from holding equities is the expected dividend yield plus expected rate of capital gain or loss. Since stocks are an alternative to money in the portfolio, an increase in the expected return on equities with all other factors unchanged would cause people to hold more stocks and less money.

4. The expected rate of return on bonds (r_b). This is the current yield on bonds plus the expected rate of capital gain or loss. Since bonds, like stocks, are an alternative to money in the portfolio, an increase in the expected return on bonds with all other factors unchanged would cause households to hold more bonds and less money.

5. The expected inflation rate (p^e). This measures the expected return from holding physical assets. During periods of high inflation, assets such as gold, real estate, and art objects appreciate in value at roughly the inflation rate. Since these are alternatives to money in the wealth portfolio, an increase in expected inflation will cause an increase in the holdings of physical assets and a reduction in money holdings.

6. Other variables influencing the demand for liquidity (u). The unique feature of money is its high degree of liquidity. Money can be used easily to buy goods and services which is a desirable property not possessed by physical assets, stocks, and bonds. For example, those who want to convert their stocks into goods and services must first sell their stocks, wait ten working days before they receive the check, convert the check into money, and then use the money to buy goods and services. Possible factors influencing the desire for liquidity include uncertainty about future economic events and institutional arrangements involving the buying and selling of stocks, bonds, and physical assets.[6]

Velocity's behavior is determined by the variables in the demand for money function. As stated before, velocity measures how frequently dollars are spent on final goods and services. For a given quantity of nominal money balances, an increase in the demand for money means that we are holding onto our dollars for a longer period of time, or spending them fewer times on final goods and services (i.e., the velocity of money declines). Therefore, changes in the variables in the money demand function that increase the demand for money—such as declines in yields on stocks or bonds, falling expected inflation, or an increase in the return on money—cause V to fall, and a given quantity of money supports less spending on final goods and services. Conversely, if yields on stocks, bonds, money, or expected inflation change to lower the demand for money, velocity rises as the dollars turn over more quickly. In this case a given quantity of money balances supports a higher level of nominal GNP.

THE DISTINCTION BETWEEN REAL AND NOMINAL INTEREST RATES

An important part of monetarism is to distinguish between real and nominal interest rates. When people refer to interest rates, they are usually describing rates we observe on bonds and bank deposits. These rates we observe are called nominal interest rates. According to the monetarists, these interest rates are determined in the loanable funds market because the interest rate is the price of credit. The supply of loanable funds comes from household and business savings, while the demand is the borrowing desires of firms and the government. Equilibrium of supply and demand determines the prevailing interest rate and quantity of funds.[7]

The nominal interest rate is composed of two factors, the real interest rate and the expected inflation rate in the form suggested by Irving Fisher:

$$r = i + p^e$$

where r is the nominal interest rate, i is the real interest rate, and p^e is the expected inflation rate.[8] The logic behind Fisher's equation of interest rates is that the interest rate charged on a loan is composed of both a real return plus the expected inflation rate. To illustrate, suppose you and I agree on the following transaction: I will loan you one dollar for one year. At the end of the year I must get back at least the expectation of the inflation rate because that is the rate that prices of goods and services are expected to rise during the year. For example, if prices are expected to rise by 10 percent during the year, then the goods and services that I can buy with one dollar today will cost $1.10 one year from today. So I must charge at least 10 percent on the loan just to stay even in terms of expected real purchasing power.

In addition to the expected inflation rate, I want to profit from this transaction. I have no desire to loan you my dollar for "free," so I seek an additional return. This return in excess of the expected inflation rate is the real interest rate. For example, if the real rate is 5 percent, then I will charge you 15 percent interest for this loan.

Unfortunately, real interest rates and expected inflation rates are difficult to observe. In theory, the real interest rate is the real marginal product of the last unit of capital employed, but since it is virtually impossible to observe this value, no one really knows what the real rate is. The expected inflation rate is society's average expectation of price increases. This too is difficult to observe, although surveys exist that measure it. What is commonly done is to take the nominal interest rate which can be observed, the survey or some other value of expected inflation, and compute the real interest rate as[9]

$$i = r - p^e$$

This distinction between real and nominal rates is important for two reasons. First, Fisher's equation of interest rates shows that if the expected inflation rate rises by X percent then nominal interest rates will also rise by X percent.[10] The second reason is that monetarists distinguish between which interest rates influence the different demand functions in the macro model. The money demand function discussed above is influenced by nominal interest rates because these rates are a component of the return on bonds—an alternative asset to money in the wealth portfolio. Real consumption and investment are assumed to depend on real interest rates. In the case of consumption, this is because our consumption decision is the other side of our saving decision. When we save, we don't care what the expected inflation rate is as long as it is reflected in the nominal rate to ensure that the future purchasing power of our savings remains independent of expected inflation. So what matters to saving and, therefore, consumption is the real return.

In the case of investment spending, a firm doesn't care about the expected inflation rate because they expect the value of their durable capital to appreciate at this rate. Expected inflation is not a cost of buying equipment because, while firms pay this amount in nominal interest cost for their loan, they expect to get it back in the form of appreciating value of their capital goods. Thus, expected inflation washes out, and the true cost of borrowing is the real interest rate. As we see later, this distinction between real and nominal interest rates is important to the monetarists because it is part of their theory of how changes in money influence GNP. It is a distinction the early Keynesians never made because expected inflation is an irrelevant concept in a fixed price model.

MONETARIST TRANSMISSION MECHANISM

The Short Run

The transmission mechanism refers to how a change in the nominal supply of money causes a change in nominal GNP. To describe this mechanism, we use Fisher's equation of exchange stated in percentage change form:[11]

$$\%\Delta \text{ in M} + \%\Delta \text{ in V} = \%\Delta \text{ in P} + \%\Delta \text{ in Y}$$

which shows that the growth rate of nominal aggregate demand (the left side) equals the growth rate of nominal GNP (the right side). Let us assume that the economy is at full employment with a real growth rate equal to a long-term trend rate of 3 percent per year; the income velocity of money is constant; and the monetary growth rate is 3 percent per year. Substituting these values into the percentage change form of the equation of exchange yields

$$3\% + 0\% = \%\Delta \text{ in } P + 3\%$$

which yields zero percent change in the price level P, or stable prices. In the loanable funds market, assume that the expected inflation rate is also zero percent, so the nominal interest rate and the real interest rate are the same.

Now suppose that the Federal Reserve initiates open market purchases of bonds that permanently drive the growth rate of the money supply from 3 percent to 5 percent. Also assume that the public did not expect this increase to occur. The Federal Reserve buys bonds from banks and individuals; the proceeds to banks go directly into their reserves, and individuals will tend to deposit their proceeds in bank deposits. As a result, bank reserves are now growing at an annual rate of 5 percent—2 points faster than before. Bank's excess reserves have risen, so they wish to increase their loans. They do so by lowering interest rates on loans to induce households and firms to increase their borrowing. As this process occurs, the increased monetary growth is ending up in the hands of the public in the form of larger deposit growth and currency holdings.

According to the monetarists, this increased monetary growth puts the public in the position of holding excess money balances (i.e., their actual holdings of money exceed their desired holdings). Excess balances exist because the public's demand for money depends on wealth (or permanent income) which hasn't changed as a result of the increased monetary growth. To illustrate, suppose that you directly sold a bond to the Federal Reserve. You exchange a $1,000 bond with the Federal Reserve for a newly printed $1,000 check made out to you which you deposit in your bank account. Has your wealth or permanent income gone up? The answer is no because all you have done is exchange one asset for another. Your wealth is the same as is your permanent income because this transaction does not increase your net worth or long-run expected income stream. The public is in a position of holding more money than they wish to hold, and they begin to dispose of the excess. According to the monetarists, the excess money will initially be used to buy financial assets such as stocks and bonds which bids up their prices and lowers their yields.

The lower yields on stocks and bonds cause several things to happen. First, they induce households to hold more money. Since returns on the alternative assets in the wealth portfolio have declined, money has become relatively more attractive to hold. The higher prices of stocks and bonds also raise household wealth which further induces the public to hold more money. As households hold larger money balances as a proportion of income, the new dollars are turning over at a slower rate meaning that the velocity of money has declined. This increase in the quantity of money demanded resulting from lower interest rates is called the liquidity effect.

Second, lower yields on financial assets mean that nonfinancial assets have become relatively more attractive. As a result, households begin purchasing more real estate, new housing, and consumer durables, which is the first channel where the increased monetary growth shows up in the output market. As these expenditures increase, nominal income begins to rise at a faster rate.

Third, since the increased monetary growth was unanticipated, people do not immediately expect prices to rise. Expected inflation is still around zero and since nominal interest rates have fallen as a result of the portfolio reshuffling, real interest rates have declined. Since real consumption and investment spending are a function of real interest rates, the lower real rates stimulate consumption and investment spending. This increase in aggregate demand growth further stimulates nominal income and is the second channel where the increased monetary growth influences aggregate demand growth.

The net result of these three effects is to raise nominal aggregate demand growth above its original level. Even though velocity has declined, it has not fallen by the same amount that monetary growth rose because some of the newly created money is being spent on final goods and services. Therefore, nominal GNP (PY) is now growing faster than 3 percent, which raises the next question: Since nominal GNP is composed of both prices and output, what are the new relative growth rates of P and Y?

Monetarists argue that most of the increase in aggregate demand growth initially shows up in output growth as opposed to inflation. Since the monetary expansion was unexpected, firms do not realize why the demand for their product has increased. In particular, firms initially perceive the increased demand to be specific to their product. They are not aware that aggregate demand for all final goods and services has increased. As a result, sellers of goods and services may be content to sell more of their product, raise prices only slightly, and place more orders from their suppliers to replenish inventories. The suppliers behave in the same manner. They don't realize why the demand for their product has increased, so they are willing to fill the orders without significantly raising prices. Workers are fooled as well. Labor suppliers observe their nominal wages rising because of increased demand, but they do not expect prices to rise as rapidly as nominal wages. Thus, workers believe that their real wages are rising and are willing to supply more labor. The net result of this process is to increase output growth while price increases stay relatively small.

This increase in output growth causes the demand for loanable funds to rise. As output grows more rapidly, firms increase their borrowing to purchase investment goods to increase capacity. This increase in the demand for loanable funds results in higher interest rates, which is called the income effect. Since interest rates have risen, the velocity of money also starts to rise as the public holds a smaller proportion of their income in the form of money and begins to spend their dollars more frequently. This further stimulates spending on final goods and services, and nominal GNP is now growing faster than 5 percent.

At some point in this chain of events firms and workers begin to realize what is happening. The rising demand for their goods and services is not specific to them but, instead, is a general increase in the demand for all goods and services. As sellers begin to realize that the increase in demand growth has been caused by a monetary expansion, they begin to charge higher prices. Workers realize that their nominal wages are not rising as rapidly as prices, thus their real wages are actually falling. Workers demand higher nominal wages to compensate for higher expected inflation, and the resulting higher real wages cause firms to cut back on their quantity of labor demanded. Output begins to grow more slowly, or even fall. Price increases are passed on to the buyers of goods and services, and the inflation rate begins to rise.

Once the inflation rate begins to rise, something the monetarists call the price expectations effect takes hold. As the public observes higher inflation, they begin to incorporate it into their expectations. Higher expected inflation raises the demand for loanable funds because people wish to borrow today to purchase goods and services to beat expected price increases and pay back the loans in future depreciated dollars. At the same time lenders are less willing to supply loanable funds at current interest rates because they expect to be paid back in future depreciated dollars. The result is a rising demand for loanable funds combined with falling supply which drives interest rates up further. This increase in interest rates causes people to demand even less money meaning that velocity rises even more, leading to even higher growth of nominal aggregate demand.

The Long Run

Eventually, the increased monetary growth results in higher nominal interest rates and a higher inflation rate but no change in real interest rates and the growth of real output. The monetarist model incorporates the natural rate hypothesis which states that the long-run economic growth rate depends on factors that affect aggregate supply: labor supply, technology, saving, and investment. In the long run the price increases are fully anticipated, and real wages (net of productivity growth) return to the level that existed before the increase in monetary growth occurred. Workers eventually realize what the new inflation rate is and demand that their nominal wages rise at the same rate to preserve their real wages. Thus, the labor market returns to a full employment level, and output returns to the natural rate, growing at 3 percent.

The velocity of money has risen to a level higher than its original value but eventually it stops growing. Following the increase in monetary growth, velocity initially declined because interest rates fell (the liquidity effect). Velocity then rose because interest rates increased due to the income and price expectations effects. But eventually the factors that influence the velocity of money stop changing, nominal interest rates settle at a final long-run value, and real permanent income achieves a long-run growth rate of 3 percent. Returning to the quantity theory in percentage change form:

$$\%\Delta \text{ in M} + \%\Delta \text{ in V} = \%\Delta \text{ in P} + \%\Delta \text{ in Y}$$

and substituting our long-run values,

$$5\% + 0\% = \%\Delta \text{ in P} + 3\%$$

The long-run effect of the increase in monetary growth from 3 percent to 5 percent is to raise the inflation rate from zero percent to 2 percent. In other words, in the long run monetary growth in excess of long-run output growth is fully reflected in the inflation rate.

Interest rates are higher than their original values by the amount of the increase in the inflation rate. Referring to Fisher's equation of interest rates, the nominal interest rate reflects the expected inflation rate. Since the inflation rate has risen 2 percentage points, and in the long run this increase is fully anticipated, nominal interest rates have risen 2 percentage points. Real interest rates are independent of monetary growth in the long run because real rates are determined by households' real savings decisions, the marginal productivity of capital, and the government's real borrowing needs—none of which have been altered in the long run as a result of the change in the monetary growth rate. The dynamics of the adjustment process of interest rates, velocity, and nominal GNP growth are shown in Figure 5.1.

Finally, if we had chosen to work our way through a decrease instead of an increase in the monetary growth rate, the effects would be exactly opposite of those just described. Interest rates would initially increase and then decrease. The velocity of money would first rise and then fall, and in the long run nominal GNP growth would decline by the amount of the decrease in the monetary growth rate. In the long run, real output would still be growing at 3 percent per year while interest rates and the inflation rate would have fallen by the amount of the decline in the monetary growth rate, although in the short run real output growth would decline for some period of time.

Short- and Long-Run Adjustment Times

The length of time it takes a change in monetary growth to work its way through the economy is an empirical issue investigated by Friedman and Schwartz (1963a, 1963b, 1982). Their general conclusions suggest that, following changes in the monetary growth rate, the liquidity effect occurs over a period of about three to six months, after which time the income and price expectation effects dominate. Interest rates return to their original levels about eighteen months following the change in the monetary growth rate. And finally, the long-run effect on interest rates, that they change by the full amount of the change in monetary growth and therefore expected inflation, is on the order of about twenty years for long-term rates and ten years for short-term rates, although this adjustment time has shortened in recent decades. A similar time frame describes

Figure 5.1
Interest Rate, Velocity, and Nominal GNP Growth Following an Increase in Monetary Growth

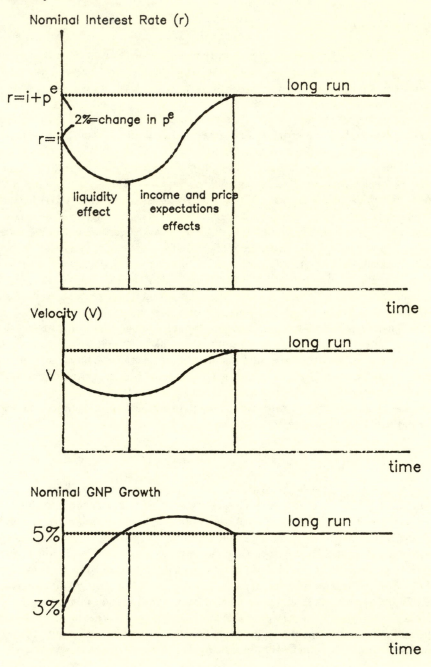

the behavior of velocity and nominal GNP growth. Since velocity and the demand for money respond to interest rates, if it takes interest rates ten to twenty years to fully reflect the change in monetary growth, then it must take this long for velocity to achieve its long-run value. Also, if it takes velocity this long to adjust, then it must take nominal GNP growth, the sum of monetary and velocity growth, a similar amount of time to fully reflect the change in monetary growth.

Monetarists argue that it takes so long to reach the long-run path because the public forms their expectations adaptively. Transactors' expectation of the inflation rate which influences nominal interest rates, velocity, and nominal GNP are based on past information (i.e., the expected inflation rate is based on previous actual inflation rates). When the public observes the inflation rate rising, they slowly incorporate this information into their expectations, and it may take many years for the public to fully realize that inflation will rise as much as it eventually does. While it may not be obvious why expectation formation should take this long, one possible explanation is that the public might not expect the rate of aggregate demand growth to be maintained over the long run.

Whatever the reason, Friedman and Schwartz cite an example where they claim expectations of inflation were being formed based on events that had occurred at least twenty years prior: the public expected inflation rates from June 1947 to the outbreak of the Korean War in 1950 to be negative. The widespread view at the time was that following World War II deflation, or falling prices, would occur because, Friedman and Schwartz claim, that had been the case following World War I, the Civil War, and the War of 1812.[12]

Finally, Friedman and Schwartz calculate the lag from money growth to output measured as the time from the peak in money growth to the peak in output, and the trough in money growth to the trough in output. They conclude that the average time from the peak in money growth to the peak in output is eighteen months, and the average time from the trough in money growth to the trough in output is twelve months. These average lags, however, have very high standard deviations (i.e., the length of the lag varies considerably from episode to episode). Friedman and Schwartz summarize the lag in monetary policy by describing it as "long and variable."

THE BUSINESS CYCLE

The source of the business cycle according to the monetarists should now be obvious: erratic nominal aggregate demand growth caused by unstable monetary growth. Since monetarists believe the demand for money varies in a predictable manner, they conclude that changes in the supply of money are the major source of aggregate demand instability. Furthermore, since monetarists believe that the Federal Reserve Bank has ultimate control over the nominal supply of money, they hold the Federal Reserve primarily responsible for observed economic instability. When the Federal Reserve significantly raises the monetary growth rate, business expansions result, and when monetary growth is significantly reduced, recessions result. This explanation begs the question: Why is monetary growth unstable?[13]

Monetarists believe that fluctuations in monetary growth have occurred because during much of the Federal Reserve's history they have pursued a policy of targeting short-term interest rates instead of the quantity of money. The Federal Reserve sets a target band around a short-term interest rate, and if market rates rise above this target, the Federal Reserve drives the rate down by creating reserves. This action has the short-run effect of lowering short-term interest rates by increasing the monetary base, leading to an increase in monetary growth.

As we have seen, however, an increase in monetary growth only lowers interest rates in the short run through the liquidity effect. After a period of months, the income and price expectations effects work to drive interest rates back up. If the Federal Reserve continues to pursue their interest rate target, they will supply reserves at an even faster rate which may be successful at lowering short-term rates in the short run, but eventually the income and price expectations effects will take over and interest rates will be driven still higher. So the Federal Reserve, in their effort to maintain a low interest rate target, eventually creates reserves at a rapid rate, and the result is accelerating monetary growth, a business expansion, and rising inflation.

At some point, the public becomes concerned with inflation. Shoppers come home from the supermarket upset with the rising prices. Households get sticker shock at auto dealers when potential new car buyers can't believe how much car prices have risen since they last shopped for one. Households become concerned that prices of the basket of goods and services they buy are rising rapidly enough to outstrip their gains in nominal income. At this point, the public demands relief from inflation and turns to the federal government for a solution.

Pressure builds on the Federal Reserve to reduce inflation. To cool off the economy requires that interest rates be driven up further, so the Federal Reserve's interest rate target is raised. The Federal Reserve slows the rate of reserve expansion which reduces the monetary growth rate and drives interest rates up. But slower monetary growth raises interest rates only in the short run. After six months or so, the income and price expectations effects work to lower interest rates, but if the Federal Reserve wants to keep rates high, they must further reduce monetary growth. This reduction in monetary growth reduces aggregate demand growth and creates a recession with lower inflation and higher unemployment. When the public starts screaming about rising unemployment, pressure builds to stimulate the economy, and the Federal Reserve lowers the interest rate target, increases reserve growth, and starts the process all over again. Milton Friedman calls it the "yoyo economy."

The monetarists' proposal to reduce the amplitude of the business cycle is to maintain stable, sustained growth of the money supply which, they contend, would minimize deviations in nominal aggregate demand and bring about a higher degree of economic stability than we have actually experienced. Friedman (1959) advocates a monetary growth rule where the Federal Reserve would be bound in some way to maintain a fixed rate of monetary growth. Proposals include requiring the Board of Governors to tender their resignations to Congress each year they do not meet a specified monetary growth target, or replacing the Federal Reserve with a computer that simply buys enough bonds on the open market to maintain a certain percentage growth rate for the monetary base.

It is important to recognize what monetarists are not promising if their monetary growth rule is implemented. They believe a monetary growth rule would help make the economy more stable than it has been. But a monetary growth rule would not completely stabilize economic activity because monetary instability is considered a major cause of economic activity, but not the only one. Factors that affect aggregate supply such as wars, technological changes, oil price shocks, or attitudes about work are also considered important determinants of economic activity. Thus, monetarists contend that a monetary growth rule would not eliminate business cycles, but help minimize them.

EVIDENCE

If the monetarist model is correct, it must be true that changes in monetary growth precede changes in nominal GNP growth. Furthermore, interest rates and the velocity of money should behave in the manner implied by the monetarists' transmission mechanism—that is, following an increase in the monetary growth rate, interest rates and velocity must first fall then rise and conversely for a decrease in the monetary growth rate.

In this section, the percentage change in the nominal quantity of M1 is used to measure monetary growth. While economists debate which measure of money is the best one, most seem to agree that the proper definition of money is either M1 or M2. For our purposes, M1 and M2 growth tend to move up and down together, so the choice of M's is not absolutely crucial over most of our sample period.

On a quarterly basis, the growth rate of M1 varies considerably, so much so that it is often difficult to discern patterns in its behavior. This point is illustrated in Figure 5.2 where the quarter-to-quarter percentage changes in M1 expressed at annual rates are plotted over the period 1953.II to 1969.IV. The gyrations in this series make it difficult to observe longer term trends in the growth rate. To avoid this problem, we smooth the series by considering a four-quarter moving average of M1 growth. This method calculates M1 growth for any given quarter as the average of that quarter and the prior three-quarter growth rates and is also plotted in Figure 5.2[14] Using a moving average has its pluses and minuses. On the plus side it smooths out the series and makes it easier to observe trends. On the minus side, it makes M1 growth appear to be much smoother than it actually is. Since both M1 growth and nominal GNP growth vary so much from quarter to quarter, in all of the figures that follow, M1 and nominal GNP growth are calculated using the four-quarter moving average.

Figures 5.3 through 5.6 plot M1 growth, nominal GNP growth, and the ninety-

Figure 5.2
Quarterly M1 Growth and M1 Growth Expressed as a Four-Quarter Moving Average

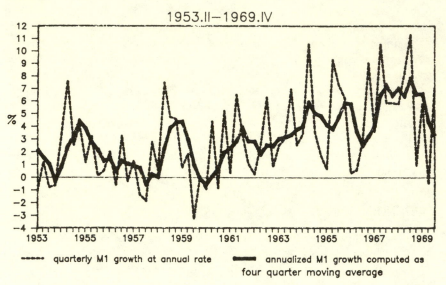

day Treasury bill rate over several business cycles which are identified by their peaks (p) and troughs (t). If the monetarists are correct in their interpretation, then money growth should lead nominal GNP growth, and interest rates should behave in the manner described earlier. Figure 5.3 covers the period 1953.II to 1960.II. Both the starting and ending quarters were peaks in real GNP, so this figure includes two complete business cycles. Figure 5.3 shows that the link between money growth and nominal GNP growth was remarkably tight during the 1950s. Both expansions during the period were preceded by sustained increases in the monetary growth rate, and both recessions were preceded by declines in M1 growth.

We can also infer velocity's behavior from Figure 5.3. Whenever M1 is growing faster than nominal GNP growth, velocity is falling. Velocity fell twice during the period, in 1954 and again in 1958, both periods of significant monetary expansion. This result is precisely what the monetarists predict: in the early stages of a monetary expansion, the public holds a large proportion of the newly created money and velocity falls. Also, when nominal GNP grows faster than M1, velocity is rising. Notice that velocity rises some time after monetary expansions. After the public holds the new money for some time, they start spending it at faster rates, and velocity rises as the monetarists predict.

The behavior of interest rates during the 1950s is also shown in Figure 5.3. In general, we see the pattern consistent with monetarism. Rising M1 growth

Figure 5.3
**Nominal GNP Growth, M1 Growth, and the 90-Day Treasury Bill Rate, 1953.II
to 1960.II**

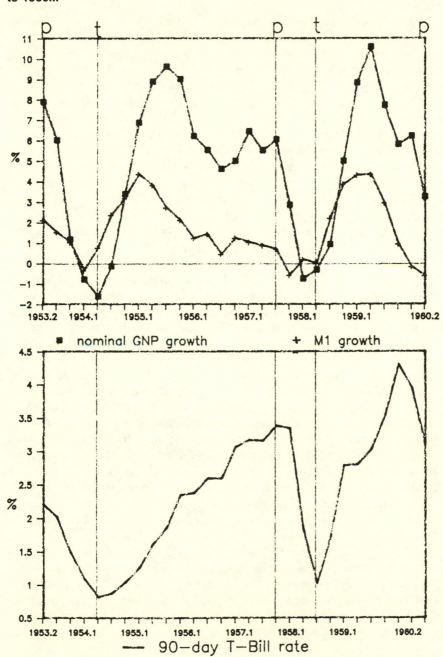

initially lowers interest rates due to the liquidity effect, but after a lag the income and price expectations effects raise interest rates. Falling money growth raises interest rates in the short term, but eventually interest rates fall as monetarism predicts.

Figure 5.4 takes us into the 1960s, a period that includes one business cycle as the economy peaked in 1960.II, reached a trough in 1961.I, and peaked again in 1969.IV. The tight link between M1 growth and nominal GNP growth continued during this period. The trough in 1961.I was preceded by a sustained decline in M1 growth (refer back to Figure 5.3), and the long expansion beginning in 1961 was certainly aided by rising money growth. Note also that we see two periods of falling velocity, 1960.IV–1961.II and 1967.III–1968.I, both during the early stages of monetary expansion and later followed by rising velocity as nominal GNP grows faster than M1. The 1966–1967 episode was the growth recession that apparently was caused in part by reduced monetary growth.

Interest rate behavior during the 1960s is also very much in line with monetarist prediction. Perhaps of special interest during the decade is the general upward trend in interest rates. In line with Fisher's equation of interest rates the general trend of inflation during the 1960s was up, which was reflected in generally rising nominal interest rates during the decade.

The period from the peak in 1969.IV to the peak in 1980.I is plotted in Figure 5.5. Again the money-nominal GNP relationship held up quite well although it is not the textbook example of monetarism provided during the 1950s and 1960s. The monetary growth rate led expansions and recessions in the manner suggested by the monetarists, although money growth was coincident with the expansion that started in 1975.II.

Velocity behaved somewhat differently during this period in the sense that it never declined, possibly because the 1970s was a decade of generally rising inflation. If the monetarists are correct that expectations are slowly adaptive, then rising inflation is consistent with rising velocity. Steadily rising expectations of inflation raise the expected return on physical assets which lowers the demand for money and raises velocity. Note, however, that during the periods of vigorous M1 growth, 1970 and 1975, the monetary growth line moves very close to the nominal GNP growth line (i.e., the growth rate of velocity declined). While we do not see the behavior of the level of velocity the monetarists predict, we do see it in the growth rate of velocity. With respect to interest rates, once again we generally see the pattern implied by monetarism as interest rates move in the same direction as M1 growth with a lag.

The final period, from 1980.I to 1986.IV, is plotted in Figure 5.6. The relationship between M1 growth and nominal GNP growth appears to have weakened considerably during the 1980s. In particular, the expansion that began in 1980.III was not preceded by any significant increase in monetary growth, although that expansion was very short. The next recession, 1981.IV to 1982.IV is entirely consistent with monetarism because it was preceded by declining

Figure 5.4
Nominal GNP Growth, M1 Growth, and the 90-Day Treasury Bill Rate, 1960.II to 1969.IV

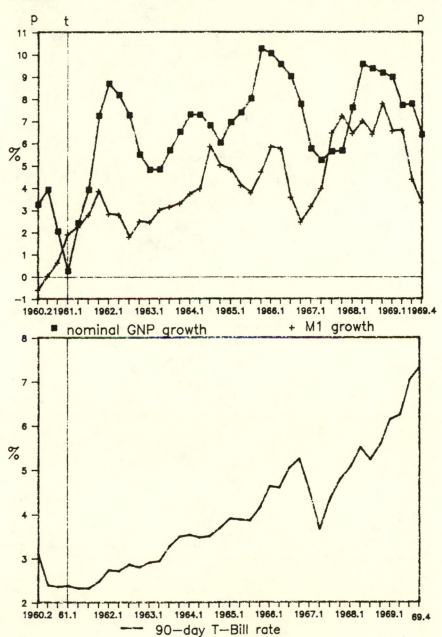

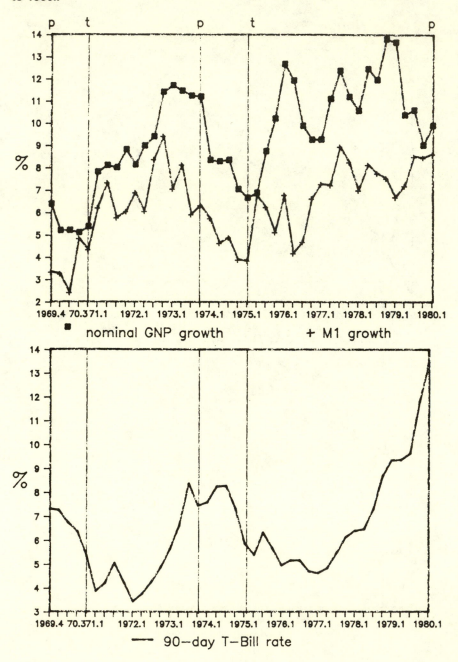

nominal GNP growth   + M1 growth

—— 90-day T-Bill rate

Figure 5.6
Nominal GNP Growth, M1 Growth, and the 90-Day Treasury Bill Rate, 1980.I to 1986.IV

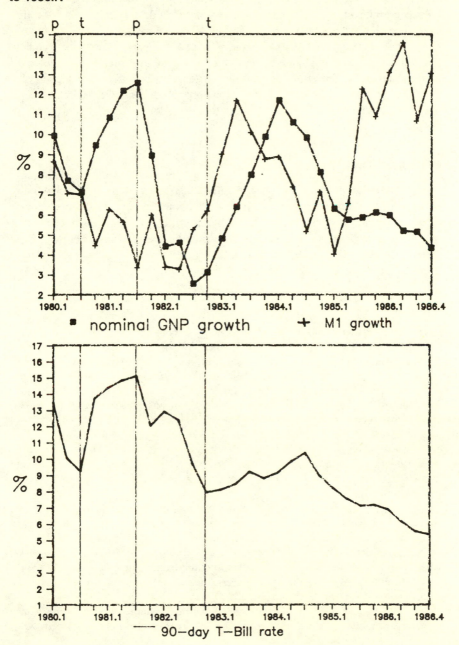

money growth over an almost two-year period, and the expansion that started in 1982.IV is preceded by rising M1 growth.

Many economists have seriously questioned monetarism because of this large divergence between money growth and nominal GNP growth in recent years.[15] Of special interest is the decline in velocity in 1982, 1983, 1985, and 1986 that weakened the M1-nominal GNP link. While monetarists predict that velocity falls when monetary growth rises rapidly as in 1985, their theory also predicts that velocity starts rising soon after. Notice that a similar picture emerges with interest rates as the Treasury Bill rate falls as monetary growth rises, but continues to fall long after the income and price expectations effect should have taken hold (based on past average behavior). This topic is addressed in greater detail in chapter 12.

CONCLUSION

The evidence considered here is generally consistent with monetarism. Money growth does tend to lead nominal GNP growth and, because prices are slow to adjust, generate business cycles. Even harsh critics of monetarism admit that monetary growth has at least exacerbated some business cycles or helped cause some of them (see chapters 10 and 11). Yet a debate continues over the relative importance of money in explaining business cycles.

NOTES

1. Other prominent monetarists include Henry Simons, Frank Knight, Jacob Viner, Phillip Cagan, Allan Meltzer, and Karl Brunner. Milton Friedman and Anna Schwartz are the most prominent due to the immense quantity of their writing in the field of monetary economics and the fact that their *Monetary History* (Friedman and Schwartz 1963a) is considered the empirical foundation of monetarism.

2. A basic reading list on monetarism includes Friedman and Schwartz (1963a, 1963b, 1982), several other papers reprinted in Friedman (1969), and Friedman's debate with his critics edited by R. J. Gordon (1974).

3. Discounting, when the Federal Reserve loans reserves to a bank, is another method of monetary control. Discounting used to be the primary tool of monetary control, but now it is minor. For several years, open market operations have been the Federal Reserve's primary tool of monetary control.

4. The case where V falls by the same proportion that M rises is the liquidity trap suggested by Keynes (1936) where the money demand schedule becomes perfectly interest rate elastic. I have never seen anyone argue that V might fall by more than M rises.

5. Permanent income can be viewed as the return on wealth in the form $Y^p = rW$, where Y^p is real permanent income, r is the return on wealth, and W is real wealth. Since it is difficult to measure both nonhuman and human wealth, Friedman uses his measure of permanent income in the money demand function.

6. This discussion ignores the ratio of human to nonhuman wealth in the money demand function because Friedman does not make clear its effect on money demand.

7. Interest rate determination in the loanable funds market contrasts to the Keynesian

model where the interest rate is determined in the money market which Keynes called the theory of liquidity preference.

8. The actual formula is $r = i + p^e + ip^e$. The last term, ip^e, has a very small numerical value so it is usually ignored which yields $r = i + p^e$.

9. Sometimes the real rate is calculated as $i = r - p$, where p is the actual inflation rate. This is not the true real rate that enters the consumption and investment functions because it measures the real rate after inflation has actually taken place. Since consumption and investment represent commitments to future activity, these decisions are based on the rate expected to prevail in the future which depends on the expected inflation rate.

10. This simple version of Fisher's equation of interest rates ignores income taxes. The effects of income taxes in Fisher's equation are discussed by Darby (1975).

11. This equation is derived from the result that the %Δ in (ab) = %Δ in a + %Δ in b.

12. The expected inflation rate cited is from the Livingston survey which asks individuals employed in business their expectation of the price level over the next six months. The responses are used to compute the expected inflation rate. An alternative explanation for the post–World War II expected deflation is that the depression was expected to return (see chapter 12).

13. Unstable monetary growth is discussed in more detail in chapter 12.

14. The formula for a four-quarter moving average, where the $t's$ are time subscripts, is

$$X_t = (x_t + x_{t-1} + x_{t-2} + x_{t-3})/4$$

For example, the M1 growth observation for 1960.II is

$$(MIG_{1960.II} + MIG_{1960.I} + MIG_{1959.IV} + MIG_{1959.III})/4$$

where *MIG* is the monetary growth rate in the designated quarter.

15. The weakening M1-nominal GNP relationship during the 1980s is discussed in more detail in chapter 12.

6 | The Rational Expectations Model

While economists have long known that expectations of future economic variables are important determinants of current economic behavior, explicit models of expectations formation are relatively new. One early attempt by Phillip Cagan (1956) incorporated adaptive expectations into the monetarist model which, as discussed in the previous chapter, results in the very long adjustment time back to the natural rate of output following a change in aggregate demand. In fact, it is this very long adjustment period in the monetarist model that some have found unrealistic.

A path-breaking article by John Muth (1961) developed the model of rational expectations. He was dissatisfied with existing models of expectation formation, including adaptive expectations, because he said they "bear [little] resemblance to the way the world works." As an alternative, Muth offered the rational expectations model which postulates that individuals base their expected future value of an economic variable on all currently available information, not just on past values of the variable itself. Muth originally applied his model to firms and specific markets, and it remained relatively obscure until the early 1970s when Robert Lucas (1972) applied rational expectations to the Friedman (1968) and Phelps (1970) natural rate hypothesis. In doing so, Lucas developed the rational expectations model of the macroeconomy and initiated a huge controversy over the model's usefulness that raged for about a decade. The debate quieted down in the early 1980s when the rational expectations model came to be viewed as a major contribution to macroeconomics, but not the complete explanation of the business cycle.

RATIONAL EXPECTATIONS

Rational expectations as formulated by Muth is based on two notions. First, the future expected value of an economic variable is based on all currently available information. This "information set" includes current and past values of all factors economic transactors believe influence the variable being forecast. Second, it assumes that economic transactors are aware of the economic relationships that exist—that is, they know the model that determines the value of the variable they are forecasting.

To illustrate rational expectations formation, suppose that individuals are interested in forecasting the future inflation rate. Furthermore, suppose that the model that determines the actual inflation rate is the equation of exchange. Individuals know that monetary growth in excess of the real output growth minus velocity growth must be reflected in the inflation rate. For the sake of simplicity, assume that velocity is constant so its growth rate is zero and that the long-term growth rate of real GNP is 3 percent. In this case, monetary growth in excess of 3 percent will be fully reflected in the inflation rate. According to the rational expectations hypothesis, if we observe an increase in the monetary growth rate that we believe is permanent, then we immediately adjust our expectation of the inflation rate according to the equation of exchange. If we observe monetary growth rise from 3 percent to 5 percent and believe this increase to be permanent, then immediately our expected inflation rate rises from zero percent to 2 percent. In contrast, the adaptive expectations model assumes that the increase in monetary growth must raise the inflation rate before people expect the inflation rate to rise. The difference between the two models is that expectations are assumed to adjust much more rapidly in a world of rational expectations than with adaptive expectations.

The rational expectations hypothesis does not claim that expectations are always correct. In the example just described it is possible that the change in monetary growth may not be observed by the public, that velocity may unexpectedly change, or that technological factors may alter output growth. In these cases, once the public realized what happened, they would adjust their expectations rationally as the new information became available.

RATIONAL EXPECTATIONS AND OUTPUT

The rational expectations macromodel is quite similar to the monetarist model in that both accept the natural rate hypothesis and assume that wages and prices are flexible. As we learned in chapter 5, the natural rate hypothesis holds that in the long run unemployment and real output return to their natural, or full employment, rates. The vast majority of economists now accept this proposition but disagree about how the economy moves from one long-run equilibrium to another and how quickly this adjustment occurs. The monetarist model postulates that the adjustment from one long-run equilibrium to another is quite slow because expectations are formed adaptively. The rational expectations model suggests a much faster speed of adjustment because expectations are formed rationally.

Lucas' rational expectations macromodel starts at the micro level by considering the problem facing an individual "worker-producer" who operates in a competitive environment. The problem this individual faces is that he or she can closely observe the price of the product he or she produces (the ''local price'') but not the aggregate price level (the ''global price''). In other words, the worker-producer has very accurate, up-to-date information about the price of his or her own product but is not as certain about the aggregate price level.

In many ways, this is a reasonable abstraction. A typical individual may have a good idea about demand conditions for the product he or she produces by regularly monitoring sales figures and price trends. Individuals would be quite interested in these numbers because, after all, their major source of income is the return on their labor from producing a particular good or service. Firms also are very interested in price and output conditions for their products as well as the inputs they purchase on a fairly regular basis. At the same time, individuals and firms may not be as aware of aggregate price trends. While households purchase some goods and services on a regular basis such as food, beverages, and gasoline, and firms buy labor, electricity, and raw materials regularly, there are many goods and services that are purchased only occasionally, such as houses, autos, and appliances by households, and structures and equipment by firms.

Suppose that these individuals and firms suddenly observe an increase in the price of the product they produce. They are interested in discerning if this price increase is due to an increase in aggregate demand or is specific to their product. If the price increase is due to an overall increase in aggregate demand, then in real terms nothing has changed; for the workers, nominal wages and prices are both rising at the same rate. Therefore, real wages are constant, and there is no incentive for workers to increase their quantity of labor supplied. For the firm, the price of its output is rising, but so are the prices of all of the inputs it purchases. Firms have no incentive to increase output because their marginal cost and demand schedules have both shifted up by equal amounts so they continue to produce the same quantity at a higher price.

Suppose instead that the increase in prices was specific to a particular product, perhaps caused by an increase in tastes for the product that raises its relative price. In this case there is an incentive to raise output because the demand schedule for the product has increased while the marginal cost schedule has not. The firm is motivated to produce more output at a higher profit per unit. Workers are also willing to increase their quantity of labor supplied because their real wage has increased; firms are willing to pay them higher nominal wages because the value of their marginal product has been raised by the amount of the increase in the product price. Since the aggregate price level has not risen, the real wage rate rises. As a result, the opportunity cost of leisure rises and the workers are willing to supply more hours.

Therefore, the crucial issue in the rational expectations macromodel is how individuals and firms interpret price changes. On the one hand, if a change in prices is viewed as solely due to a change in aggregate demand, then firms do not change output and workers keep their hours constant because all nominal values rise in equal proportion and all real values are unchanged. In this case, the economy moves along the long-run aggregate supply schedule, and output remains at the natural rate. On the other hand, if the price change is viewed as solely specific to individual products, then firms do change output, and workers, believing that their real wages have changed, are willing to alter their hours. This case refers to a movement along an upward sloping short-run aggregate supply schedule.

Therefore, the rational expectations macromodel postulates a positive relationship between prices and output, but it is only a relationship between unexpected changes in prices and output. Changes in aggregate demand that are fully anticipated cause price changes that are universally viewed as global, and output does not change. However, changes in aggregate demand that are not anticipated cause changes in prices that are viewed as local which causes output to fluctuate. This relationship between unexpected price changes and output is summarized at the aggregate level with the "Lucas type" output equation:

$$Y_t - Y_{nt} = \alpha(P_t - P_t^e) + u_t$$

where Y is real output, Y_n is natural real output, P is the actual price level, P^e is the rationally expected price level, u is a random error term picking up shocks to aggregate supply, and the subscripted t's represent the time period.[1] The coefficient α measures the responsiveness of output to mistakes in forecasting prices. This equation tells us that deviations in real output from the natural rate are caused by either mistakes in forecasting prices or random shocks to aggregate supply. There is no relationship between prices and output in the long run because the natural rate hypothesis assumes that in the long run expectations of the price level are correct.

An interesting and controversial application of the model is the policy neutrality result suggested by Sargent and Wallace (1975). They consider the case of a central bank that attempts to control aggregate demand in a systematic manner. If the monetary authority responds in a systematic way to variables like the unemployment rate, the inflation rate, and interest rates, then eventually people will realize it and incorporate this information into their rational expectation of the price level. Since observations of economic variables like unemployment, inflation, and interest rates are very easy to obtain, individuals will gather this data and, based on the systematic way the monetary authority reacts, predict how the monetary authority will respond. For example, suppose the public knew that whenever the interest rate rose by 1 percentage point the monetary authority reduces the monetary growth rate by 1 percentage point. If the public observed interest rates rise by 1 percentage point, they would rationally expect money growth, aggregate demand growth, and therefore the inflation rate to fall by 1 percentage point. In this case, the decline in the inflation rate would be universally viewed as global, and output would not deviate from the natural rate. In this way, systematic monetary policy designed to influence real output is doomed to fail because everyone anticipates the central bank's reaction.

THE RATIONAL EXPECTATIONS VERSION OF THE BUSINESS CYCLE

The rational expectations model suggests that business cycles are caused by unexpected changes in aggregate demand largely caused by changes in money. If the Federal Reserve increases the money supply and people don't realize it, then prices will begin to rise. Once the price level begins to rise, firms and workers are left to decide if this price rise is local or global. It seems likely that agents will interpret the price change to be some combination of the two, the relative proportions depending on the past average value and variance of the price level. If individuals live in a country with a long history of variable prices, then it is likely that the current price increase will be largely viewed as global. If they live in a country where prices have been very stable, then it is possible that the current price increase will be viewed as largely local.

Let us assume that the price increase is viewed as partly local and partly global. Since some of it is local, the discussion in the previous section suggests that firms will raise output and workers will supply more hours. But this increase in both output and the price level is only temporary because once the firms and workers realize that the price increase was caused by rising aggregate demand, they will adjust their expectations and view the entire price increase as global. At that point, firms adjust by returning output to the natural rate, and workers return to their original number of labor hours.

If aggregate demand declines and prices fall, the scenario works in reverse. Firms and workers observe declining prices and if part of this decline is viewed as local, firms reduce output because they think that their product price is falling more rapidly than their input costs. At the same time, workers believe that their real wages are falling and reduce their quantity of labor supplied. An interesting aspect of this process is that workers voluntarily reduce their hours of work because they believe that the opportunity cost of leisure has fallen. As a result, the unemployment that we associate with recessions is voluntary and is described as an "aggregate holiday." But eventually the firms and workers realize that the price decline is global; firms realize that their input costs are falling by the same proportion as their output prices, and workers come to believe that their nominal wages are falling by the same proportion as the general price level and that the opportunity cost of leisure has not, in fact, changed. Once everyone realizes that the price change is global, firms raise output back to the natural rate, and workers increase their hours to a level consistent with the natural rate of unemployment.

Therefore, according to the rational expectations model, business cycles are temporary deviations of output from the natural rate caused by unanticipated changes in aggregate demand. If aggregate demand unexpectedly rises, output rises above the natural rate but only temporarily because, once expectations adjust, output returns to its natural rate. If aggregate demand unexpectedly falls, a recession results as output declines below the natural rate. But once expectations adjust, a business expansion occurs as output rises back to the natural rate.

A question naturally arises here: Why are monetary-induced changes in aggregate demand ever unexpected if money supply data are so easy to obtain? There are two explanations. First, it is not obvious that the public acquires accurate up-to-date data on the money supply. Money supply figures are often revised several weeks after their initial appearance which suggests that measures of the money stock are somewhat imprecise. The second reason is that the public must distinguish between a permanent and temporary change in money. If we observe a one-week increase in the monetary growth rate, does this indicate a permanent change? Of course not. We must observe monetary figures over several weeks before we can identify trends. Therefore, if the Federal Reserve changes the monetary growth rate and intends to pursue this policy for the foreseeable future, the public has to observe the raw numbers for several periods before they believe the change to be permanent. During that time, the public would be unable to discern if price changes were caused by changes in aggregate demand or local factors, and the monetary policy would affect output.

It should now be clear why the model is so controversial. The implications that rising unemployment during recessions is voluntary, that systematic monetary changes may not alter real output, that deviations of output from the natural rate are quite short, and that the public is busy checking on the values of key economic data all fly in the face of Keynesian economics. Later in this chapter we discuss why the rational expectations macromodel has fallen into disfavor, but first we explore the empirical evidence for the model.

EVIDENCE

The starting point for our investigation is the issue of whether or not individuals form their expectations rationally. If, in fact, individuals form their expectations of the price level (or any other variable) rationally, then forecasted values should possess three characteristics. The first is unbiasedness. On average, the error of the forecast should be zero (i.e., on average, forecasts should be correct). The second characteristic is that the forecast error cannot be improved upon by considering any information that is available at the time the forecast was made (i.e., forecasters should be efficiently using all information that is available at the time the forecast is made). Third, rational expectations implies that forecasting errors must be serially uncorrelated, which means that errors in one direction cannot persist through time. In other words, participants cannot overpredict or underpredict the variable they are forecasting for several consecutive periods. Instead, the forecast errors should be randomly positive or negative over time although the unbiasedness condition tells us that they must average zero.

To test if expectations are formed rationally, several economists have investigated survey data of expected prices to see if the rationality conditions are satisfied.[2] Survey data are generated by asking individuals what they expect the price level or inflation rate to be over a future period. Two commonly used series are checked for rationality: the Livingston survey where economists are asked what they think the price level will be in the future, and the Michigan survey where households are asked what they think the future inflation rate will be.

The evidence on rationality is best described as mixed. Several studies have rejected the rationality conditions for the Livingston data because the forecasts are biased and appear to be consistent with adaptive expectations formation.[3] In contrast, several studies (e.g., Bryan and Gavin 1986) have found that the Michigan data satisfy the conditions for rationality which leads to the interesting conclusion that households appear to form their forecasts more rationally than well-informed economists.

There are reasons, however, to discount the mixed results found in these studies. One reason is that there may be an aggregation problem in that the survey observations are the average of several responses, thus an observation way out of line with the others could distort the average. A second reason is that rejecting the assumptions of a theory does not necessarily invalidate the theory because the acid test is whether or not the model predicts actual outcomes. In other words, so what if forecasts are not formed rationally? The important issue is if the outcomes predicted by the rational expectations macromodel do, in fact, occur.[4]

This last point refers us to studies that test the predicted outcomes of the theory. One line of research that tends to support the model is Lucas' (1973) study that compares output deviations across countries. Remember that output deviates from the natural rate because individuals are unable to discern whether a price change is particular to their product or caused by a general inflation. As stated earlier, countries with long histories of both high and variable inflation should show a relatively large price response and small output response to a change in aggregate demand. Countries with histories of low and stable inflation should show a relatively small price response and large output response to a change in aggregate demand. Lucas compared countries with different degrees of aggregate demand and inflation variability—Argentina, Canada, West Germany, Italy, and the United States—and reported the following results with π being the short-run responsiveness of output to the growth in aggregate demand, $var(p)$ the variance of the inflation rate, and $var(AD)$ the variance of nominal aggregate demand.

	π	$var(p)$	$var(AD)$
Argentina	.011	.01998	.01555
Canada	.759	.00018	.00139

W. Germany	.820	.00026	.00073
Italy	.622	.00044	.00040
United States	.910	.00007	.00064

The evidence is convincingly in favor of the rational expectations model for Argentina and the United States. Argentina has had a much higher degree of variability of both aggregate demand and inflation than the United States. As the rational expectations model predicts, the responsiveness of output to aggregate demand in the United States is noticeably higher than in Argentina. Therefore, the short-run price response is lower in the United States than in Argentina. The evidence is not quite as convincing for the intermediate case of Italy. Italy experienced a lower degree of aggregate demand variability than either Canada or West Germany but has a lower short-run output response than either as well.

Sargent (1986) presents more evidence by considering the end of some European hyperinflations when the inflation rate was at incredible heights and then fell dramatically. In the context of the original Phillips curve, as the inflation rate gets higher and higher, unemployment should continue to fall. Conversely, when the inflation rate declines, unemployment should increase. In the expectations augmented version of the Phillips curve with adaptive expectations, a significant reduction in the inflation rate should cause falling output and rising unemployment for some time before expectations adjust and output and unemployment return to their natural rates. In contrast, the rational expectations version of the Phillips curve predicts that if the inflation rate declines and people expect this decline to occur, the short-run Phillips curve will shift to the left, and output and unemployment will remain at their natural rates.

One case Sargent considers is Germany after World War I. Ordered to pay huge reparations by the victors of the war, Germany essentially printed the money to pay them. As a result, the inflation rate grew by leaps and bounds, especially in 1923, and then ground to a halt in 1924. What the rational expectations macromodel predicts is very consistent with events in Germany:

	inflation rate	index of production
1921	155%	77
1922	7,488%	86
1923	$4.2 \times 10^{10}\%$	54
1924	12%	77

As we see, the hyperinflation was over in 1924, and output, instead of declining significantly, rose. According to the rational expectations macromodel, German citizens anticipated that the hyperinflation was going to cease and incorporated this into their expectations (i.e., the decline in the inflation rate was very widely interpreted as global).

Another case is Poland after World War I. Consider the behavior of inflation and unemployment in that country during the early 1920s:

	inflation rate	number of unemployed
1921	136%	98,000
1922	819%	116,255
1923	44,359%	86,003
1924	0.19%	127,936

Here, the evidence is not quite as convincing as in the case of Germany. The significant increase in inflation in 1922 is associated with an increase in the number of unemployed, and when the hyperinflation takes off in 1923, unemployment declines. The hyperinflation ends in 1924, and while the number of unemployed increases significantly in that year, it does not appear to be associated with a disastrous increase in unemployment predicted by the Phillips curve with backward looking expectations formation.[5]

Yet another line of empirical work that supports the rational expectations hypothesis is from Barro and Rush (1980). They specify an equation where money growth depends on variables the Federal Reserve considers when making monetary policy. This information set consists of lagged money growth, lagged unemployment, and a measure of government expenditures. The equation is estimated with post–World War II data, and the predicted values of money growth from the equation are designated as expected money growth—the idea being they could have been easily predicted given the information available at the time. In effect, Barro and Rush assume that individuals generate their expectation of money growth as if they are estimating equations of this sort. The authors then test if the expected money growth series helps explain deviations of the actual unemployment rate from the natural rate. They report that expected money growth does not influence deviations in the unemployment rate. Next, they generate an unexpected money growth series by subtracting expected money growth from the actual money growth. Barro and Rush find that this series does help explain unemployment deviations and therefore conclude that only unexpected money growth influences the unemployment gap as the rational expectations hypothesis predicts.

This is only a brief sketch of the empirical literature in support of the rational expectations version of the macromodel. A fair assessment is that the hypothesis does a reasonably good job of explaining extreme cases like hyperinflations and the difference between the United States and Argentina. However, an alternative set of empirical literature suggests that the rational expectations version of the macromodel does a poor job of predicting economic outcomes. Studies by Gordon

(1982), Mishkin (1983), and Hall and Fields (1987) generate series on expected changes in aggregate demand by estimating models where aggregate demand is based on variables that are easily available at the time of the forecast such as lagged money growth, interest rates, and unemployment. The predicted values of aggregate demand growth are designated as expected and are found to influence output deviations in the short run while the natural rate hypothesis holds in the long run. These studies generally conclude that an expected change in aggregate demand growth causes output to deviate from the natural rate for a period of about three to five years which seriously discredits the rational expectations macromodel. Mishkin (1983) reports this result while at the same time finds support for the hypothesis that expectations of aggregate demand changes are formed rationally.

The model was also discredited by events during the early years of the Reagan administration. When Reagan was elected President, he promised to pursue moderate rates of monetary growth in an effort to reduce the inflation rate. Here was a preannounced policy that perhaps should have been anticipated and, according to the rational expectations macromodel, should not have caused a recession. Of course, a recession did result, and right or wrong it posed serious questions about the hypothesis. The proponents were "embarrassed" (Sheffrin 1983, p. 181) by the episode, and critics considered it a serious blow to the model.

CONCLUSION

It would be wrong to state that the rational expectations revolution is over. Instead, it is important to make the distinction between the notion that expectations are formed rationally and the outcomes predicted by the rational expectations macromodel. On the one hand, rational expectations has replaced adaptive expectations as the accepted model of expectation formation. Thus, the rational expectations revolution has succeeded in the sense that many economists now believe that individuals form their expectations of future economic variables in a forward-looking, rational way. On the other hand, most economists have lost enthusiasm for the rational expectations version of the macroeconomy because of the empirical studies suggesting that expected changes in aggregate demand cause output to deviate from the natural rate for a period of a few years. The reason why expected changes in aggregate demand cause output deviations is open to debate. It may be because expectations are adaptive, as the monetarists claim, or that prices and wages are not flexible as the Keynesians assume (see chapter 7).

NOTES

1. The Lucas supply equation can also be written in terms of actual and expected inflation rates.

2. Studies that investigate the rationality of survey data include Noble and Fields (1982), Bryan and Gavin (1986), and Williams (1987).

3. Figlewski and Wachtel (1981) present evidence that the Livingston data are formed adaptively.

4. Perhaps the classic exposition of this methodological point is found in Friedman (1935).

5. Sargent (1986, p. 78) states, "Unemployment is not . . . anywhere nearly as bad as would be predicted by application of the same method of analysis that was used to fabricate the prediction for the contemporary United States that each percentage point reduction in inflation would require a reduction of $220 billion in real GNP."

7 | The New-Keynesian Model

By the late 1960s the fixed price Keynesian model was being seriously questioned, largely because three of the model's major features were found lacking. First was the assumption of fixed prices and wages. As inflation became an increasingly serious problem, the assumption was untenable. Second was the fact that the Keynesian model did not make a short-run–long-run distinction. Even when the model allowed prices to fluctuate, as it did in the context of the Phillips curve, the model implied that policy-induced expansions in aggregate demand could continuously stimulate real output in the long run—an idea discredited by the natural rate hypothesis. Third, the lack of emphasis on money as a source of aggregate demand instability was difficult to accept given the close relationship between money and nominal GNP throughout the 1950s and 1960s. So by the early 1970s the Keynesian model was falling by the wayside, and the natural rate–monetarist model was coming to the forefront to become the dominant model.

By the mid-1970s, however, monetarism began to show some cracks in its armor. One contributing factor to the model's decline was the 1974 recession. Caused in part by reduced monetary growth and rising food and oil prices, it demonstrated that factors other than money have a significant effect on output. A second problem was the monetarists' assumption of flexible prices. While few economists believe that prices are completely fixed, the assumption of completely flexible wages and prices that ensure equilibrium trading seemed too unbelievable for many. Finally, the most serious blow was the long decline in the velocity of money starting in 1982. Monetarism, with its predicted close relationship between monetary growth and nominal income growth assumes that velocity behaves in a predictable manner. The erratic behavior of velocity in the 1980s appeared to destroy the link between money and nominal income.

The rational expectations model was popular during the late 1970s. But as we learned in the previous chapter, empirical evidence does not support the model's macroeconomic predictions. The rational expectations model lost considerable support as a result.

While economists were questioning the monetarist and rational expectations models, Keynesian economists were busy modifying their old model so it could better explain modern events. The result, the new-Keynesian model, is very appealing because it incorporates elements of the old Keynesian, monetarist, and classical supply-side models. It predicts that unstable aggregate demand and supply cause business cycles, views both money and autonomous private spending as major contributors to aggregate demand instability, incorporates the natural rate hypothesis, and gives theoretical reasons for the existence of short-run wage and price inflexibilities. This new-Keynesian model may be the most widely accepted macroeconomic model at this time.

SOURCES OF SHORT-RUN WAGE AND PRICE INFLEXIBILITIES

The main complaint with the old-Keynesian model was the assumption of fixed wages and prices. The model never had a good explanation of why they might be fixed, and, more important, real world observations make it obvious that prices and wages change over time. Modern Keynesians have relaxed this old assumption by arguing that, in the short run, prices are neither fixed nor completely flexible, but instead less than perfectly flexible. Furthermore, in the long run, prices are assumed to be perfectly flexible. With respect to wages, modern Keynesians assume that nominal wages are very sticky—perhaps even fixed—in the short run and perfectly flexible in the long run. Given these assumptions, changes in aggregate demand cause output to deviate from the natural rate in the short run, but not in the long run because wage and price flexibility ensures that output returns to the natural rate.

If the Keynesians are correct that wages and prices are inflexible over a period as long as a few years, then output fluctuations caused by aggregate demand might be avoided if wages and prices were perfectly flexible. This raises an interesting question: If inflexible wages and prices are the reason why demand-induced recessions occur, then why does a system of inflexible wages and prices exist? The Keynesians respond that there are private incentives to having a system of inflexible wages and prices. In the short run, these private incentives cause rigidities that result in a macroeconomic externality in the form of demand-caused output fluctuations. Many of the new-Keynesian model's predictions depend on the existence of private incentives for wage and price rigidities.

The Existence of Listed Prices

Modern Keynesians argue that prices are not completely flexible in the short run because complete price flexibility requires that all prices be determined in auction settings where buyers and sellers negotiate prices. Keynesians argue that while some prices are determined in auction settings, most prices are not because there are economic incentives not to conduct auctions. As a result, our economy is characterized by listed prices where sellers post prices for particular goods and services and buyers either make the purchase at the listed price or choose not to without ever attempting to negotiate, or "haggle," over the price.

The pervasity of listed prices is evident when you consider the goods and services we buy. Ask yourself which ones have prices that are listed and normally not negotiated and which ones have prices that typically are negotiated with the seller? The vast majority of goods and services you buy have listed prices. You walk into a store or restaurant and pay the listed price without attempting to negotiate. If you consider the listed price too high, you choose not to buy the good or service instead of trying to talk the seller down. In these cases, the listed prices are fixed over the short run, although the duration of the short run can vary quite a bit. Some listed retail prices often change on a weekly or even daily basis such as prices of gasoline, fruits, and vegetables, while prices of other goods and services change infrequently, such as prices of books, haircuts, movie tickets, and prices listed in catalogs.

At the same time, a large number of prices, some listed, are regularly subject to negotiation between buyers and sellers. Examples include prices of real estate, new and used cars, appliances, stocks, and bonds. These prices are flexible because they are determined in an auction setting where prices respond quickly to supply and demand.

Why is our economy characterized by products with inflexible listed prices and by products with flexible prices determined in auction settings? The answer revolves around the characteristics of different goods and services which determine if their prices are listed and not typically negotiated, or normally subject to negotiation.[1] One important characteristic of goods and services is pervasive heterogeneity—in other words, we are faced with a vast array of different types and qualities of products. If we were negotiating prices for each individual product, it would take an incredible number of auctions. Since auctions take valuable time and space, we tend to avoid price negotiations unless the expected benefit (the expected price reduction) exceeds the expected cost (the time commitment).

The second characteristic is that some purchases require immediate physical contact between the buyer and seller. Examples include restaurant meals, movie tickets, and haircuts. Since the buyers' time is valuable and they must be present to make the purchase, time-consuming auctions typically do not take place. Note that some of the products that are auctioned, such as stocks and bonds, do not require the ultimate buyer to actually be there. Instead, we call stockbrokers to buy the stocks for us, and they send us the certificates in the mail. But appointing agents to purchase meals, haircuts, or attend movies for us is ridiculous because the ultimate consumers must be physically present.

The third characteristic of the things we buy is that most bear a price that is relatively small in proportion to our income. Why bother negotiating for a box of cereal, a tank of gasoline, or a six-pack of beer when the amount you save might be, perhaps, only 10 percent below list price? We're only talking about saving a few cents which is very small in relation to most incomes. This amount is very different from saving 10 percent on a house or a car, which is why prices of very expensive goods and services tend to be negotiated in an auction setting.

To see how these characteristics come into play, consider your weekly trip to the supermarket. You enter a store that has literally thousands of different products and even among specific types of products such as corn flakes, several different brands to choose from. While the total cost of your purchases at the supermarket is probably a significant proportion of your income, the price of no one individual product is. Furthermore, since this is your weekly food you're buying, you intend to consume it in the relatively near future so you want it now.

The reasons why supermarket food prices are not auctioned should be quite clear. The average grocery shopper probably spends at least an hour each week shopping, so the time involvement is not trivial. Consider the time spent if auctions or negotiations with the sellers were conducted for every individual type and brand of product sold in that store. Furthermore, the store itself would have to be enormous to hold all of the negotiators representing the sellers. Even though we might be able to save a small amount of money for every product we purchased, and perhaps make a substantial saving on our total grocery bill, the time involvement would be so large that it would not be worth it. We could send a representative to the supermarket to negotiate for us, but this is impractical because we would not expect another individual to know all about our tastes and make choices based on our own demand schedules. Furthermore, the cost of hiring an agent for such a time-consuming task as grocery shopping may well exceed the benefits.

This discussion explains at least two interesting phenomena. One is the dramatic increase in convenience stores over the past few decades. Almost everyone knows that convenience stores charge high prices. Yet convenience stores have been quite successful because customers know that they can make their purchases very quickly. This "quick purchase" feature has become increasingly important over time as our incomes have grown to make our time increasingly valuable. Our discussion also explains why price negotiation is more prevalent in less developed countries. In those countries individuals are poor; the value of their time is low. Therefore, it is in their interest to bargain over prices for a wide variety of products because the potential savings may be a significant proportion of their incomes.

Do Listed Prices Imply Price Inflexibility?

Now that we have established why listed prices are so prevalent, we address the next issue: Does the existence of listed prices necessarily imply price inflexibility? The answer is no according to the monetarists, yes according to the Keynesians. Monetarists point out that during hyperinflations prices are listed but change so frequently (more than once a day) that they are very flexible. Therefore, listed prices are not necessarily inflexible. Keynesians agree that flexible listed prices exist during hyperinflations, but argue that hyperinflations are rare, extreme cases. In the absence of hyperinflation they claim that there are several good reasons why listed prices and price inflexibilities go hand in hand.

According to some Keynesians, an important source of price inflexibilities is the existence of menu costs. This term, referring to restaurant menus, applies to situations where firms incur costs when changing prices. In the case of restaurants, since meal prices are printed on menus, changing prices involves printing a new set of menus. Since these printing costs may be significant, restaurants are reluctant to change prices unless faced with a significant change in demand. In other cases, the menu costs may be trivial: changing the price of lettuce at the supermarket requires changing the sign above the display, and changing the retail price of gasoline involves the simple task of altering the setting on the gasoline pumps. According to the menu cost argument, firms will not incur the cost of changing prices unless the increased revenue from doing so exceeds the cost of changing the prices. Therefore, firms faced with a small change in demand may not change their prices because of menu costs. This lack of price adjustment in the face of a small change in demand may cause a significant change in output (Mankiw 1985).

Another explanation for price stickiness is the notion that many firms routinely engage in markup pricing, basing their pricing decisions more on cost than demand considerations (Okun 1981). Consistent with the Keynesian belief that very few markets are perfectly competitive in the short run, markup pricing assumes that most firms are able to act as price setters in the short run. According to the advocates of markup pricing, firms set prices according to

$$P = (1 + Z)(C^w + C^m)$$

where P is the price charged by sellers, Z is the markup fraction, C^w is the average labor cost, and C^m is the average cost of materials. According to this equation, prices change if either average variable costs of labor or materials change, or if firms choose to change the markup fraction. According to the Keynesians, the markup fraction depends on demand conditions—during periods of rising demand, firms are more likely to raise the markup over cost, and conversely during periods of falling demand.

The main feature of markup pricing is the suggestion that if the markup fraction (Z) is constant, then firms routinely adjust prices to changes in costs. Markup pricing is attractive to firms because of its simplicity. It allows firms' top management to allocate pricing decisions to lower-level management by telling them to simply apply the formula and pass on cost changes in the form of price changes. Furthermore, this behavior allows businesses to be perceived as being fair because they can blame any price increases on costs and not give the impression that they are greedy and charging the highest prices the market will bear.

Another reason suggested by the Keynesians for the existence of price rigidities is that some prices are fixed by contracts. These price contracts include arrangements between firms and their suppliers specifying prices to be paid over the duration of the contract as well as prices of regulated goods such as public transportation and utilities. These prices are not responsive to changes in demand because in the case of contracts between firms and suppliers, the prices will not change until the contracts expire, and in the case of regulated goods, suppliers must undertake the time-consuming process of applying to regulatory agencies for rate changes.

Finally, Keynesians suggest that prices are inflexible because firms believe that customers dislike frequent price changes. Stable prices are assumed to be good for customer relations; therefore, in the short run, firms faced with changes in demand are more likely to hold the line on prices and allow quantities to adjust.

Gradual Price Adjustment

A significant body of empirical evidence (discussed later in this chapter) suggests that following an expected change in aggregate demand growth, it takes around three to five years for prices to fully adjust and output to return to the natural rate. The existence of price rigidities is not sufficient to explain this fact because price inflexibilities could be consistent with a much shorter adjustment time. For example, following an expected 10 percent increase in aggregate demand over and above trend growth, firms could wait some time because of factors that hinder price adjustment and then raise their prices by 10 percent all at once. However, this is not what we observe in actuality. Following expected changes in demand, prices change slowly over a period of years until they reach their new long-run level. However, we cannot provide a complete description of this phenomena until we have discussed nominal wage behavior.

Sources of Nominal Wage Inflexibilities

The Keynesians believe that nominal wages are quite inflexible in the short run, in many cases even fixed. As we already mentioned, since wage rigidities result in involuntary unemployment during recessions, there must be some private incentives to have wage rigidities or this system would not exist. In the labor market, the private incentives take the form of implicit and explicit labor contracts.

Keynesians argue that most workers are under some sort of explicit or implicit contract that determines their nominal wage rate for a given period of time. These contracts may be explicit as in the case of union contracts, or implicit as in the case of many private firms and governments that periodically review their employees' job performance. While these contracts exist in the short run, over long periods of time, labor contracts are renegotiated. Therefore, over a period of several years wages are completely flexible.

The union sector that works under explicit contracts accounts for only about 20 percent of the labor force, and the proportion has been declining for several years. These union wage contracts, however, influence wage rates in several nonunion industries as well. For example, in heavily unionized areas it is not uncommon for firms that hire nonunion labor to base wage rates on what union workers are receiving. If the union in the area negotiates a new contract, it influences wages of nonunion workers over the same period.

These union contracts are typically three years in length, tending to be this long for two reasons: the cost of negotiating them, and the fact that every time a contract comes up for renewal, there is a possibility of a strike. The negotiation costs arise because both the firms and workers involved in the negotiations carry on extensive research about wage rates in other industries, company profitability, costs of fringe benefits, and any other factors the parties think are relevant. The possibility of a strike is important because strikes are very costly to both workers and firms. Therefore, the contracts tend to cover periods of a few years because both parties wish to avoid costly negotiations and strikes as often as possible, but not too often because of the risk of changing economic conditions.

In the case of implicit labor contracts, although nonunion workers are not likely to strike, the costs of employee reviews and altering relative wage structures is important. Most workers under implicit contracts work with the understanding that their wages will be stable from one employee review to the next—a time frame ranging from six months to one year. Firms wish to avoid these reviews because they are costly, involve considerable paperwork and time expense by management, and cause inevitable conflicts with some employees who are disappointed with their evaluations or raises.

The determination of university faculty salaries illustrates the costs of employee review. Each spring, individual faculty present their cases to the university administration about their accomplishments that the faculty members secretly hope and dream will get them on the short list for a Nobel Prize. This process involves a significant time involvement as each faculty member presents a written report on all accomplishments during the academic year in classroom teaching, research projects, and service to the university and community. These annual reports are then reviewed by each department chair and dean of the school who then write a short report on each faculty member and make salary determinations for the upcoming year. Considerable time is spent on this by all parties involved, and some bruised egos inevitably result.

Many firms and governments conduct this costly, time-consuming employee review process in a similar manner.[2] It is because of the significant costs involved that these reviews are done only periodically. Between reviews, employee nominal wage rates are usually fixed. Therefore, the costly nature of changing wages rates under both implicit and explicit labor contracts is the basic reason why nominal wages are rigid in the short run.

A related issue is the question of why wage contracts are fixed in nominal as opposed to real terms. An alternative to fixed nominal wages is to provide cost of living adjustments (COLA) contracts where the nominal wage rate automatically adjusts to changes in the price level. In the United States, COLA contracts are fairly rare, and 100 percent COLAs, where nominal wages change by the full amount of a change in the price level, are almost nonexistent.

There are a number of reasons for the paucity of COLA contracts in the United States. One factor is that the United States has rarely been subjected to extremely high inflation over an extended period of time. In contrast to several South American countries where severe inflation has existed for decades and wages are fully indexed, the United States has not had this problem, and, as a result, workers have not demanded full COLA protection. Another reason is that full COLAs present a significant risk to firms. The risk is not from general demand-induced inflation that raises prices for all products in equal proportion because full COLAs would keep real wages constant and minimize fluctuations in employment and output. Instead, the risk occurs when demand is not rising equally in all industries. Suppose that demand in one industry is falling while general aggregate demand growth is raising the average price level. In the industry experiencing declining demand, output prices would fall, yet a COLA agreement would dictate that the firm raise its workers' nominal wages in response to the rise in the general price level. This real wage increase would further reduce profits of the firm facing declining demand and put the company into an even deeper hole. Yet another risk associated with COLAs is from general increases in input costs. If energy prices suddenly jumped and raised the aggregate price level, as occurred during the mid-1970s, then firms would be forced to raise nominal wages during a period of contraction. The resulting nominal wage increase would be very counterproductive, causing still further declines in employment and output.

THE BUSINESS CYCLE IN THE NEW-KEYNESIAN MODEL

One of the new-Keynesian model's major contributions is the prediction that unstable aggregate demand and supply are important determinants of the business cycle. Aggregate demand instability causes business cycles because wages and prices are assumed to be less than perfectly flexible in the short run. Aggregate supply effects cause business cycles for the same reasons that the classical model suggests: real changes in the labor market and/or the production function alter the quantity of output firms are willing to produce at a given price level.

Aggregate Demand

With respect to aggregate demand instability, the new-Keynesian model is very similar to the old-Keynesian model. Both view erratic private expectations of consumption and investment spending as major sources of aggregate demand instability. New-Keynesians also stress unstable money demand and, in a major break from the old version, monetary instability to be additional sources of economic instability.

The new-Keynesian model's predictions following changes in aggregate demand are very similar to those of the monetarist model, although for different reasons. If the economy experiences an increase in aggregate demand, the initial response will be an increase in both prices and output. The increase in demand, even if it is expected, causes prices to rise but only modestly relative to the change in demand because Keynesians argue that private incentives such as menu costs and markup pricing keep prices from being completely flexible in the short run. With the markup pricing, prices rise in the short run by the full amount of the change in aggregate demand only if costs also rise by the full amount of the change in aggregate demand. But Keynesians claim that short-run coBinsensitive to demand changes.

Rigid short-run nominal wages are the major reason why costs are insensitive to changes in demand. Labor costs average around 75 percent to the total cost of producing output. The existence of implicit and explicit labor contracts makes wages very inflexible in the short run. Therefore, a large proportion of business costs are unresponsive to changes in demand.

The second reason for slow cost adjustment is the existence of price contracts between firms and their suppliers. Firms buy some inputs from suppliers under specified contracts that state the prices. Following an increase in demand, firms place more orders from their suppliers who are bound to provide the inputs at the specified contract prices. Therefore, input prices agreed to in contracts are inflexible until the contracts come up for renewal.

The third reason for slow cost adjustment is firms' practice of FIFO (first in, first out) cost accounting, basing accounting costs on historical costs as opposed to replacement costs. With FIFO accounting, a change in demand that affects current costs will not influence historical costs by an equal proportion. Therefore, perceived costs will not change by the full amount of the change in demand.

Therefore, because costs, especially labor costs, are slow to adjust, an increase in aggregate demand causes prices to rise in the short run, but not by the full amount of the increase in demand. The increase in the price level drives down real wages which allows firms to employ more labor and produce more output. Therefore, both prices and output rise as the economy moves along an upward sloping short-run aggregate supply schedule.

The predicted pattern of price adjustment following the change in aggregate demand is gradual, slowly rising over a period of years to the final long-run level. As mentioned earlier, price and wage rigidities are not necessarily consistent with the gradual adjustment of prices because prices and wages could adjust all at once some time after the change in demand. But in fact we observe prices and wages adjusting slowly over a period of several years. According to the Keynesians this price adjustment pattern emerges because price contracts between firms and their suppliers and wage contracts tend to be staggered (i.e., all contracts do not expire at the same time). Keynesians argue that staggered wage contracts are an especially important source of gradual price adjustment. To understand why, consider the case of explicit union wage contracts which tend to be three years in duration. In the same period as the change in aggregate demand, wages are influenced only for workers whose contracts expire that period. The following year when the next three-year contracts are renegotiated, wages for workers whose contracts expire that year will be influenced, and the same process will occur the following year when yet another group of three-year contracts are negotiated. In this way, it will take at least three years for wages and, therefore, prices to fully adjust to the change in aggregate demand.

The new-Keynesian model assumes that in the long run all contracts can be renegotiated, and, therefore, wages and prices are perfectly flexible. Over time, all price contracts between firms and their suppliers and wage contracts between workers and employers are renegotiated. Thus, in the long run all contracts fully reflect supply and demand conditions. Furthermore, the other factor hindering price adjustment, FIFO accounting, is not as important in the long run because over time as prices rise, most business equipment and structures eventually get replaced, thus historical costs tend to move closer to replacement costs. Perfectly flexible wages and prices in the long run ensure that prices and wages fully reflect changes in aggregate demand and that output returns to the natural rate.

Supply Shocks

From the 1930s to the mid-1970s, macroeconomics focused almost exclusively on aggregate demand instability. The 1973–1975 recession, caused in part by rising food and oil prices, was an important event because it led macroeconomists to consider changes in aggregate supply as an important cause of business cycles. The new-Keynesian model has been a leader in incorporating supply-side effects in macroeconomic modeling. Our discussion here on this aspect of the model is relatively brief because this topic is discussed at length in the next chapter in the context of the real business cycle model.

Supply shocks are events that cause firms in the aggregate to change the amount of output they are willing to produce at a given price level. Examples include changes in relative input costs, changes in the level of unionization that lead to changes in the aggregate wage rate, and the application of new technologies into the production process. Supply shocks can be positive or negative. The outstanding example of a negative supply shock is the rise in the relative prices of food and oil during the mid-1970s, and an example of a positive supply shock is the rapid pace of advancements in computer technology during the 1980s.

A negative supply shock such as the rise in oil and food prices raises the marginal costs of production for virtually all firms because agricultural and petroleum products are important inputs in so many production processes. Rising input prices affect firms that use these inputs by shifting their marginal cost schedules to the left. In the aggregate, the short- and long-run aggregate supply schedules shift to the left, causing less output to be produced at existing prices. Assuming constant aggregate demand growth, the negative supply shock causes a reduction in output growth, or even a recession, along with a higher inflation rate.

Because nominal wages are assumed to be sticky, the rise in prices lowers real wages. Labor is placed in a quandary; their real wages have declined, yet if they demand higher nominal wages, further reductions in output and rises in prices would occur. Instead, labor must receive lower real returns for output to return to the full employment level. Incidentally, this example points out the dangers of 100 percent COLA contracts. Workers fully protected from inflation by COLAs would automatically have their real wages maintained in the event of a negative supply shock. If nominal wages rise by the full amount of the price increase, further unemployment would occur in the industries with COLAs.

A positive supply shock such as the aging of the baby boomers into highly productive workers shifts the short- and long-run aggregate supply schedules to the right. Wages rise and, for a given level of aggregate demand growth, more rapid economic growth and lower inflation result.

EVIDENCE

The new-Keynesian predictions we examine here are price and wage inflexibility, and the existence of gradual price adjustment following expected changes in aggregate demand. We do not discuss the evidence on nominal wage inflexibilities here because there is actually very little argument about nominal wages—a large number of economists agree that nominal wages are inflexible over periods that may be several months long. The evidence on supply shocks is discussed in the next chapter.

Cecchetti (1986) conducted an excellent study of price rigidity at the microeconomic level by investigating the pricing behavior of thirty-eight magazines from 1953 to 1979. He postulates that the prices of magazines at the newsstand are relatively sticky because the market is monopolistically competitive. Each specific magazine has some degree of monopoly power due to subject coverage and consumer loyalty, but at the same time close substitutes for most magazines exist. In other words, the demand schedule facing each magazine publisher is very price elastic; as a result, each publisher may be reluctant to raise the price of its magazine because they might be the first to do so and lose a large quantity of sales.

Cecchetti reports that prices did change very infrequently—only about once every four years. Furthermore, he finds that publishers allowed their magazine prices to erode by about 25 percent in real terms before raising their prices. He also mentions that the frequency of price changes increased during periods of high inflation, while at the same time the result that prices were changed when real prices had changed by 25 percent continued to hold. Cecchetti interprets his results as supporting the monopolistic competition model of price changes and argues that the pricing behavior he found in newsstand magazines may describe a large number of other markets in the economy.

Several economists, including prominent Keynesians, have interpreted Cecchetti's results as unsupportive of the menu cost argument of price stickiness.[3] They note that newsstand prices of magazines present a good illustration of a case where the cost of changing prices is really quite small—too small to explain the existence of sticky prices. The cost of changing magazine prices is trivial. It's a matter of simply changing the type for the next issue. Hence, the result that magazine publishers change their prices only about once every four years is cited as evidence that the menu cost argument is not an important part of price stickiness. Critics of the menu cost argument also note that prices appear to change much more quickly in response to changes in costs than to changes in demand—an asymmetry that is inconsistent with menu costs but consistent with markup pricing.

Perhaps the strongest evidence in favor of the new-Keynesian model comes from the studies of price adjustment following expected changes in aggregate demand (discussed in chapter 6). The new-Keynesian model argues that changes in aggregate demand, whether expected or unexpected, cause output deviations because of assumed wage and price rigidities. Several studies decompose aggregate demand growth into expected and unexpected components by predicting the growth of aggregate demand based on easily identifiable variables at the time of the forecast.[4] This exercise involves setting up an equation where aggregate demand growth depends on current and past period values of monetary growth, interest rates, unemployment rates, and anything else that might influence the current period level of aggregate demand growth. The expected demand growth is generated by estimating the equation and using the predicted value of demand growth as a measure of expected demand growth. The difference between the actual value and the estimated value is the residual and is designated to be unexpected demand growth.

The next step in the process is to study the effects of expected and unexpected demand growth on output and prices. This exercise is carried out by specifying an equation where the inflation rate is a function of current and lagged expected and unexpected nominal aggregate demand growth, both measured net of trend output growth. The equations are estimated, and the lagged response of the inflation rate to changes in the two components of demand growth is studied. These studies generally find that even when demand growth is expected, prices do not respond quickly (i.e., changes in expected demand growth cause output to deviate from the natural rate), and it takes a few years for the inflation rate to fully adjust and output to return to the natural rate.

CONCLUSION

The new-Keynesian model is widely accepted for a number of reasons: it explains sources of wage and price inflexibilities, incorporates both supply-side and demand-side influences into one model, and has empirical support. The supply-side feature of the model is expanded upon in the real business cycle model discussed in the next chapter. That model argues that changes in aggregate supply are the major source of economic fluctuations.

NOTES

1. This discussion draws heavily from R. J. Gordon (1981).

2. While working for the U.S. State Department as a visiting economist, I served on a merit pay board. The government's procedure for reviewing employees is every bit as complicated and costly as university systems, perhaps even more so.

3. See Ball, Mankiw, and Romer (1988), especially the comments at the end of the article.

4. Studies reporting strong support for the hypothesis that prices adjust gradually following expected changes in aggregate demand include R. J. Gordon (1982), Mishkin (1983), and Hall and Fields (1987).

8 | Real Business Cycles

The classical economists' focus on supply-side effects as the major source of changes in aggregate economic activity dominated macroeconomics until the 1930s when Keynes' *General Theory* (Keynes 1936) changed macroeconomic thinking. Keynes focused attention on the role of aggregate demand in the business cycle. His revolution was successful because for the past fifty-plus years the major business cycle theories have been based on the instability of aggregate demand.

The modern demand-side theories (monetarist, rational expectations, and new-Keynesian) discussed in the preceding three chapters have two important features: the reversion of real GNP to its trend value, and the prediction that real wages are countercyclical following changes in aggregate demand. GNP reversion to trend is formalized in the widely accepted natural rate hypothesis which argues that in the long run output returns to the natural rate. Whenever output deviates from the natural rate, in the long run forces work to return output to its natural rate. These modern demand-side models also postulate that real wages are countercyclical over the business cycle (except in the case of the new-Keynesian model following supply shocks), because of incorrect price expectations by labor suppliers (monetarist and rational expectations) or rigid nominal wages (new-Keynesian). Although a thorough discussion of real wage behavior is postponed until chapter 12, let us note here that real wages tend to be procyclical or acyclical, not countercyclical. This inability to explain actual real wage behavior has been an especially thorny problem for modern theories discussing the effects of changes in aggregate demand.

Largely because of the appearance of supply shocks in the 1970s, some economists began to question these two basic results of demand-side models and during the early 1980s developed the real business cycle model as an alternative.[1] This new theory holds that the predominant cause of business cycles is not unstable aggregate demand causing output to fluctuate around a trend but, instead, changes in aggregate supply causing the trend line to shift up and down. In effect, this model is a throwback to the classical model by downplaying the role of aggregate demand and stressing the role of aggregate supply in the business cycle. It has the added feature of predicting procyclical real wages. While the number of adherents to this real business cycle theory is currently fairly small, the model has attracted an enormous amount of attention during a relatively short period of time.

SOURCES OF SUPPLY-SIDE DISTURBANCES

The real business cycle model postulates that exogenous shocks to aggregate supply are the major source of output fluctuations. These shocks can be caused by a wide array of factors including demographic changes, technology shocks, changes in relative input prices such as the oil price shocks of the 1970s, and changes in consumer preferences. The real business cycle model does not argue that aggregate demand is completely irrelevant but emphasizes instead the role of aggregate supply.

Supply-side effects can be represented with the following production function:

$$Y_t = f(L_t, K_t, z_t)$$

where Y is real GNP, f is the functional form, L is labor input, K is the capital stock, z is a term that picks up shocks to the production function, and the subscripted $t's$ represent the time period. The shock term is assumed to evolve according to the following process:

$$z_t = \alpha + z_{t-1} + e_t$$

where α is a constant term and e is a random error term with an expected value of zero. It is illustrative to rewrite the equation for the shock term as

$$\Delta z_t = \alpha + e_t \qquad \alpha > 0$$

which tells us that technology increases at a constant rate, α, plus any innovations in the random error term, e.

Random shocks occur in the economy that affect the production function itself (f) or the inputs into the production process (K and L). An example of a factor that would affect the form of the production function is an advancement in technology such as the introduction of computer microchips. While microchips would not affect production functions in all industries, they would be very beneficial to several, including publishing and financial services, by allowing information to be processed much more quickly and at greatly reduced cost. This would represent a positive shock to the economy because in the affected industries the existing stock of capital and labor could produce more output for a given price level.

Shocks to the inputs into the production function involve changes in the available quantities of labor or capital. Examples of factors influencing the quantity of labor resources include changes in marginal tax rates on labor income and demographic shifts. In fact, a current issue in economics is the potential effects of the 1960s and 1970s "baby-bust" on labor force growth in the late 1980s and 1990s. The quantity of capital available is affected by factors such as changes in the relative price of energy or new governmental regulations that affect which units of capital can be used in the economy—for example, increased restrictions on noise pollution that force airlines to take older jets out of service.

According to the real business cycle model, an economy is constantly receiving exogenous shocks to the production function. These might be major shocks like a plague or a war, but more likely they are a series of smaller shocks to labor, capital, and technology that have a positive trend value (α) plus a random component (e). The positive trend reflects the fact that, over time, positive influences on aggregate supply lead to economic growth. The random component provides the characteristic that, net of trend growth, these shocks are on average neither good nor bad for economic activity, but instead neutral.

The random nature of the shock term does not mean that shocks offset each other on a period-to-period basis. In other words, a positive shock is not necessarily followed by a negative shock followed by a positive shock; instead, shocks can accumulate in the sense that negative shocks can occur for several consecutive periods followed by consecutive positive shocks. In a probabilistic sense, this is the same as the random nature inherent in flipping a coin. We know that after a large number of flips half of the outcomes will be heads and the other half tails, but at the same time this does not mean that we obtain a sequence of head-tail-head-tail-head-tail. Instead we may obtain a random series that includes consecutive series of heads and then tails.

If consecutive shocks occur in the same direction, then output growth changes. These shocks are viewed as persisting over time because they are permanent for the foreseeable future. For example, the baby-bust decline in labor force growth will persist for at least a decade, and the introduction of computers has provided us with technology that we will be using for a great many years. When several of these negative shocks accumulate, output growth declines and a recession may result. On the other hand, if several positive shocks occur, then output grows more rapidly.

SUPPLY SHOCKS AND THE REAL BUSINESS CYCLE

One fact about aggregate economic behavior that the real business cycle model must be able to explain is the persistence of output changes. Persistence simply means that during expansion output tends to grow more rapidly than trend for several consecutive quarters. During growth recessions output grows more slowly than trend for several consecutive quarters, and during recession output falls for several consecutive quarters. In other words, we do not observe output, in levels or in growth rates, behaving in a purely random manner from quarter to quarter.

The real business cycle theory argues that changes in economic growth are caused by either a series of shocks in the same direction or a single significant random shock. Both cases are consistent with persistent changes in output. In the case of a series of shocks in the same direction, we can easily see how this causes persistent changes in output because the shocks put the same expansionary or contractionary pressure on output for several periods.

In the case of a single significant random shock, the source of output persistence may not be obvious. The result follows from the model's three important assumptions. First, after new capital goods are ordered, they take several periods to build.[2] Second, following changes in income, households gradually adjust their consumption patterns over time. In other words, if households experience a change in their real wage and income growth, they do not immediately alter their current consumption by the full amount that they eventually will over time. Instead, households spread out the changes over several periods. Finally, the model assumes that wages and prices are perfectly flexible which ensures that all trading takes place in equilibrium.

To describe the transmission of a single exogenous shock to changes in aggregate output, we begin with an economy in a steady state. Both the shock parameter and output are growing at the long-term economic growth rate of 3 percent, and there are no random shocks (i.e., $\alpha = 3\%$ and $e = 0$). Now suppose a positive shock occurs: high-speed assembly line robots are introduced. Initially, firms that can gain from this new technology, such as auto manufacturers and food processing firms, will demand these new capital goods from the firms that produce them. The increased demand for these new investment goods causes output of the robotics producers to rise as the industry starts to fill the new orders. During this period more labor is demanded, and, because wage rigidities are assumed not to exist, both employment and real wages rise. The shock that initially was important to only a subset of all industries begins to spread throughout the aggregate economy because employees of the robotics-producing firms and employees of firms that sell inputs to these manufacturers are earning higher real incomes that are partly spent on general consumption goods.

This one-time shock generates persistent changes in output because of the time-to-build feature of capital goods and the assumed consumption smoothing. The time-to-build feature is important because once the demand for the new capital goods rises, it takes several periods to fill the new orders, and during that time, workers continue to earn higher incomes. Households enjoying higher incomes spread their increased consumption over several periods which causes aggregate output and employment to grow more rapidly than trend for a number of periods.

Real wages are procyclical because the technology shock raises the marginal products of both labor and capital, and the resulting increase in labor demand raises both employment and real wages. If the shock had been negative, the demand for labor would have fallen, causing real wages and employment to decline. Thus, output and real wages move in the same direction. Also, all changes in employment are voluntary. Assuming flexible wages and prices, if the demand for labor falls, then real wages decline as well. As a result, the quantity of labor supplied declines—that is, fewer individuals offer their labor services because the opportunity cost of leisure has fallen.

It is important to realize that real wages are not restricted to be only procyclical. Real wages are countercyclical if the shock is to labor supply. A negative shock like the baby-bust will reduce labor supply growth and raise real wages, while a positive shock to labor supply such as increased immigration lowers real wages. Therefore, the real business cycle model allows countercyclical real wages, but this point is not emphasized. Instead, the model attempts to explain procyclical real wages because this is what we observe more often.

A random supply shock affects the money market because of the relationship between real GNP and the demand for real money balances. Rising income and employment cause the demand for money to rise as households demand more money for transactions purposes and as firms demand new loans to finance purchases of capital goods that incorporate the new technology. If either the Federal Reserve Bank is willing to create new money to meet the higher demand, or the interest elasticity of the money supply is greater than zero, more money is forthcoming. According to the real business cycle model, this is the source of the positive relationship between money and output—rising output growth raises the growth of the demand for money which causes an increase in the monetary growth rate. The causality here is completely different from the monetarist, rational expectations, and new-Keynesian models where changes in monetary growth may cause temporary changes in real GNP growth.

Over time, the effect of the shock works its way through the economy. Eventually, the capital incorporating the new technology is in place and the economy returns to a new steady state equilibrium with a 3 percent growth rate. But more importantly, the 3 percent growth rate takes place at a higher base level of output than was the case before the productivity shock occurred. In other words, once the new robots are in place and the adjustments are complete, the economy resumes its 3 percent growth but at a higher starting point because the robotic technology allows existing labor and capital to produce more output at a given price level.

Recessions, both growth recessions and declines in the level of real GNP, occur when the whole process works in reverse. A sequence of negative shocks such as a series of new government regulations that reduces the productive stock of capital cause output to grow slower than the trend rate, and are recessionary if output actually falls. The initial effect of a negative shock shows up in the industries forced to take capital out of service because of the new regulation. These firms reduce their demand for labor and produce less output. The shock spreads throughout the economy as workers with lower incomes reduce their consumption spending. Declining consumption combined with the decline in demand for productive inputs cause the negative shock to spread throughout the aggregate economy. The decline in income growth causes the growth of the demand for money to decline, and the rate of monetary growth falls, giving us a positive correlation between monetary growth and output growth. Finally, over time the effects of the shock work themselves out, and eventually the economy returns to the long-run growth rate of 3 percent but this time from a lower base.

The real business cycle model is best thought of as a business growth cycle model. While random aggregate supply shocks cause the trend line to shift up and down, in the long run the economy returns to its trend growth. Aggregate supply is the main driving force in the model, but aggregate demand is not totally irrelevant. In particular, changes in aggregate demand caused by real factors can cause output fluctuations, such as changes in real government spending because they alter the real interest rate and, therefore, affect the rate of capital accumulation or changes in tastes for consumption versus saving which influences the real interest rate.

One factor the model does not consider a cause of business cycles is money—an important determinant of output fluctuations in all modern demand-side theories. Money is neutral even in the short run. Changes in monetary growth only change the inflation rate. This denial of monetary influences on output is perhaps the most controversial aspect of the model and a major reason why many economists remain skeptical about the model's ability to predict events.

EVIDENCE

The empirical debate between the real business cycle economists and demand-side economists involves two issues. First, are changes in output permanent or temporary? On the one hand, traditional demand-side models stress that most changes in real GNP are temporary deviations from the natural rate. Unstable aggregate demand causes output to deviate from its natural rate, but, in the long run, wage and price flexibility cause real GNP to return to the natural rate. On the other hand, proponents of the real business cycle model argue that most output changes are permanent and just happen to give the appearance of being transitory business cycle fluctuations around trend.

The second empirical issue is whether or not changes in money cause changes in real GNP. Demand-side models, especially the monetarist and rational expectations versions, consider changes in money to be a very important cause of output fluctuations, and we saw some evidence of this relationship in chapter 5. However, the real business cycle model considers money irrelevant in determining real output. According to real business cycle economists, the positive correlation between monetary growth and output growth reflects causality from output to money, not from money to output.

These issues can only be settled empirically. With respect to the debate about whether output changes are permanent or transitory, economists study the time series properties of real GNP (and other aggregate measures of output). In the controversy over whether or not money causes output, we have already seen in chapter 5 why the monetarists believe money causes GNP. In this chapter we examine evidence that supports the contention that money does not cause output.

Changes in Real GNP: Permanent or Transitory?

This debate utilizes a methodology called time series analysis which involves specifying equations that characterize a variable's past history. Here we focus on real GNP. While several possible time series representations for real GNP exist, the debate focuses on two types: a trend reversion model which is consistent with natural rate demand-side theories and a random walk model that corresponds to the real business cycle theory.

We begin with a trend reversion model. For the moment, let us ignore deviations of output from the natural rate and model just the pattern of long-run natural real GNP. The natural rate hypothesis assumes that natural real GNP grows at a constant rate over time which can be represented by the following equation:

$$\ln Y_{n,t} = \ln Y_{n,o} + gT$$

where ln indicates natural logarithm, Y_n is natural real GNP, g is the trend rate of growth of natural real GNP, T is time, and the subscripted t represents the time period. The equation tells us that the log of natural real GNP at time t equals the log of natural real GNP at some starting point, time o, plus the trend growth. Natural logs are used because they have the property that if a variable has a constant growth rate, then changes in the variable's natural logarithm will be constant. This can be seen by taking the derivative of the equation with respect to time:

$$d \ln Y_n/d T = g$$

showing us that g, the coefficient on the time trend, is the constant long-term growth rate, and $ln Y_{n,o}$ is the initial starting value for the log of natural real GNP. For example if we start with 1950.I by assuming that actual real GNP was at the natural rate during that quarter, then $Y_{n,o}$ is the log of real GNP in 1950 which is about 7.0 (ln of 1264.6 billions of 1982$). Since 1950.I, real GNP has grown at an average rate of about 3.2 percent per year, or about .75 percent per quarter. In terms of the equation determining the natural rate of real GNP,

$$\ln Y_{n,t} = 7.000 + .0075 T$$

The time term (T) takes on a value of zero in 1950.I, 1 in 1950.II, 2 in 1950.III and so on. So the equation says that the log of real GNP in 1950.I is 7.00,

7.0075 in 1950.II, 7.0255 in 1950.III and so on, which can be extrapolated out to, say, 1980.I when the value would be 7.90 (7.0, the base in 1950.I, plus .0075 times 120 because 120 quarters would have passed). Graphically, the time trend is shown in the top half of Figure 8.1 as the dotted straight line that has a slope of .0075 per quarter.

In line with the natural rate hypothesis we model the pattern of actual GNP where it is allowed to deviate from the natural rate in the short run but restricted to equal the natural rate in the long run. An equation that describes this process is

$$\ln Y_t = \ln Y_{n,t} + \beta(\ln Y_{t-1} - \ln Y_{n,t-1}) + u_t$$

where Y is actual real GNP, β is a coefficient that lies between zero and 1, and u is a random shock term with a finite variance and an expected value of zero. The values of natural real GNP, Y_n, are determined according to the process

$$\ln Y_{n,t} = \ln Y_{n,o} + gT$$

The value of β, the coefficient on lagged output deviations, is important in the debate. The traditional trend reversion model claims that β lies between zero and 1 which ensures that whenever real GNP is not on the trend line the tendency is for output to return to the trend line. To see this, suppose that the log of real GNP was moving along the trend line and no shocks are hitting the economy (i.e., the error term equals zero for several consecutive periods). Then, perhaps because of an expansion in monetary growth, the error term takes a positive value consistent with real GNP being several billion dollars above long-term trend. The equation tells us that if u at time t jumps from zero to some positive value, then the log of real GNP at time t rises by that same amount above trend.

This is where the value of β becomes important. β represents the amount that lnY_t changes following a change in lnY_{t-1} which can be seen by taking the derivative of the trend reversion equation with respect to lnY_{t-1}:

$$d \ln Y_t/d \ln Y_{t-1} = \beta$$

Suppose that β equals 0.5. If the random shock raised real GNP $50 billion above trend, then next period the $50 billion corresponds to period $t-1$ and real GNP in period t will lie $25 billion (0.5 x $50 billion) above trend. The following period, real GNP will be $12.5 billion (0.5 x $25 billion) above trend, and so on. The essential point is that the effect of the shock dissipates over time—real GNP rises above the trend line but returns to trend over time. This is shown in the top half of Figure 8.1 where the solid line is the log of actual real GNP

Figure 8.1
Trend Reversion versus Random Walk

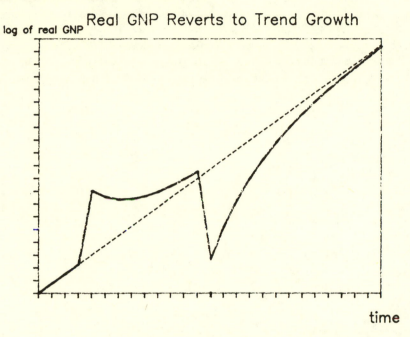

Real GNP Reverts to Trend Growth

log of real GNP

time

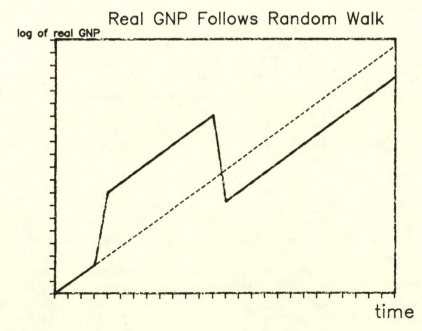

Real GNP Follows Random Walk

log of real GNP

time

being subjected to first a positive and then a negative shock. In both cases (after several periods have passed), real GNP reverts back to trend.[3]

Suppose, as the real business cycle model suggests, that the log of real GNP does not revert to a fixed trend line, but instead random shocks shift the trend line up and down, although the trend line may have the same slope as in the trend reversion case. This process predicted by the real business cycle model follows a random walk which can be shown to be a special case of the trend reversion model with β equal to 1. Let us write the trend reversion model again,

$$\ln Y_t = \ln Y_{n,t} + \beta (\ln Y_{t-1} - \ln Y_{n,t-1}) + u_t$$

and set β equal to 1,

$$\ln Y_t = \ln Y_{n,t} + \ln Y_{t-1} - \ln Y_{n,t-1} + u_t$$

and rearranging terms,

$$\ln Y_t - \ln Y_{t-1} = \ln Y_{n,t} - \ln Y_{n,t-1} + u_t$$

and noting that $\ln Y_{n,t} - \ln Y_{n,t-1}$ represents the long-run economic growth rate g,

$$\ln Y_t - \ln Y_{t-1} = g + u_t$$

This is the random walk model, a special case of the trend reversion model when β equals 1. It states that the change in the log of actual real GNP (the rate of change) equals a constant growth rate, g, plus a random shock term. The constant term g is called the drift in the series and in this case is the long-run growth rate of positive supply shocks. The random walk is demonstrated in the bottom half of Figure 8.1 where the series grows at rate g but shifts around depending on the value of the error term u. A positive shock to the economy raises the level of real GNP and shifts the trend line up by the amount of the shock. GNP continues on this new path until a new shock—in this example, negative—shifts the trend line down. The permanent nature of output changes results from the fact that random shocks change the long-run growth path of real GNP—for example, a positive shock shifts the trend line up, and the trend line stays there until another shock shifts it again. Since there is no reversion to any fixed trend line, output changes are said to be permanent instead of transitory.

According to advocates of the real business cycle model, the log of real GNP actually follows a random walk while giving the appearance of a business cycle with trend reversion. This is because of the random nature of the shocks. They are equally likely to be positive as negative (i.e., the trend line is equally as likely to shift up as down). The random behavior allows shocks to occur in the same direction over a number of consecutive periods, and because a single shock takes several periods to work its way through the economy, what we think is a business cycle with trend reversion is, in fact, the trend line randomly shifting up and down.[4]

One of the ways economists attempt to find out if the natural logarithm of real GNP follows a random walk is by estimating equations like

$$\ln Y_t = \alpha + \beta \ln Y_{t-1} + u_t$$

and testing if the coefficient β is significantly different from 1. Results show that you cannot reject the hypothesis that β equals 1 which supports the random walk version. This conclusion, however, has been criticized by Bennett Mc-Callum (1986) who points out that the random walk is true only when β exactly equals 1. If the true value of β is as close as 0.98, we would reject the random walk hypothesis in favor of the trend reversion model. McCallum's point is quite valid because estimated parameters, in this case β, have confidence intervals—we can say with some degree of probability that the true value's confidence interval includes unity. But it may also include 0.99, 0.98, and 0.97. Therefore, being unable to reject the real business cycle claim that β equals 1 does not necessarily mean that we can reject the trend reversion model with β slightly less than 1.[5] As a result, the empirical evidence is not conclusive about whether real GNP follows a random walk or a trend reversion model because neither claim can be rejected.[6]

Does Money Influence Output?

The real business cycle model argues that, even in the short run, money does not influence output. This contention is extremely controversial because it conflicts with modern demand-side theories that consider changes in money to be an important cause of business cycles. As is the case with the time series properties of real GNP, the evidence about money causing real GNP is somewhat inconclusive, although most economists continue to believe that monetary factors are an important determinant of short-run economic activity.

From the early 1970s until the early 1980s there was very little debate about the money-income issue because economists were generally convinced that changes in money cause changes in output. Two important events helped bring about this belief: the appearance of Friedman and Schwartz's book on monetary history, and results from time series causality tests. Friedman and Schwartz's *Monetary History of the United States* (1963a) argues that over the period 1867–1960, every major economic expansion was associated with a sustained rise in the monetary growth rate, and every contraction associated with a significant monetary contraction. This book, considered by many to be one of this century's great works in macroeconomics, convinced many people and helped bring monetarism to the forefront of macroeconomic thinking. The second important development was the Granger causality time series tests that attempted to determine causal relationships between money and income. Christopher Sims (1972) applied the Granger test to the causal relationship between money and nominal GNP which involves specifying two equations:

$$PY_t = c1 + \sum_{i=1}^{J}\beta_{1i}PY_{t-i} + \sum_{i=1}^{J}\beta_{2i}M_{t-i} + u_{1t}$$

$$M_t = c2 = \sum_{i=1}^{J}\beta_{3i}PY_{t-i} + \sum_{i=1}^{J}\beta_{4i}M_{t-i} + u_{2t}$$

where *PY* is nominal GNP, *M* is the nominal quantity of money, the *c's* are constant terms, the *u's* are error terms, and the subscripted values represent time periods. The number of lags of each variable (the value of *J*) can be varied; typically lags of four or eight quarters are used. The first equation specifies nominal GNP as a function of lagged nominal GNP and lagged money, while the second equation specifies nominal money balances to be a function of lagged nominal GNP and lagged nominal money balances. The idea is to determine if money causes income and if income causes money. In the first equation the lagged values of nominal GNP pick up the variability in nominal GNP that can be explained by its own past history, and any variability left over is unexplained. If lagged values of money are statistically significant in the equation, then money is explaining some of the remaining variability of nominal GNP. Therefore, money is said to "Granger cause" nominal GNP. Likewise for the second equation. If nominal GNP is statistically significant, then the conclusion is that nominal GNP causes money.

Sims' tests of the money-income relationship concluded that a two-way causality existed (i.e., money causes nominal income and nominal income causes money). While Sims had not shown that money caused real GNP, the results can be interpreted as such because monetarism argues that there is a strong causality between money and nominal GNP in both the short and long runs and between money and real GNP in the short run.

Following the appearance of Friedman and Schwartz's *Monetary History* and Sims' causality results, plus some time for it all to "soak in," by the early 1970s macroeconomists were in fairly wide agreement that money has a causal effect on output. That belief was questioned in the early 1980s when Sims (1980a, 1980b, 1982) expanded the Granger causality method by adding more causal variables. The expanded version of the Granger test is called a vector autoregression model, or VAR, and is based on the notion that because economists don't know much about the specific form of structural macroeconomic models, a reasonable alternative is to estimate small reduced form models in an effort to identify statistical relationships among economic aggregates. A VAR specifies each variable in the system as a function of its own past history and lagged values of the other variables in the system. Here is a vector autoregression model for output (Y), money (M), prices (P), and interest rates (r):

$$Y_t = c1 + \sum_{i=1}^{J}\beta_{1i}Y_{t-i} + \sum_{i=1}^{J}\beta_{2i}M_{t-i} + \sum_{i=1}^{J}\beta_{3i}P_{t-i} + \sum_{i=1}^{J}\beta_{4i}r_{t-i} + u_{1t}$$

$$M_t = c2 + \sum_{i=1}^{J}\beta_{5i}Y_{t-i} + \sum_{i=1}^{J}\beta_{6i}M_{t-i} + \sum_{i=1}^{J}\beta_{7i}P_{t-i} + \sum_{i=1}^{J}\beta_{8i}r_{t-i} + u_{2t}$$

$$P_t = c3 + \sum_{i=1}^{J}\beta_{9i}Y_{t-i} + \sum_{i=1}^{J}\beta_{10i}M_{t-i} + \sum_{i=1}^{J}\beta_{11i}P_{t-i} + \sum_{i=1}^{J}\beta_{12i}r_{t-i} + u_{3t}$$

$$r_t = c4 + \sum_{i=1}^{J}\beta_{13i}Y_{t-i} + \sum_{i=1}^{J}\beta_{14i}M_{t-i} + \sum_{i=1}^{J}\beta_{15i}P_{t-i} + \sum_{i=1}^{J}\beta_{16i}r_{t-i} + u_{4t}$$

The intuition behind the VAR system is very similar to that of the Granger causality test. The first equation in the system specifies real GNP as a function of lagged values of real GNP, money, prices, and interest rates. The lagged values of real GNP pick up what that variable's own past history can explain about its current value, and any variance left over is the component of real GNP that cannot be explained by its own past history. The VAR model attempts to determine if this unexplained portion can be explained by money, and/or prices, and/or interest rates. For example, if the results showed the interest rate variables to be statistically significant in the top equation, then the conclusion would be that interest rates have a causal influence on output. Similar logic applies to the other equations in the system. Also, several causality combinations are possible since each equation allows up to three causal factors to influence the variable on the left side of the equals sign.

A potential problem exists with both VAR and Granger tests. Suppose we estimated this system of equations and found out that interest rates influence output. This gives us two possible "truths," one being that interest rates do, in fact, influence output, and the other possibility being that something else besides interest rates influences output, but this other factor is correlated with interest rates so that estimation of this system gives the appearance that interest rates influence output.[7]

Sims estimated a system like the four variable version above and found that when interest rates are included in the output equation, interest rates influence real GNP, but money does not, which contradicted his earlier results (Sims 1972). Sims also reported that real GNP influences money. Furthermore, other researchers have found similar results using vector autoregression models (e.g., Litterman and Weiss 1985). This apparent conflict between the results of the two-variable Granger causality tests and multivariate VAR tests may indicate that either money does not influence output, or that money does but money is not significant in the equation because the interest rate variable may be picking up the effect if interest rates are correlated with money.

Sims' results are very controversial, so it is not surprising that they have been questioned. One notable challenge is by McCallum (1986) who argues that Sims' findings are predictable because he uses U.S. data that cover a period when the Federal Reserve was conducting monetary policy by targeting interest rates. Under interest rate targeting, when a monetary authority intends to reduce monetary growth, their policy variable is an interest rate. In the case of the Federal Reserve it is the Federal Funds rate. To reduce monetary growth, the Federal Reserve raises this rate which causes a movement along the money demand schedule that induces the public to hold less money. As the public reduces their quantity of money demanded, the quantity of money outstanding falls which lowers real GNP in the short run. Therefore, McCallum concludes that because the Federal Reserve uses interest rate targets to attempt monetary control, we find a correlation between interest rates and output when in fact the true relationship is between money and output.

So here again, as is the case with the random walk versus trend reversion models, the evidence conflicts. At this point macroeconomists don't really know what the truth is, but in the case of money and output, it appears that a significant majority of macroeconomists remain convinced that money does influence output in the short run.

CONCLUSIONS

The real business cycle model has the potential to stand macroeconomics on its head. If the model is correct that real shocks are the dominant cause of output changes, then the conventional wisdom of models stressing the role of aggregate demand is largely wrong, and the profession will have to rewrite most of the textbooks. However, the real business cycle model is currently viewed with doubt. While few economists would disagree that aggregate supply considerations are important, the denial of a role for money is too much for many economists to swallow. The debate continues and probably will for several more years.

The real business cycle model has forced macroeconomists to reconsider the role of aggregate supply, and this may be the model's significant contribution. It is possible that macroeconomics had swung too far toward demand-side theories and ignored supply considerations, although the new-Keynesian model explicitly incorporates aggregate supply considerations. Perhaps macroeconomics is moving toward a consensus that business cycles can be caused by either demand or supply instability. Unfortunately, at this time no one can identify the relative importance of the two.[8]

NOTES

1. Two articles originally set forth the real business cycle model: Kydland and Prescott (1982) and Long and Plosser (1983).

2. The time-to-build feature of capital goods was discussed in chapter 4.

3. β was set equal to 0.5 to obtain the simulated pattern in the trend reversion plot of Figure 8.1. Note that as β gets closer to 1, it takes longer real GNP to return to trend.

4. An interesting article by Mark Rush (1987) shows that a series generated from a random walk equation subjected to purely random shocks bears a very strong resemblance to the actual plot of the natural logarithm of real GNP.

5. McCallum (1986) also shows that if the true value of β is 0.98, then temporary changes in output are twenty-five times more important and permanent changes twenty-five times less important than when β equals 1.

6. Studies that examine the time series properties of aggregate output measures and find a large random walk component (and therefore conclude that output changes are largely permanent) include Beveridge and Nelson (1981), Nelson and Plosser (1982), and Campbell and Mankiw (1987). Studies that find a small random walk component and therefore conclude that output deviations are largely temporary include Watson (1986), P. Clark (1987), and Cochrane (1988).

7. For a discussion of the potential problems with causality tests, see Jacobs, Leamer, and Ward (1979).

8. Both demand- and supply-side economists have estimates of the importance of permanent versus transitory changes in output. The real business cycle economists estimate that about 75 percent of the variance in output is permanent while the demand-side economists estimate that about 90 percent of output variance is transitory. For a discussion of how these estimates are obtained, see Hall, Fields and Fields (1989).

9 | Important Features of Modern Models

Now that we have discussed the four main competing theories of the business cycle—monetarist, rational expectations, new-Keynesian, and real business cycle—we can compare and contrast them. Specifically, we are interested in examining how the models treat the main issues in the business cycle: the role of price and wage adjustment, the nature of cyclical unemployment, the relative roles of aggregate supply and aggregate demand in economic fluctuations, and the importance of aggregate demand's different components as sources of instability. This discussion sets the stage for chapters 10 and 11 where we describe twentieth-century business cycles in some detail. Our ultimate goal is to identify which features of the four models help explain specific recessions and expansions.

THE NATURE OF UNEMPLOYMENT

All four models offer different interpretations of the nature of recessionary unemployment. The natural rate monetarist, rational expectations, and new-Keynesian models recognize that unemployment associated with changes in aggregate demand represents lost output, but the models differ considerably on why more workers are unemployed during economic downturns. In the case of the monetarist and rational expectations models, cyclical unemployment is viewed as voluntary: individuals are unemployed because they misperceive real wage offers. In the monetarist model, workers have adaptive expectations so when the growth rates of prices and nominal wages fall, workers mistakenly interpret this as a decline in their real wages. They see nominal wages growing more slowly but don't realize that prices are rising more slowly as well. As a result, the perceived decline in real wages causes individuals to search for longer periods of time before they are offered their reservation wage and accept employment. As a result, unemployment exists because of mistaken expectations and is voluntary in the sense that it is frictional.

The rational expectations view is similar to the monetarist's in the sense that unemployment results from mistaken price expectations. When aggregate demand growth unexpectedly declines, downward pressure is placed on wage and price growth. Workers observe wage and price growth declining but believe that the decline is in part local as well as global. Because of this mistake, they perceive their real wages as falling and voluntarily take more leisure and less work; thus observed employment falls.

Keynesians adamantly dispute the idea that recessionary unemployment is voluntary. According to their model, the existence of rigid nominal wages means that when aggregate demand declines, the resulting decline in quantity of labor demand causes an excess supply of labor at the existing wage rate. This excess supply of labor represents involuntary unemployment where the number of unemployed individuals exceeds the number of job vacancies.

The real business cycle model differs from the natural rate models in that declines in output are not "lost." Since observed changes in output are caused by external shocks influencing aggregate supply, there is no foregone output associated with deviations from a fixed trend. Also, the model postulates that unemployment associated with recessions is voluntary, but not because of mistaken expectations. Instead, workers voluntarily take leisure when their real wage temporarily declines as a result of a negative productivity shock that reduces labor demand. Mistakes in price expectations are not important; instead, workers take more leisure when real wages fall because the opportunity cost of leisure has fallen.

All three models that predict voluntary recessionary unemployment (monetarist, rational expectations, and real business cycle) are open to the "aggregate holiday" charge—the idea that during severe recessions a large part of the labor force is voluntarily taking leave from work. Proponents of this notion argue that during recessions a large number of low-skill, low-wage jobs go unfilled. These are jobs that unemployed individuals are certainly qualified to fill. This description fits that of frictional unemployment: existing unemployed workers coexist with vacancies, and the unemployed possess the skills to fill those vacancies.

To some extent, existing empirical evidence seems to favor the Keynesian view that falling employment and rising unemployment associated with recessions is involuntary. This is because most of the observed U.S. cyclical unemployment is due to changes in the employment rate as opposed to the labor force participation rate. The labor force participation rate—the percentage of the working age population that is working or actively seeking work—measures labor supply and remains fairly steady during recessions. However, the employment rate, which is the proportion of the labor force that is actually working, measures labor demand and falls during recessions. Therefore, changes in labor demand, not supply, are associated with much of the change in employment over the business cycle. In other words, recessionary unemployment may be largely involuntary.

Proponents of voluntary cyclical unemployment argue that this conclusion, consistent with the Keynesian view, is based on misleading statistics. Specifically, they claim that the employment and unemployment statistics gathered by the U.S. Department of Labor count as unemployed and in the labor force those people who really are neither in the labor force nor unemployed. These individuals in question are not working, but are also not willing to accept existing vacancies they are qualified for at the going wage rate. However, these individuals would be willing to take their old job back at the previous wage rate, but that job is no longer available. Therefore, individuals who fit this description should not be counted as unemployed because they do not constitute excess supply of labor at existing wage rates, which is what we normally think of as unemployment.

To some extent the debate over whether cyclical unemployment is voluntary or involuntary boils down to a judgment call. Consider the following case and ask yourself if this person is voluntarily or involuntarily unemployed. Suppose that a well-paid stock-analyst in Manhattan is laid off during a recession. This individual would like to continue working at a similar job on Wall Street, but no vacancies exist because all of the brokerage houses are laying off workers. At the same time, many vacancies exist for hamburger fryers at fast-food restaurants that pay the minimum wage. The unemployed analyst is certainly capable of filling these vacancies, yet for a variety of reasons, perhaps including the belief that the brokerages will be hiring again soon, or a preference to sit at home rather than fry hamburgers for the minimum wage, the analyst chooses not to apply for (or accept) a job at the restaurant. Is the analyst voluntarily or involuntarily unemployed? Should the analyst even be counted in the labor force? It is really a matter of opinion. If you think that this individual is voluntarily unemployed or shouldn't even be counted in the labor force, then you agree with models that view cyclical unemployment as being voluntary. However, if you consider this person involuntarily unemployed, then you agree with the Keynesian model view of involuntary recessionary unemployment.

AGGREGATE PRICE ADJUSTMENT

An important issue in any model that considers unstable aggregate demand to be a source of output fluctuations is the speed of price adjustment. This was discussed in chapter 4 where we pointed out an important difference between the Keynesians and classicals: the speed of price adjustment. At one extreme, the classical model argues that prices are perfectly flexible, therefore changes in aggregate demand do not cause output to deviate from the full employment rate. At the other extreme, the early Keynesian model assumes fixed prices so that output changes by the full amount of a change in aggregate demand.

Modern models argue that in the short run prices are either flexible (monetarist, rational expectations, and real business cycle) or inflexible (new-Keynesian). The empirical evidence mentioned in chapter 7 on price flexibility suggests that prices adjust gradually: the time it takes following an expected change in aggregate demand growth to be fully reflected in the inflation rate is something like three to five years. While this evidence is entirely consistent with the new-Keynesian model that assumes short-run wage and price inflexibility, does this evidence necessarily contradict models that assume flexible prices?

The answer is no. Flexible prices can be consistent with gradual price adjustment. The existence of slow price adjustment following changes in aggregate demand is consistent with the monetarist and real business cycle models, the difference being why the models predict slow price adjustment. Monetarists believe that prices adjust slowly because adaptively formed price expectations adjust slowly. In the real business cycle model, the output persistence caused by time-to-build capital and consumers' spreading out changes in consumption spending over time could cause prices to take time to adjust to new long-run levels along with the economic growth rate. The evidence on gradual price adjustment does, however, cast serious doubt on the rational expectations model; in fact, these empirical studies have probably done more to discredit that model than anything else.

AGGREGATE DEMAND AND SUPPLY

One common feature of all four models is that unstable aggregate demand is a contributing factor to the business cycle although this point is not emphasized in the real business cycle model. Each model has its own story about which components of aggregate demand are the sources of instability: the monetarists argue that erratic monetary growth is the major source of aggregate demand instability; the rational expectations model argues that unexpected changes in money are important; the modern Keynesian model argues that changes in money supply, money demand, and private-sector expectations cause aggregate demand instability; and the real business cycle model claims that nonmonetary (real) factors influencing aggregate demand can cause output fluctuations.

Therefore, all four models indicate that aggregate demand can cause economic fluctuations but disagree about exactly which components of aggregate demand are the major cause of instability. In previous chapters we investigated the role of the different components by considering some empirical evidence and saw that the same macroeconomic data are not inconsistent with competing models. Therefore, while economists agree that aggregate demand is important, at this point we simply cannot conclude which component(s) of aggregate demand is (are) the major cause of business cycles.

What about aggregate supply? While all economists recognize that a major shock such as a war or massive immigration would influence output, only two of the models stress the role of supply shocks: the modern Keynesian and the real business cycle models. The monetarist and rational expectations models largely ignore supply considerations because aggregate demand instability is considered much more important. The new-Keynesian model stresses supply shock effects on the short- and long-run aggregate supply schedules, and the real business cycle model is a supply-side-dominated model that argues that shocks to aggregate supply are the predominant cause of business cycles. This raises the question: If aggregate supply considerations are important, how important are they? Unfortunately we cannot answer this question. Both aggregate demand and aggregate supply are factors, but the relative importance of the two is not clear at this time.

One way to distinguish business cycles caused from the demands versus supply-side is by studying the initial movement of output and inflation. Demand-side fluctuations are distinguished by output and prices initially moving in the same direction. Supply-side fluctuations can be recognized when output and inflation initially move in opposite directions. Keep this distinction in mind when we study historical episodes in the next two chapters.

WHAT CAUSES BUSINESS CYCLES?

Given the brief discussion in this chapter, it seems reasonable to assume that no one particular factor causes business cycles. Each of the four theories has something to offer to the explanation of business cycles. Therefore, we should not take these competing theories as being mutually exclusive; instead, consider information from each. If we take this approach, then the models seem in general agreement that prices adjust gradually, both aggregate demand and supply are important, and aggregate demand instability can come from any one of its components, including money. The debate over nature of cyclical unemployment may be largely a matter of judgment.

In the next chapter, we examine historical business cycles, address the issue of the relative importance of aggregate demand and supply, and look at the importance of individual components of aggregate demand. It appears that, over a long period, all of the factors considered important by the four competing models show up as causal factors.

10 | Historical Episodes before World War II

We now examine selected historical episodes to study past business cycles and evaluate the nature and causes of these economic fluctuations. We begin with the Panic of 1907, notable for its severity, brevity, and the fact that it provided the impetus for Congress to pass the Federal Reserve Act in 1913. This recession is considered among the five or six most severe since 1879 (Friedman and Schwartz 1963a, p. 157).

THE PANIC OF 1907

By all accounts, 1906 was a great year. It was the year of peak growth during the expansion that ran from August 1904 to May 1907. Real GNP in 1906 was up 11.6 percent over the 1905 level; the unemployment rate fell from 4.3 percent to 1.7 percent even as the economy absorbed over a million new immigrants; and (by modern standards) inflation was not especially serious as the GNP deflator rose 2.7 percent.

Throughout the expansion, and especially in 1906, economic growth was led by construction of new railroads, urban electric streetcars, and the electrical generating and transmission systems required to power the streetcars. The building of these transportation goods involved significant gains in output of steel for the rails and copper wiring for the electric train systems. In fact, it was during the early 1900s that copper became a very important metal as an input into the new electrical systems. Copper price and output data reflect this fact: from 1903 to 1906, production rose 30 percent and prices 60 percent, although part of the price rise has been attributed to an attempt to form a copper trust and monopolize the industry (Flamant and Singer-Kerel 1970, p. 34). Also, from 1902 to 1907, 950 new electrical power plants were built, enough to increase generating capacity by 129 percent. And from 1900 to 1910 the number of individuals classified as electricians went from 51,000 to 108,000 (U.S. Department of Commerce 1976).

The economy began to grow more slowly in early 1907, and it is not precisely clear why. One explanation revolves around the fact that prices of raw inputs, including copper, were rising rapidly enough to significantly reduce profits of the electrical streetcar lines. As a result, there was a severe enough decline in new orders for streetcars and the accompanying inputs that production of new streetcars essentially halted. The decline spread through the economy and lowered the economic growth rate which was accompanied by falls in common stock prices of 5.2 percent in the first quarter and 6.5 percent in the second quarter. In May 1907 the growth slowdown turned into a recession that was not severe— only a mild slump lasting through the summer and into early fall accompanied by a significant decline in copper prices. However, a sequence of events in October 1907 initiated a series of bank runs that turned the mild slump into a severe recession.

To understand how a mild recession could turn into an economic rout (something that would be repeated in 1929–1933), it is necessary to realize that in those days the public's confidence in the banking system was very fragile. Deposit insurance did not exist, and virtually everyone had at least a rudimentary understanding of the fractional reserve banking system. The public knew that if a large number of a bank's depositors lost confidence in a bank and began to withdraw their deposits, it was important for individual depositors to get to the bank very quickly to be one of the lucky ones to take home some of the fractional reserves. The unfortunate ones who arrived too late would often lose their entire deposits. The term *panic* is not an exaggeration when the incentives were for every depositor to withdraw his or her funds as quickly as possible during a crisis of confidence in banks.

Bank runs were fairly common in the United States prior to the advent of deposit insurance. The literature of the day suggests that it did not take much to start a bank run. A negative rumor about a particular bank, or even something as innocuous as a minor scuffle between two individuals that just happened to take place outside of a bank was enough to start a bank run.[1] If a lender of last resort had existed to provide funds to solvent banks experiencing runs, the problem probably would not have been as serious. Indeed, England had not experienced any major financial panics affecting general economic activity since 1866 because the Bank of England had adopted the role of lender of last resort (Grossman 1988). A central bank had not existed in the United States since the Second Bank of the United States. In the absence of a central bank the logical institution to serve in the role was the U.S. Treasury, but they had never done so in any systematic way. Therefore, the situation was ripe for banking panics to break out.

The October 1907 panic was precipitated by the actions of F. A. Heinze who had organized a pool of individuals that attempted to corner the shares of United Copper Company. For a brief time, the pool achieved its objective: on October

14, the price of a share of United Copper rose from 37 1/4 to 60. But unfortunately for Heinze, and most everyone else as it turned out, by October 16 the price of United Copper had fallen to $10/share. The next day, a firm controlled by Heinze's brother, who was also involved in the pool, failed (Mitchell 1941, p. 75).

F. A. Heinz was the president of the Mercantile National Bank of New York. When the public learned of his involvement in the failed copper pool, depositors of Mercantile National Bank, apparently suspecting Heinze of risking bank funds, began to withdraw their deposits. At the same time, depositors lost confidence in seven other New York banks controlled by Heinze's business associates and began withdrawing deposits from those banks. A developing crisis was temporarily averted when a clearinghouse, in which several banks had interest, pledged aid to those banks experiencing runs. The pledged aid included the stipulation that Heinze and his business associates sell their interests. This agreement was reached on Sunday, October 20, and the situation appeared to be under control.

On Monday, however, the situation deteriorated. The president of Knickerbocker Trust Company reportedly wanted to gain control of some of the banks previously controlled by Heinze and his associates. The depositors of Knickerbocker Trust were not pleased with this development, and the run on Knickerbocker started when it opened for business on Tuesday morning. Knickerbocker Trust lasted three hours that day and suspended operations after paying out around $8 million to depositors (Mitchell 1941, p. 75).

The panic spread quickly. Their confidence rattled, the public ran on several other large New York banks, and within a few days more had failed amid a wild scramble for cash. In an effort to stop the bank runs, the U.S. Treasury and a consortium headed by J. P. Morgan provided liquidity. The Treasury deposited $25 million with national banks, and the Morgan group added $25 million in reserves. This aid, however, did not stem the tide as the runs spread to rural banks—a situation made worse by the fact that the demand for currency was normally strong in the autumn as farmers sold their crops. New York banks began instituting payment restrictions on deposits, and the moratorium spread across the country, lasting until January 1908.

When the moratorium ended, the banking panic was over, but the damage to the overall economy had already been done. Since the public had lost confidence in the banking system, they chose to increase their holdings of currency and reduce their holdings of deposits. This behavior is important because when the public converts deposits into currency, the reserves in the banking system decline. With fractional reserve banking, the decline in reserves implies that banks must call in loans which lowers the money stock via the money multiplier. Furthermore, during panics banks would raise their reserves on their own accord to place themselves in a stronger position to handle any future bank runs. These two effects are demonstrated by the fact that from September 1907 to May 1908 the monetary base rose by 10 percent, yet the quantity of money fell by 5 percent

(Friedman and Schwartz 1963a, p. 158). Short-term interest rates jumped during the crisis but returned to pre-panic levels by January.[2]

The recession lasted a total of thirteen months with general economic activity bottoming out in June 1908. The recession is notable not only for its brevity but for its severity as well. Annual output in 1908 was 11 percent lower than in 1907, an extremely large decline for so short a period. While the implicit GNP deflator declined only 1 percent during the recession, monthly wholesale prices fell by about 5 percent (Friedman and Schwartz 1963a, p. 156). The simultaneous decline in inflation and output suggests that it was largely a demand-side recession.

.The Panic of 1907 had a lasting effect. It clearly demonstrated the need for a lender of last resort, an institution that would stand by to quickly lend reserves to financial institutions experiencing runs. While some individuals and organizations did serve this function in the Panic of 1907, they were ad hoc in the sense of putting together arrangements that were not part of their normal operating function. What was needed was an institution whose purpose was to serve as a lender of last resort, not only to serve the function but also to assure the public that bank runs need not cause the loss of their deposits. The Panic of 1907 was the impetus for Congress to pass the Federal Reserve Act in 1913, establishing the Federal Reserve Banks whose purpose was to be the lender of last resort.

THE "ROARING '20s," 1921–1929

The United States experienced four complete business cycles from the trough in June 1908 to the trough in July 1921. Perhaps most notable during that period is the severe recession from January 1920 to July 1921 that featured a collapse in prices: wholesale prices fell 56 percent from May 1920 to June 1921, three-quarters of which took place between August 1920 and February 1921 (Friedman and Schwartz 1963a, p. 232).

In the summer of 1921 the economy was poised for a wonderful decade near the end of which the United States seemed on the brink of genuine economic prosperity. The period from 1921 to 1929 was not, as some people think, one continual economic expansion. In fact it included two recessions with the first from May 1923 to July 1924 and the second from October 1926 to November 1927. But since both of those recessions were very mild, it is not wrong to think of the entire period from 1921 to 1929 as one of considerable prosperity as significant gains in output occurred with relatively stable prices. From the trough in 1921.III to the eventual peak in 1929.III, the average annual rate of real GNP growth was a remarkable 5.9 percent which includes the two minor recessions. The GNP deflator inflation rate averaged −0.5 percent annually, and, not surprisingly, nominal long-term interest rates trended down. According to one estimate, the actual unemployment rate was below the natural rate during six of the nine years from 1921 to 1929.[3]

In many ways, the 1920s was the decade of the urban middle-class working family. This was the time when significant numbers of urban working people acquired their own homes, electrical service in those homes, electrical home appliances, and automobiles. Potter (1974, p. 47) cites several examples of the gains in living standards including these: from 1920 to 1929 the number of registered automobiles went from 9 million to 23 million, electrical generation from 41 billion kilowatt hours to 97 billion kilowatt hours, the number of miles of surface roads almost doubled from 388,000 to 626,000, and 40 percent of U.S. households had radios by 1929.[4]

The economic expansion was, however, largely an urban phenomenon as the 1920s were generally years of despair on the farm. Farmers had done very well during the period including World War I as food prices more than doubled from 1914 and 1919. This prosperity bred optimism, and many farmers acquired more debt to purchase land and machinery. Unfortunately for many farmers, however, the 1921 collapse in farm prices caused serious problems as net farm income declined by almost half. It took ten years before the measure reached levels achieved in 1920. While farm prices and output did recover, farm income remained low because of the interest service on farmers' debt, no unexpected inflation to erode the real value of those debts, plus the fact that real estate taxes rose steadily throughout the decade, in part due to assessments for road paving (Hughes 1987, pp. 432–434). Many farmers sold out to developers of the new suburbs, and for many where this was not an option, bankruptcy and migration to the prosperous cities was the best available course of action.

This prosperous decade started with the expansion that ran from July 1921 to May 1923. Prior to the July 1921 trough the real money supply was rising because prices were falling faster than the nominal money supply was declining. Both long- and short-term interest rates declined sharply, and the expansion was under way by summer. Investment in both residential and nonresidential structures began to grow before the trough and then exploded once the expansion began. By early 1922 consumers joined in, acquiring new durable goods at rapid rates. Over the expansion, the average annual rates of growth were as follows: real GNP 14 percent, nonresidential structures 39 percent, producer durable equipment 31 percent, residential structures 19 percent, and consumer durables 18 percent. The economy was growing very rapidly, at a rate that simply could not be sustained over a prolonged period of time.

These growth rates point out the central feature of the 1920s prosperity: the boom was driven by production of consumer durables and investment goods, particularly business and residential structures. Consumer durables grew rapidly because of a number of factors such as pent up demand still remaining from World War I, significant gains in household income which must have been partly viewed as transitory, wide availability of a number of exciting products such as automobiles and electrical appliances, large numbers of young families, and the rapid spread of buying durables on time such that, by the late 1920s, 15 percent of all retail sales were on installment (Allen 1931, p. 140).

The enormous expansion of residential structures was also due to unsatisfied demand left over from World War I, rapid income growth, the high family formation rate and the corresponding large number of young families, migration from the farms to the cities, and migration to the new suburbs made so much easier by the automobile. In addition, the new housing market appeared to have a speculative element to it, especially from 1924 to 1927 when the ratio of residential construction to GNP was "by far the highest in the 20th century" (Gordon and Veitch 1986, p. 326).

The huge gains in producer equipment and structures have been widely discussed. One interesting hypothesis that is consistent with the real business cycle model holds that the boom in fixed business investment was caused by a "Schumpeter style" wave of innovations.[5] Several important innovations, developed prior to World War I, came to fruition during the 1920s—the two most important being a rugged and reliable automobile engine and improvements in the technique of mass production. The internal combustion engine was first introduced in the 1860s but was an unreliable machine until after World War I when advancements allowed these engines to perform for long durations without repairs. Mass production, an even older idea, was applied to automobile manufacturing by Henry Ford and quickly spread to other industries as well. The combination of mass production of automobiles and increased performance of their engines caused major changes in American lifestyles and significant gains in living standards.

Ford revolutionized the automobile industry in 1913–1914 by altering the method of mass production. Previously, auto workers moved parts to several different work stations, with an individual automobile being built at each station. Ford changed things around by assigning workers to spots along a mechanical conveyer that moved the unfinished automobiles along while workers attached parts. In other words, Ford changed from a system where the workers moved and the automobiles being assembled were stationary, to a system where the workers were stationary and the unfinished automobiles moved. This novel development allowed Ford Motor to achieve enormous gains in labor productivity— for example, labor required for chassis assembly was reduced from twelve manhours to two manhours. These huge gains in productivity and corresponding reductions in costs allowed Ford Motor to raise its workers' wages to $5 per day, a very high wage for assembly workers, to reduce the workday by one hour, and to lower the price of the Model T from $950 in 1908 to $290 by 1924 (Williamson 1951, p. 728). At $290 per auto, many middle-class working families were able to afford one.

The mass production technique was applied to several other industries as well, notably electrical appliances including radios, telephones, mechanical refrigerators, and washing machines, as well as the food and tobacco industries. The widespread application of mass production explains in large part the fact that from 1920 to 1929 total employment in manufacturing was roughly constant while output grew over 60 percent. The resulting cost reductions are a major reason why output gains were accompanied by stable or falling prices in many industries.[6]

This wave of innovations and the accompanying growth of output in these directly affected industries spread throughout the economy. In particular, it is difficult to overemphasize the importance of the increased production and use of motor vehicles. The ever-increasing numbers of cars, trucks, and buses on the roads required more gasoline, tires, roads, and service stations to serve the vehicle owners. Furthermore, the automobile allowed urbanites to move to the suburbs which stimulated construction of new homes and businesses outside of the central city. In this way, technological innovations raised output of a vast array of goods and services and helped spread general prosperity throughout urban America.

It is interesting to note that overly expansionary monetary and fiscal policies were not an important cause of output gains in the 1920s. Monetary growth remained relatively stable throughout the period at rates consistent with stable prices. In fact, Friedman and Schwartz (1963a) term the period the "high tide of the Federal Reserve," as the central bank was successfully able to control monetary growth and keep the economy from overexpanding at rates that would have caused accelerating inflation. With respect to fiscal policy, the level of real government purchases, which at the time constituted only 14 percent of GNP, grew at a 2.5 percent average annual rate from 1921.III to 1929.III—far less than the overall economic growth rate.

The central feature of the period from 1921 to 1929, then, was rapid economic growth not induced by overly expansionary monetary and fiscal policies. The fact that economic growth was significantly above the longer-run historical average while prices declined slightly suggests that the period was one of an economic expansion greatly aided by the supply side. The technological innovations developed earlier and the spread of mass production constituted a series of enormous positive supply shocks that allowed significant gains in living standards without inflation.

The two recessions during this period were quite mild. The first started in the spring of 1923 and lasted until July 1924 with output falling a total of 4.1 percent. Friedman and Schwartz (1963a) attribute this output decline to an attempt by the Federal Reserve, concerned by the continuing rapid pace of output gains, to keep the economy from overheating. The rate of monetary growth declined throughout much of 1923. Over the course of the recession, investment was the only component of aggregate demand to decline.

Monetary growth picked up again in early 1924, and an expansion was under way by summer. This expansion lasted more than two years and was vigorous, though not as strong as the previous one. Real GNP grew at an annual rate of 5.6 percent, once again led by investment spending, especially business equipment and residential structures which grew at rates of 12.9 and 15.3 percent, respectively. Consumer durables grew at a rate of 10.9 percent.

During this middle expansion, speculative excesses began to appear. In 1925 the hot item was Florida land. Florida was increasingly becoming a popular tourist spot; land there was viewed as a good investment. By 1925, Florida land had become so desirable as a capital gains investment that Northerners were paying exorbitant prices for land, often everglades wetland, they had never seen. In some cases buyers paid $20,000 per homebuilding lot several miles inland from Miami, and genuine oceanfront lots sold for up to $75,000 (Allen 1931, p. 231). Prices started to decline in early 1926, and the bubble burst when land prices collapsed following a severe hurricane in the autumn of 1926.

The Federal Reserve again moved to slow the expansion by keeping monetary growth low throughout 1926. The economy peaked in October 1926 and moved into another mild recession lasting until the end of 1927. Once again, investment was the laggard, but this time consumer durables fell slightly. Real GNP declined only 2 percent from peak to trough, and apparently most U.S. households never even knew a recession had occurred.

One contributing factor to this recession was the temporary closing of the Ford Motor assembly plant. Ford Motor had not altered the Model T since 1913 and was losing market share to competitors, most notably Chevrolet. Competitors offered several features not available on the Model T including a closed body that the Model T chassis was not strong enough to handle and a choice of colors. In spring 1927 Ford Motor stopped production, throwing thousands out of work, and began retooling to produce the Model A that would more effectively compete in the marketplace. In the fall of 1927 Ford rehired the auto workers and began production in the mammoth new Rouge River Complex in Dearborn, Michigan. The Model A appeared on showroom floors on December 2. As an indication of the public interest in the car, 1 million people reportedly mobbed Ford's New York headquarters to see the car, and police were needed to control crowds attempting to view the car in Kansas City and Cleveland (Allen 1931, p. 135).

The resumption of production by Ford Motor helped usher in the final expansion of the decade that lasted from the trough in November 1927 to the peak in August 1929. During this period the average annual rate of output growth was 6.9 percent with especially strong gains in industrial production. Once again spending on consumer durables was a major driving force, growing at an annual rate of 9.2 percent. Investment spending, however, was running out of steam as from the trough to the peak business structures were flat, and residential structures fell by around $3.5 billion in 1972 dollars. Only business equipment rose, at a 16 percent average annual rate. The other contributors to growth included consumer services and nondurables and government purchases which grew at average annual rates of 3.4 and 4.2 percent, respectively.

The economy continued to expand in 1929, and from the first to the second quarter real GNP grew at a 16 percent annual rate although almost a quarter of that gain was inventory investment. Overcapacity had developed in several industries including textiles, tires, and autos.[7] The auto market appeared to be oversold given existing prices and household incomes. The expansion slowed significantly in the third quarter when real GNP was up $2 billion (1972$), but inventories had been added at the rate of $12 billion (1972$). The economy peaked in August 1929.

It is impossible to discuss the latter stages of the decade without mentioning the behavior of stock prices. Equity values rose vigorously throughout much of the decade, and there were good fundamental reasons why: corporate profits were growing rapidly, and nominal interest rates were falling. In fact, few contemporary observers seemed concerned about the stock market until 1928 when the *New York Times* Industrial Average of 25 "good, sound stocks" rose 35 percent, followed by another 36 percent gain from January to August 1929 (Galbraith 1961). Many observers expressed concern over "speculative excess" in the stock market including the Federal Reserve which moved to slow the advance of stock prices by raising the discount rate three times during 1928 and in February 1929 warned banks not to issue loans for speculative purposes.

Despite the doomsday economic forecasters in the late 1920s (they are always around), the general consensus was that prosperity would continue, and this optimism was reflected in the stock market.[8] The 1928–1929 stock market advance occurred despite the fact that both short- and long-term interest rates had bottomed out in late 1927 and early 1928, respectively. In fact, by 1929, short-term rates had risen over 200 basis points above 1927 levels.

A debate continues to this day about the 1928–1929 rise in stock prices: Was it based on sound fundamentals or was it nothing more than a speculative bubble waiting to burst? Those claiming sound fundamentals were the cause note that dividends had grown along with stock prices to keep yields on stocks roughly in line with yields on government bonds. Therefore, stocks were earning about the same as the best available alternative asset (Hughes 1987, pp. 426–428).

Galbraith (1961) was among those who advocated the "bubble ready to burst" view. He argued that a large proportion of the rise in stock prices was generated with borrowed funds and therefore constituted a house of cards. One contributing factor was that many stock purchases were on margin—a system where brokers borrowed funds from banks and re-lent them to individuals to purchase stocks.[9] The Federal Reserve recognized this fact and made a series of moves which helped cause a decline in bank loans to brokers in 1928. However, nonbank corporations more than took up the slack by funneling excess cash to the brokerages so that by 1928 nonbanks accounted for over 60 percent of brokerages' funds. Thus, attempts by the Federal Reserve to slow speculation in the stock market were effectively bypassed by nonbank firms.

Galbraith discussed a second important source of the stock market increase: the investment trusts. These companies would issue both stocks and bonds to the public and use the proceeds to buy stocks in other companies, in many cases other investment trusts. During periods of rising stock prices, the values of the common shares of an investment trust rise faster than the overall market, and when overall stock prices fall, the common shares of investment trusts fall faster than the overall market. For example, suppose an investment trust was originally formed by issuing one-half debt and one-half equity. If the trust's asset value rises, this increase would show up only in the equity portion since the value of the debt remains the same. Therefore, the value of the investment trust's outstanding common stock rises proportionately more than the value of the trust's assets.

To illustrate this point, suppose that an investment trust were formed by selling $50 million of common stock and taking on $50 million of debt by issuing bonds. The trust would have $100 million to invest in the stock market. If stock prices rose 25 percent, then the assets of the investment trust have risen $25 million dollars. Since the value of the debt remains constant, the entire $25 million increase accrues to the equity holders. Thus, the value of the investment trust's outstanding stock, originally worth $50 million, would now be worth $75 million, a 50 percent gain.

According to Galbraith, the gains were further enhanced when investment trusts held shares in other investment trusts. In our example, if the shares in the investment trust were invested in shares of a similar investment trust, then the 25 percent gain in overall stock prices would raise the value of the first investment trust by $50 million and the second investment trust, which holds the first investment trust's stock as its assets, would rise in value by $100 million. If several investment trusts were holding the equity of each other, the gains during periods of rising stock prices could be mind boggling. According to Galbraith (1961, p. 61), "In 1929 the discovery of the wonders of geometric series struck Wall Street with a force comparable to the invention of the wheel. There was a rush to sponsor investment trusts which would sponsor investment trusts, which would, in turn, sponsor investment trusts." As long as stock prices were rising, the investment trusts worked the geometric miracles and helped move the market up. However, the numbers could work just as quickly in reverse, as occurred in the autumn of 1929.

THE GREAT DEPRESSION, 1929–1941

The period from 1929 to 1941, known as the Great Depression, probably led to more profound changes in macroeconomics than any other historical event in recent history. It was the impetus for Keynes to write *The General Theory* (Keynes 1936) which, as discussed in chapter 4, essentially marks the birth of modern macroeconomics. There Keynes argues that the massive unemployment and human misery associated with the 1930s demonstrated the need for stimulative monetary and fiscal policies to help return the economy to full employment. Keynes' ideas set off a debate over the desirability of macroeconomic fine tuning that exists to this day. Furthermore, his policy prescriptions were consistent with parts of the Roosevelt administration's New Deal legislation that were designed to stimulate aggregate demand and also led to a greatly expanded role for the federal government in the economy.

Economists are interested in the depression largely because of its severity and length. It includes two major recessions that were so severe the economy didn't recover in the sense of producing at the natural rate of output until 1941. The worst recession was the first one from August 1929 to March 1933, coined "The Great Contraction" by Friedman and Schwartz. It started out innocently enough: a mild recession characterized by declining expenditures on investment goods and consumer durables. By the time it was over, the United States had experienced three separate waves of bank runs, a 22 percentage point rise in the unemployment rate, and a 53 percent decline in nominal GNP which was associated with huge declines in both output and prices. The second recession that occurred in 1937–1938 was shorter and less severe, but the recovery that followed was weak until 1940.

Given the depression's severity and length, it is not surprising that economists have spent considerable resources trying to identify its causes. Originally, the prevailing opinion was that the Keynesian model provided the explanation: falling autonomous expenditures amplified by the spending multiplier caused the large declines in output. However, this view was later attacked by Friedman and Schwartz (1963a) who argue that the depression largely resulted from deflationary monetary policies conducted by the Federal Reserve. Still other explanations focused on international considerations, especially the adverse effects of the Smoot-Hawley Tariff passed in 1930 (Kindleberger 1973). Only in recent years has something of a consensus emerged that considers several factors important.

The Great Contraction, 1929–1933

The depression started from the economic peak in August 1929. At first the downturn was relatively mild as economic growth slowed during the second quarter and then turned negative in the third quarter when spending on investment goods and consumer durables flattened. The apparent causes of the initial reduction in output were a combination of overcapacity in several industries that led to declines in investment spending, and contractionary pressures from declining monetary growth as from 1928.III to 1929.III M2 rose by only 0.8 percent after growing in the 4 to 5 percent range from the start of 1927 to mid-1928.[10] Initially, no one seemed too concerned about the economic downturn because the previous two recessions had been relatively short and mild. There was no reason to expect the 1929 downturn to be different.

The situation grew more serious following the stock market crash in October. In early October stock prices were 15 percent below their peak in early September. Following a brief rally stock prices began to plummet and did so for nineteen days as prices fell 35 percent with the worst days being October 28 and 29 when prices declined 23 percent. Since much of the stock had been purchased on margin, with the stock as collateral on the brokers' loans, shareholders received margin calls from their brokers to put up more collateral or sell their stocks to raise cash. The resulting panic selling drove prices down rapidly, and the investment trusts worked their geometric magic in reverse.

There are at least three possible explanations for why the stock market crash exacerbated the recession. First, the decline in equity values (approximately $20 billion) reduced household wealth which is consistent with falling consumption expenditures. Second, the decline in stock prices reduced the value of existing capital relative to new capital goods to reduce the demand for new investment goods. Third, and perhaps most important, was the rise in household and business uncertainty caused by the crash. This increase in uncertainty, which Romer (1988) documents by citing forecasters of the day, is consistent with rising precautionary demand for money and further reductions in purchases of consumer goods, especially durables given households' concern with their ability to meet future payments.

While it is difficult to quantify the effect of the stock market crash on the output decline, economists are certain that it was important because the recession worsened noticeably after the crash. Seasonally adjusted industrial production declined 1.8 percent from August to September, 9.8 percent from October to December, and then another 23.9 percent from December 1929 to December 1930 (Romer 1988). During the first year following the crash, expenditures on consumer durables declined 19 percent while spending on services and nondurables fell 7.4 percent. M2 velocity declined 13 percent from 1929 to 1930.

The situation was made even worse in October 1930 when the first wave of bank runs started.[11] The failures began in the U.S. farm belt and spread to the urban areas. During November, 256 banks with deposits of $180 million failed, and in December, another 352 banks with $370 million of deposits failed. Most important was the December 11 failure involving mismanagement of the Bank of the United States in New York with $200 million in deposits. Not only was it the largest bank ever to fail but the name confused many into thinking that it was an "official" bank which caused further declines in confidence.[12]

Another negative factor was the 1930 passage of the Smoot-Hawley Tariff. Designed to benefit U.S. farmers and manufacturers, the law raised average tariff rates from just under 20 percent to 45 percent. Farmers and manufacturers did not benefit because within two years more than sixty other countries raised their own tariffs in retaliation. Smoot-Hawley was a factor in the declining volume of world trade and "probably one of the most damaging pieces of legislation ever signed in the United States" (Council of Economic Advisors 1988, p. 147).

Despite the bank failures and Smoot-Hawley, the economy did not slide further into depression. In fact, by early 1931 there were some signs of recovery as factory employment declined much more slowly and personal income rose 6 percent from February to March (Friedman and Schwartz 1963a, p. 313). Friedman and Schwartz contend that this was the time when vigorous action by the Federal Reserve might have averted the depression that was to come. If the Federal Reserve had engineered a significant increase in the monetary base to offset the rising currency-deposit ratio and falling velocity, the economy might have entered a period of expansion. But this was not to be as the monetary base continued to grow slowly and by early 1931 was still below the levels of late 1929.

Two events in late 1931 caused the pace of economic activity to deteriorate further: a second wave of bank failures and Great Britain's decision to leave the gold standard. The second wave of bank failures began in March 1931 and had more serious effects than the first wave since banks and the public had experienced the same thing only a short time ago. During 1931, 2,293 U.S. banks failed, along with others in Europe as the panic spread overseas. By January 1932 the second wave of bank failures was over, but just from August 1931 to January 1932, 1,860 banks with deposits of just under $1.5 billion dollars failed, and the deposits of many surviving banks declined. The public reacted by vigorously raising the currency-deposit ratio while banks raised their excess-reserve ratio. The combination of these two factors allowed the existing monetary base to support a much smaller stock of money.

Britain's decision in September 1931 to abandon the gold standard was the result of a serious drain on its gold stock and had important ramifications for the United States. The world financial community became concerned that the United States would follow Britain's lead, so transactors began selling dollars for U.S. gold which started a gold outflow from the United States. The Federal Reserve, concerned about the gold outflow, raised the discount rate which put further contractionary pressure on monetary growth. The stock of money (M2) fell 14 percent during 1931 and, just from August to January 1932, declined 12 percent—the fastest decline over such a short period in U.S. history since 1860 (Friedman and Schwartz 1963a, pp. 317–318). This combination of falling monetary growth and falling velocity dragged down aggregate demand growth, and the United States economy spiraled downward.

Yet another negative influence on aggregate demand growth was a 1932 legislated rise in income tax rates. The state of macroeconomic knowledge was not as complete as it is today, evidenced by the Hoover administration's belief that the emerging federal budget deficit had somehow helped "cause" the severe recession. Therefore, it became a federal goal to balance the budget which resulted in the Revenue Act of 1932 that raised income tax rates. While the income tax only applied to households with incomes of $5,000 or more per year, effectively exempting something like 90 percent of all households, high-income families incurred sizable jumps in their tax liabilities.[13] Although total income tax liabilities were small by today's standards, the Revenue Act was precisely the wrong medicine at the wrong time.

The situation slightly improved following a Federal Reserve policy of vigorous open market purchases of government securities from April 1932 to August 1932. During those five months the Federal Reserve raised its bond holdings by about $1 billion, and the base grew rapidly throughout 1932 and into early 1933. However, it wasn't enough. The decline in the money multiplier offset the rise in the base, and the stock of money declined during the first nine months of

1932 before rising in the fourth quarter. Real GNP continued to decline although at a slower pace. There was actually some indication of an economic revival during summer 1932 as production and wholesale prices began to rise.

Unfortunately, a third wave of bank panics started in late 1932, first in the Midwest and then spreading out to the Western states. Once again, the currency-deposit ratio rose and the money stock declined. Banking moratoriums spread across the country and existed in about half of the states by March 1933. On March 6, President Roosevelt declared a national banking "holiday." When the holiday was suspended, 5,000 banks that had been open for business prior to the moratorium did not reopen, and, of those, 2,000 never did (Friedman and Schwartz 1963a, p. 330).

The effects of the three waves of bank failures are shown by the following facts: from June 1930 to February 1933 currency holdings of the public rose 51 percent, bank deposits fell 33 percent, and the currency-deposit ratio rose by 129 percent. Furthermore, the bank reserve-deposit ratio rose 47 percent, partly a result of banks holding excess reserves as a buffer against possible future bank runs. The important result of this behavior is that from the economic peak in August 1929 to the trough in March 1933 the stock of M1 fell by 28 percent and the stock of M2 by 35 percent, despite the fact that the monetary base grew by about 23 percent (Degen 1987, pp. 65–68).

March 1933 was the trough of the Great Contraction. Relative to what had been the case in August 1929, nominal GNP was about 50 percent lower and that decline was divided about equally between output and prices. The March unemployment rate stood near 25 percent as the United States and many other countries experienced widespread misery.

Recovery, 1933–1937

Following the deep trough in March 1933, the economy began one of the longest peacetime expansions ever—a fifty-month revival that lasted until May 1937. While the expansion was long, it was somewhat weak in the sense that despite large gains in output, several measures of real spending at the 1937 peak were still below levels achieved in 1929. Furthermore, wages and prices grew rapidly over the expansion, especially during 1936 and 1937, despite the existence of a large pool of unemployed labor.

The economy actually showed preliminary signs of revival in late 1932 as industrial production, largely in response to increased spending on producer durable equipment, reversed its downward trend. The recovery did not start in earnest until the spring of 1933, and many writers associate the upturn with both improved confidence associated with the inauguration of Franklin D. Roosevelt, and the end of the last banking crisis in March 1933 (e.g., Allen 1940). One indication of this increased confidence was the public's returning trust in the banking system. Starting in mid-March after the banking moratorium (holiday) ended, the currency-deposit ratio began to fall as the public held relatively more of their money in the form of bank deposits and less in the form of currency. This pattern continued with the introduction of the Federal Deposit Insurance Corporation at the start of 1934.

Rapid monetary growth and stimulative fiscal policy were two major sources of aggregate demand growth during the expansion. The monetary base grew rapidly, the result of large gold inflows caused by both increased domestic production of gold following the revaluation from $23 per ounce to $35 per ounce in 1933–1934, and inflows from Europe, especially Germany, as citizens there sought safe havens for their wealth. The Federal Reserve was a passive force, choosing not to sterilize the gold inflows, and the monetary base grew a total of 60 percent over the expansion. The fact that the public was holding relatively more of their money in the form of bank deposits would have raised the money multiplier, but banks increased their excess reserve position in part because short-term interest rates were falling over the period. The rising excess-reserve ratio actually offset the falling currency-deposit ratio, and the money multiplier fell throughout much of the period. But since the base was rising rapidly, the money stock rose—M2 at an average annual rate of 11 percent (Friedman and Schwartz 1963a, pp. 499–501).

Fiscal policy was stimulative during the period as the New Deal programs were designed to raise aggregate demand with the aid of the multiplier process (Roosevelt called it "pump priming"). The New Deal programs certainly stimulated demand, but in retrospect the magnitudes were too small to bring about a fully employed economy. Nominal federal spending went from $4.7 billion in 1932 to a peak of $8.5 billion in 1936 while nominal GNP was still about $20 billion below its full employment rate during the mid-1930s.

One of the expansion's interesting features was the behavior of nominal interest rates. Partly the result of the rapid monetary growth, short-term interest rates fell throughout the period to very low levels. From early 1934 to the expansion's end, yields on both commercial paper and short-term Treasury Bills were less than 1 percentage point and the spread between the two was fairly narrow—not surprising since commercial paper is very low risk. The behavior of long-term rates is also interesting, in particular the fact that the spread between yields on long-term government bonds and Baa rated corporate bonds became quite wide—over 600 basis points in 1932—then narrowing to around 200 basis points by 1937. One obvious implication of this spread is that confidence in business conditions was still low—investors had a strong preference toward low-risk instruments and against higher risk instruments. The yields were bid accordingly.

Perhaps the outstanding feature of the expansion was the fact that in real terms neither investment spending (with the exception of durable equipment) nor consumer durable spending ever reached 1929 levels, which is apparently why the unemployment rate remained high. At the 1937 peak, real spending on nonresidential structures, residential construction, and consumer durables were just 65 percent, 62 percent, and 92 percent, respectively, of their 1929 levels. Only real consumer nondurables and services, and government purchases were above their 1929 levels.

While firms' unwillingness to engage in long-term investment projects was probably due in part to a low degree of optimism, several prominent writers also blame the New Deal programs.[14] New Deal programs had the effects of raising wage rates, reducing corporate after-tax profits, and involving the federal government in the production of several goods and services previously provided only by the private sector. Wages were driven up by the enactment of minimum wage laws, social security taxes, unemployment compensation, and the wage codes of the National Industrial Recovery Act (NIRA). When NIRA was declared unconstitutional in 1935, it was replaced with the National Labor Relations Act (also known as the Wagner Act) that made it significantly easier for workers to unionize. Corporate profits were reduced by the enactment of an undistributed profits tax in 1936. The government expanded into areas previously handled solely by the private sector including electrical generation, old-age insurance, and issuing mortgages. Since the government was now a "competitor" in these industries, less private expansion and, therefore, investment was necessary.

Whatever the reasons for the low levels of investment spending, the fact is that private net investment was negative through 1935, and when it become positive in 1936 and 1937, much of the increase was in inventories (Friedman and Schwartz 1963a, p. 495). As a result, a large pool of unemployed labor remained idle; indeed, the unemployment rate averaged 14.3 percent during the peak year 1937. At the economic peak in May, real GNP was 3 percent higher than the level at the peak in 1929, but since the population had grown by about 6 percent, per capita living standards were lower. The price level rose about 11 percent, in part due to the New Deal's increased regulation of several industries and farm price support system. An expansion had taken place, but much more was needed to return living standards to those that existed in 1929.

The Second Recession, 1937–1938

Although the 1933–1937 expansion was relatively weak, growth was strong in 1936–1937. Stock prices roughly doubled between 1935 and the end of 1936. Industrial production grew almost 30 percent from March 1936 to March 1937. Yet high labor unemployment continued, and inflation accelerated as food prices, raw-material prices, and wages grew rapidly in 1936 and 1937.

During the expansion, banks built up excess reserves, partly because of very low short-term interest rates and uncertainty as memories lingered of the bank panics a few years earlier. By late 1935 the Federal Reserve was concerned because banks were holding around $3 billion—about one-third of the monetary base—as excess reserves. The concern was that if those excess reserves were suddenly lent out and spent on goods and services, a severe inflation acceleration would result. When inflation began to show up in 1936, the Federal Reserve became convinced of the necessity of somehow removing these "idle" excess reserves from the banking system. Their attempt to accomplish this goal proved to be a major policy mistake.

The Federal Reserve tried to remove the excess reserves by raising the required-reserve ratio, believing that this action would cause banks to simply reclassify their reserves from excess to required and that would take care of the problem. From August 1936 to May 1937 the Board of Governors raised the required-reserve ratio three times which had a total effect of doubling the ratio. It never occurred to most members of the Board of Governors that because of low short-term interest rates and economic uncertainty banks were choosing to hold large excess reserves and would continue to do so regardless of the required-reserve ratio.

Meanwhile, in December 1936 the Treasury decided to begin sterilizing the gold inflows by selling bonds which essentially stopped the growth of the monetary base. Zero base growth, combined with banks' efforts to rebuild their excess reserve positions following the rise in the required-reserve ratio, had the effect of causing a slowdown of monetary growth in late 1936, followed by a decline in the level of the money stock by mid-1937. Economists generally consider this contraction in monetary growth to be a major cause of the downturn in economic activity that began in May 1937.[15]

Fiscal policy also contributed to the economy's decline. A combination of falling spending in 1937 relative to 1936 and a large increase in social security tax revenue reduced the federal deficit (including the social security surplus) from $3.4 billion in 1936 to $0.2 billion in 1937 to put further downward pressure on aggregate demand.

Therefore, the recession was largely policy induced. While Friedman and Schwartz consider the decision to reduce monetary growth "entirely understandable," given the buildup of inflationary pressures, the policymakers clearly went overboard (Friedman and Schwartz 1963a, p. 525). The resulting recession was relatively short—thirteen months—and mild until September 1937 when output measures declined sharply. Over the entire recession, real GNP declined a total of 10 percent, and almost all of this decline occurred from September to the trough in June 1938. Industrial production fell about one-third, the unemployment rate reached over 19 percent at the trough, and the price level fell by about 3.5 percent.

Final Stages of the Depression, 1938–1941

By summer's end 1937, the Federal Reserve realized what a costly error they had made and attempted to reverse the effects. From August 1937 to April 1938 the Board of Governors carried out three moves designed to stimulate the economy: authorizing open market purchases, persuading the Treasury to release $300 million of sterilized gold, and lowering the required reserve ratio (Eastburn 1965, p. 72). The monetary base bottomed out in 1937.III, and then the policy actions began to take hold. Soon afterward monetary growth became rapid; from the second quarter of 1938 and lasting for two years, M2 grew a total of 22 percent. An economic recovery was under way by the summer of 1938.

The recovery was robust, yet the unemployment rate remained high during the first two years. Over the two years following the trough, real GNP grew 17 percent, but the unemployment rate averaged 14.6 percent in 1940. The price level was stable, the GNP deflator rising by a total of only 1 percent during the first two years of the recovery. One encouraging feature during those first two years was the comeback of investment spending and consumer durables. Both components of aggregate demand had been exceedingly weak since autumn 1929, and their reemergence suggests returning business confidence. During the expansion's first two years, real producer durable spending rose 60 percent, residential structures 41 percent, and consumer durables 41 percent. Despite these gains, by early 1940 these three aggregates were still below their respective levels in 1929.

If Adolph Hitler had not attempted to conquer Europe, it is debatable what course the U.S. economy would have followed next. Quite possibly the expansion would have continued and the United States would have reached full employment within a few years. This conjecture is a moot point: in May 1940, Germany invaded France, and in short order France surrendered and the British Army was forced into a humiliating retreat from the European continent at Dunkirk. France's surrender made it apparent to all that the United States' close ally Great Britain was next on Hitler's to-be-conquered list, and so in the summer of 1940 the United States began to militarize.

The early stages of militarization involved an enormous rise in spending on defense goods. Total government purchases, which had grown 4.1 percent during the first two years of the recovery, grew 59 percent from 1940.II to 1941.II, and with the multiplier process adding further stimulus to aggregate demand growth, the expansion really gathered steam. During that twelve-month period, real GNP rose 17 percent; with the exceptions of net exports and consumer services and nondurables, all spending components experienced double digit growth. The price level rose 6 percent, and in 1941 the unemployment rate fell below double digits for the first time since 1930. By 1941.III the economy was producing at full employment, and the depression was finally over.

The depression was very costly. Just in terms of lost output (measured as the cumulative output gap from 1930–1940) the depression cost over $2 trillion in 1972 dollars, roughly equivalent to three times a single year's GNP in the mid-1930s. Other costs include the unmeasurable negative effects on the health and welfare of the American public. The entire episode was a macroeconomic tragedy.

The events of the last few years of the depression had a profound influence on macroeconomic thought. Rapid monetary growth in the late 1930s and relatively weak expansion until the defense buildup started convinced many that fiscal policy was the dominant influence on aggregate demand and that monetary policy was relatively impotent. As a result, the Keynesian model with its emphasis on the potency of fiscal policy moved to the forefront of macroeconomics where it remained for almost thirty years.

NOTES

1. For an example, see Sinclair (1906).

2. Waldo (1985) presents a formal analysis of the behavior of short-term interest rates and the currency-deposit ratio during bank panics.

3. These estimates are based on Robert J. Gordon's natural rate of unemployment series.

4. Allen (1931, p. 137) reports that radio sales went from $60 million in 1922 to $842.5 million in 1929.

5. This thesis is convincingly developed by R. A. Gordon (1961, chap. 14).

6. Potter (1974) notes that another important innovation was electric service to households. As mentioned earlier in the context of the Panic of 1907, the electrical industry was growing in the early 1900s, and this growth continued through the 1920s as homes were increasingly wired up to electricity. Also, important innovations were occurring in the chemical industry including the development of rayon and cosmetics.

7. Mercer and Morgan (1972) challenge the argument that overcapacity had developed in the automobile industry.

8. Allen (1931, p. 269) notes that on the eve of the stock market crash there were several optimists, including the famous economist Irving Fisher (Fisher's equation of exchange, Fisher's equation of real and nominal interest rates) who stated on October 17 that stock prices had reached "what looks like a permanently high plateau" and expected within a few months that the stock market would be "a good deal higher than it is today."

9. Margin requirements were low in 1929 which probably amplified the stock market advance. An individual could put up 10 cents as collateral to borrow 90 cents from a broker. Today, an individual must put up 50 cents in collateral to borrow another 50 cents.

10. R. A. Gordon (1961, pp. 426–427) stresses the view that overcapacity was an important cause of the initial decline in output. Friedman and Schwartz (1963a) stress monetary causes.

11. Bernanke (1983) suggests that the contractionary effect of widespread bank failures may not be the associated reduction in the money stock, but instead the severe reduction in the amount of financial intermediation that occurs. In related work, Grossman (1989) estimates that, based on data from 1863 to 1914, widespread banking panics are associated with a 40 percent decline in investment spending.

12. See Temin (1976, pp. 90–94) for a detailed discussion of the Bank of the United States' failure.

13. In 1929 about 9 percent of U.S. households had incomes of $5,000 or more. See Level, Moulton and Warburton (1934, p. 54).

14. See, for example, Friedman and Schwartz (1963a) and R. A. Gordon (1961).

15. The argument that reduced monetary growth was largely responsible for the 1937–1938 recession is advanced by Haberler (1976), Roose (1954), Friedman and Schwartz (1963a), and R. A. Gordon (1961).

11 | World War II to 1989

WORLD WAR II, 1941–1945

World War II was associated with a great expansion in U.S. economic activity. Several factors contributed to the rise: both fiscal and monetary policy were highly stimulative, price controls kept measured inflation from becoming disruptive, and a combination of patriotic fervor and rising real wages raised labor participation rates of several demographic groups well above their normal peacetime rates. The result was an economy experiencing huge gains in household income with virtually no involuntary unemployment.

Fiscal policy was expansionary for the obvious reason that defense expenditures rose significantly, from $2.3 billion in 1940 to $73.3 billion in 1945 (the peak was $87.5 billion in 1944). Income tax rates were also raised, but the deficit widened from $3.5 billion in 1940 to $48.7 billion by 1945. In an effort to help hold down the Treasury's borrowing costs, an agreement was reached between the Treasury and the Federal Reserve where the central bank agreed to maintain interest rates at low levels. Rates on short-term Treasury Bills were pegged at 0.375 percent and long-term Treasuries at 2.5 percent. Maintaining these low interest rates amid increasing federal borrowing and rising income required the Federal Reserve to fully accommodate any increases in credit demand. The nominal stock of money more than doubled between 1940 and 1945 as a result.

These fiscal and monetary stimuli were associated with large output gains and little inflation because a system of strong price controls existed. Furthermore, employment gains were large enough to produce the larger quantities of goods and services being demanded as demographic groups, who normally would not have worked in such large numbers, more than made up for the exit of the millions of young men and women who entered the armed services. Teenagers, women, and older Americans (who normally would have been retired) either remained at work or reentered the labor force. During the war, labor force participation rates rose 57 percent for teenage males, 80 percent for teenage females, 30 percent for all females, and half of all males over the age of 65 were employed (Hughes 1987, p. 480).

The resulting output gains were enormous. From 1941 to 1944 real GNP grew 64 percent, per capita real GNP 45 percent, and relative to what had been the case during the depression, virtually anyone who wanted to work did. As employment and output rose to new heights, total wage income did too. From 1940 to 1944 average weekly earnings in manufacturing rose more than 80 percent, and mean household income 64 percent (Hughes 1987, p. 479). Working people enjoyed significant income gains but there wasn't much to spend it on. Very few consumer durables were available because factories had been converted for weapons production, and often goods that were available were rationed. As a result, households saved large proportions of their incomes during the period, in most cases contributing to the war effort by buying U.S. government bonds.

When the war ended in 1945, the United States was by far the largest economic power in the world. Unlike most other major countries, the United States enjoyed two very important advantages: the conflict had not been fought on U.S. soil which left the U.S. capital stock intact, and manpower losses were not as large a proportion of the nation's population as in Germany, Japan, or the Soviet Union. Despite the tragic deaths of more than 400,000 young Americans who certainly would have had many productive working years had they not been war casualties, the United States economy was in fine shape at the end of the war.

RELATIVE ECONOMIC STABILITY, 1946–1960

The prevailing attitude among economists during the war was that the economic expansion was a temporary aberration from the depressed conditions of the 1930s. The consensus forecast maintained that the end of the war would bring back the depression with millions of returning soldiers facing massive unemployment. These forecasts were based on the belief that expanding defense purchases had ended the depression; therefore, when demobilization occurred at the end of the war, the depression would return because nothing fundamental had changed in the U.S. economy since 1939. As it turned out, of course, this forecast was completely wrong. In fact, it is identified as one of the greatest economic forecast errors of all time (Moore 1983, p. 402). Economists of the day were ignoring the accumulation of liquid assets by households during the war and the pent-up demand for all kinds of goods that were unavailable during the conflict.

Thus, the end of the war brought economic prosperity, not depression. During an eight-month contraction in 1945 and further output declines in 1946 and 1947 associated with demilitarization, the economy successfully converted to a peacetime footing as factories changed from producing weapons to consumer and investment goods. Households were eager to purchase consumer durables such as automobiles and appliances, and when these goods became available, Americans used their savings and bought them in droves. Residential construction, very limited during the war, rebounded as the development of the suburbs picked up again. The U.S. economy successfully absorbed the millions of returning soldiers into the labor force because large numbers of teenagers, women, and the elderly made room by returning to their normal nonworking pursuits. Also, many returning soldiers chose not to work and instead went off to college for a heavily subsidized education under the GI Bill.

The output decline immediately following the war, 19 percent during 1946, and another 2.8 percent in 1947, were movements back toward full employment output. Given that output was still above full employment, especially in 1946, considerable inflationary pressures existed which were released when the price controls expired on June 30, 1946. During 1946 the GNP deflator rose 22.1 percent, almost all of which occurred after June and the inflation continued. GNP deflator inflation in 1947 was 13.9 percent, followed by 7 percent in 1948. Despite this inflation, the 1947 consensus forecast still reflected the "return to depression" mentality. The Livingston Panel Forecast of annual CPI price changes from June 1947 was 6.64 percent deflation. The actual CPI inflation over the forecast period turned out to be 8.09 percent (R. J. Gordon 1980).

The Federal Reserve was concerned about inflation and knew that their agreement with the Treasury to peg interest rates did not allow monetary control. Beginning in 1947 the Federal Reserve began to allow short-term rates to rise while still maintaining the peg on long-term rates, and in early 1948 raised the required-reserve ratio three times to absorb some of the excess reserves in the banking system. While the monetary base continued to rise, albeit slowly, the resulting decline in the money multiplier caused the nominal stock of money to decline, which apparently precipitated the mild recession that took place from November 1948 to October 1949. Output declined a total of 1.2 percent and the GNP deflator fell about 2.5 percent. Incidentally, this is the last time the GNP deflator declined over any significant period of time (more on this in chapter 12). Almost all of this output decline was associated with falling inventories— that is, the dollar decline in real GNP almost exactly matched the real quantity of inventory disinvestment.

In large part, the recession was mild because automobile sales soared in 1949. Immediately after the war, U.S. automobile manufacturers stopped producing military hardware and began producing the same car models they had been making before the outbreak of hostilities. Given the public's high demand for new cars, the lost revenue during a period of retooling would have been significant. In 1949 the three major U.S. auto makers finally retooled and came out with new models which were very successful. In 1949 real personal consumption expenditures on vehicles and parts were 28 percent above 1948 levels.

When the excess inventories were run down by late 1949, another expansion began. The notable event during this expansion was the outbreak of the Korean War. On June 24, 1950, North Korea invaded South Korea and three days later

U.S. troops were sent into this action. This event had major consequences for the U.S. economy. The public still had fresh memories of the unavailability of many goods during World War II and were afraid that a similar situation would emerge during this conflict which had the potential to turn into World War III. The American public rushed to buy consumer durables which rose 25 percent from 1950.II to 1950.III. By 1951 consumer spending had fallen off, but government defense purchases for the war took up the slack, and the federal budget moved from a surplus of $4.3 billion in 1951 to a deficit of $8.3 billion in 1953.

Expansion in aggregate demand during the early 1950s led to considerable price inflation—a problem that has plagued the U.S. economy ever since. After being relatively stable from 1948 to early 1950, the GNP deflator rose 8.8 percent in 1950, 4.5 percent in 1951, then leveled off with the reimposition of price controls. Prior to the price controls, monetary growth was not the major source of the rapid nominal aggregate demand growth; instead, rising velocity growth was the cause. Friedman and Schwartz (1963a, pp. 597–598) contend that by the late 1940s and early 1950s the American public had finally caught on that inflation, not deflation, was the order of the day. This realization led households to hold smaller amounts of money relative to their incomes, and M2 velocity rose 20 percent from 1949 to 1951.

Economic activity peaked in July 1953, the same month fighting in Korea ceased with a truce establishing the line of demarkation between North and South Korea. At least three factors apparently caused this recession. First, government purchases were essentially flat from the second to fourth quarters of 1953 as the Korean War wound down. Second, the Federal Reserve, concerned about inflation, finally abandoned the agreement with the Treasury to peg long-term rates and in early 1953 raised the discount rate. Both short- and long-term rates rose and monetary growth declined, although it remained positive. Third, some argue that the boom in consumer durables simply ran out of gas. After adjustments from the unusual conditions during and after World War II and the Korean War, households returned to more normal patterns of durables purchased in relation to their income.

This recession was relatively mild, although more severe than the 1948–1949 downturn. Real GNP declined by a total of 2.8 percent, and the unemployment rate rose from 2.7 percent to 5.8 percent. This recession lasted until May 1954 when an expansion began that was led by purchases of consumer services and nondurables, and residential construction, both of which had bottomed out in 1953.IV, the same quarter that long-term interest rates peaked.

This expansion began despite the fact that government purchases were still declining, as they had been since the end of the Korean War. Output growth during this expansion, which was especially strong in 1955, was largely the result of investment spending, purchases of new automobiles, and net export growth. One possible source of the turnaround was a revival of optimism about the future, reflected by rising stock prices from their trough in 1953.III and strong fixed business investment growth throughout the mid-1950s. Once the expansion began, spending on consumer durables picked up steam; automobile sales rose from around 5.5 million units in 1954 to almost 8 million in 1955. No one has provided a complete explanation for this auto boom, but two factors are important—the 1955 models were quite different and exciting relative to what had been produced before (the 1955 Chevrolet is now considered a classic automobile), and three-year auto installment loans were introduced that year.

Real GNP rose 5.6 percent in 1955 and the unemployment rate fell to just above 4 percent. But during the remainder of the expansion, which would last until August 1957, output growth was weak, and the unemployment rate remained stuck at around 4 percent. Real GNP grew 2.1 percent in 1956 and 1.3 percent through the first three quarters of 1957. Meanwhile, GNP deflator inflation was edging up, from 1.6 percent in 1954 to 3.6 percent by 1957, despite the stable unemployment rate that was considered high at the time.

Monetary growth had peaked in 1955 but rising velocity sustained nominal GNP growth. As inflation accelerated, the real money supply started to decline in late 1955. Short-term interest rates rose, and eventually this monetary contraction helped cause an economic downturn. This recession was short and severe, lasting until April 1958 (eight months) but featuring a 3.2 percent jump in the unemployment rate, a 3 percent decline in output, and little noticeable reduction in the inflation rate. It was this relatively severe recession without a significant decline in inflation that led many economists to begin questioning the compatability of full employment and price stability.

The recession was short because in early 1958 the Federal Reserve took a series of steps to raise the monetary growth rate: three reductions in the discount rate, two reductions in the required-reserve ratio, and moderate open market purchases. The monetary expansion's effects on aggregate demand were amplified by rising velocity such that nominal GNP growth rose considerably, from 1.3 percent in 1958 to 8.5 percent in 1959. The resulting expansion was relatively short, two years, but robust. Real GNP rose 10.3 percent over the expansion and the inflation rate remained stable in the 2 percent range. Much of the increase in output occurred from spring 1958 to summer 1959. Output flattened in the summer of 1959 because of a strike in the U.S. steel industry that began on July 15, 1959, and lasted for 116 days. The strike affected firms producing 95 percent of all domestically produced steel and spread to industries that use steel as an input. Industrial production declined sharply. Foreign competition in the steel industry was not nearly as significant then as it is now.

The flat output growth had another proximate cause as well, yet another significant decline in monetary growth. The Federal Reserve had kept the monetary base approximately constant since mid-1958 and raised the discount rate five times between August 1958 and September 1959. M2 growth peaked in 1959.I and briefly turned negative during mid-1959. The result was a decline in nominal GNP growth, and output flattened from the last half of 1959 to early 1960. The recession began in April 1960, another short and relatively mild recession, lasting until February 1961 and featuring a 1.2 percent decline in output and a 1.6 percentage point rise in the unemployment rate. This recession had one notable consequence: it is often cited as the major factor costing the 1960 election for the Republican candidate for president, Richard Nixon.

Comments on the Early Postwar Period

Business cycles from World War II to 1960 appear to have been caused by movements in aggregate demand growth. Of the four recessions from 1948 to 1960, monetarists argue that reduced monetary growth was partly responsible for all of them, and Keynesian economists (e.g., R. A. Gordon 1961, Romer and Romer 1989) agree that monetary forces played at least some role in the 1948–1949 and 1953–1954 recessions.

The period exhibits little of the positive supply-side phenomena that existed during the 1920s. If anything, negative supply influences are suggested given the economy's inability to grow rapidly without experiencing accelerating inflation. It is not clear what negative supply influences existed, but there are two possible candidates. One is the rise in the minimum wage from 75 cents to $1 in 1956. This 33 percent rise was the first increase since 1950 and raised the real minimum wage by about 15 percent. Second is the increased strength of labor unions. Union membership as a proportion of the labor force peaked in the mid-1950s, and union activity was high from 1946 to 1959 as work stoppages as a percentage of total working time reached proportions not seen again until the late 1960s (U.S. Department of Commerce 1976).

In some respects, the economy's course during the fifteen years following World War II was disappointing. After the transition to a peacetime economy, there was hope that living standards would grow at rates such as those of the 1920s, but this was not to be. While living standards rose, the pace was rather slow. If we consider only the peacetime period starting with the end of the Korean War (1953.III) to the end of the decade (1959.IV), the average annual rate of real GNP growth was 2.1 percent—a far cry from the 5.9 percent achieved from 1921 to 1929. Furthermore, the postwar period was characterized by relatively short business cycles where recessions, while minor, appeared with considerable regularity.

There were two other disturbing features during the period: the secular rise in prices and unemployment. Prices rose continuously after 1949 and while the rates of increase were low by modern standards, the inflation was nonetheless disturbing given that it was combined with relatively slow economic growth. The secular rise, albeit slow, of the unemployment rate occurred with rates of around 3 percent in the early 1950s rising to about 4 percent by the end of the decade. Of course both of these trends would continue for decades, but they caused concern at the time.

One source of considerable optimism during the early postwar period was the reduced amplitude of the business cycle relative to the 1930s. In particular, recessions were more mild, and economists credited automatic stabilizers such as graduated income tax rates, unemployment compensation, the welfare system, and deposit insurance as the chief reason. At the same time, Keynes' ideas on the usefulness of stabilization policy were moving into the mainstream and would be wholeheartedly adopted during the 1960s. In other words, the seed of thought was being planted that maybe, just maybe, economists could eliminate business cycles.

THE 1960s EXPANSION

The 1960s were the heyday of Keynesian economics. President Kennedy, who firmly embraced the Keynesian economic principles he had learned while a student at Harvard, campaigned for office on the pledge to "get the economy moving again." Once elected, he appointed several prominent Keynesian economists, including James Tobin, Walter Heller, and Gardner Ackley, to economic advisory positions in his administration. The Keynesians arrived in Washington with a firm belief in the potency of fiscal policy and went to work thinking up ways to stimulate the economy.[1]

These Keynesians believed that proper demand management policies could reduce the amplitude of the business cycle and promote economic growth. When many of the Keynesians' ideas were implemented early in the decade and the resulting expansion turned out to be rapid, especially through 1966, and long (106 months), the Keynesians were almost giddy with delight. A few began to think the business cycle had actually been eliminated. Of course the business cycle was alive and well and the public would later pay for overly expansionary policies that were carried out (against the advice of many Keynesians) when inflationary pressures were evident during the latter half of the decade.

Monetary growth turned expansionary in 1960.III, and by the spring of 1961 the expansion began that would continue until 1969—the longest expansion in U.S. history since 1834 when records begin. We divide the expansion into two parts: the first phase from 1961–1966 when economic growth was rapid and inflation low, averaging 4.8 percent and 2.1 percent, respectively, and the second phase from 1967–1969 when output growth slowed and inflation rose, averaging 3.1 percent, 4.4 percent respectively.

The Growth Phase, 1961–1966

The 1961–1966 period of rapid economic growth was accompanied by relatively stimulative monetary and fiscal policies. M2 growth reached 5 percent by mid-1961, 7.4 percent in 1962, and remained above 8 percent from 1963–1965 before declining in 1966. This monetary growth provided the basis of much of the nominal GNP growth over the period as from 1961 to 1966, M2 growth averaged 7.4 percent per year while nominal GNP growth averaged 7 percent per year—a very close fit indicating relatively stable M2 velocity. Government spending was erratic in light of President Kennedy's New Frontier and later President Johnson's Great Society that called for increased federal expenditures on social programs. Real federal purchases jumped $16 billion from 1961–1962, working with monetary policy to help start the expansion in 1961, declined through to 1965, and then rose almost $30 billion in 1966 when the Vietnam War heated up. It is also interesting to note that from 1961 to 1966 state and local purchases grew faster than federal purchases; real state and local purchases averaged 5.9 percent annual growth and real federal purchases averaged 3.3 percent growth.

Federal tax policy was expansionary as President Kennedy supported an experiment in Keynesian economics: tax changes designed to stimulate aggregate demand including a cut in income tax rates, establishment of the investment tax credit, and more liberal depreciation allowances for businesses. The investment policies were enacted in 1962 and, after a lag, were a stimulus to investment and economic growth (Hall and Jorgenson 1967). The income tax rate reduction was not enacted until 1964 and is credited with helping stimulate the economy although it is questionable if the economy required additional stimulation at the time.

From 1961 to 1966 all components of aggregate demand grew, with investment spending and consumer durables especially strong. Total real investment spending and consumer durable purchases grew at average annual rates of 8 percent and 9 percent, respectively. The 7 percent average annual growth of nominal GNP showed up mostly in output growth instead of inflation; real GNP growth averaged 4.8 percent per year with the peak growth years being 1965 and 1966 when GNP rose 5.8 each year. GNP deflator inflation averaged 2.1 percent from 1961–1966, but this average rate masks the inflation acceleration. From 1964 the inflation rate started to rise by about 1 percentage point per year, from 1.5 percent in 1964 to 3.6 percent by 1966.

The Inflation Phase, 1967–1969

By late 1965 the Federal Reserve was concerned about the overheating economy. M2 growth fell sharply, from 8.1 percent in 1965 to 4.5 percent in 1966. Short-term interest rates rose from around 4 percent in 1965 to 5 percent in 1966, and stock prices fell 13 percent from 1964.IV to 1965.IV. Economic growth declined to 2.1 percent in 1967, then rebounded to 4.1 percent in 1968 with much of that growth coming in the latter part of the year. Real aggregate investment spending, particularly residential construction, actually declined in 1967, but a recession was avoided because consumption of services and nondurables, and government purchases (due to further U.S. military escalation in Vietnam) rose enough to offset the declining components.

In contrast to modern estimates, which place the economy at full employment in 1964, President Johnson's economic advisers did not consider the economy to be at full employment until 1966 when they issued a warning that federal financing of both social programs and the war were adding unneeded expansionary pressures. They advised Johnson to support a tax increase to cool off the economy which he initially resisted but later agreed to. Johnson persuaded Congress to enact a temporary income tax surcharge that took effect in 1968. This tax surcharge, the "Waterloo of activist fiscal stabilization policy" (Gordon 1980, p. 136), was an utter failure. The tax was announced as temporary so it did not change households' permanent disposable income. Households simply paid the tax out of personal savings, and consumption as a percentage of personal income remained about the same during the period the surcharge was in effect. Thus, the tax change did not reduce aggregate demand growth, and real GNP grew 4.1 percent in 1968 and the inflation rate rose to 5 percent.

The 5 percent inflation rate was a source of concern, enough so that the Federal Reserve set out to reduce it by contracting monetary growth. Beginning in early 1969 both M1 and M2 growth declined significantly. Compared to 1968 growth rates, M1 went from 7.7 percent to 3.2 percent, M2 from 8 percent to 4.1 percent. Short-term interest rates rose about 250 basis points and the recession began in December 1969. A contributing factor to this slowdown was the declining level of federal purchases since their peak in 1967–1968 (corresponding to peak U.S. military involvement in Vietnam).

This recession, which lasted until November 1970, was very mild. Real GNP fell only 1 percent, largely the result of falling investment spending and declining government purchases. There was, however, an unusual twist: the inflation rate hardly budged. The GNP deflator rose 5.6 percent in 1969 and 5.5 percent in 1970 while the unemployment rate went from 3.6 percent at the economic peak to 5.8 percent at the trough. This occurrence, recession without declining inflation, was termed *stagflation* and many economists were at a loss to explain this apparent contradiction of the traditional Phillips curve.

Comments on the 1960s

The 1960s was a decade of significant economic growth. From the trough in 1961 to the peak in 1969, real GNP grew a total of 44 percent—an average annual rate of 4.5 percent which is the best performance over a sustained period since 1938–1945. However, unlike the 1920s when supply influences were a major source of growth, the demand-side gains of the 1960s imposed a significant cost on American society in the form of rising inflation that turned out to be very difficult to eliminate.

In macroeconomic thought, the 1960s witnessed the peak and decline of Keynesian economics. The policy activists went to Washington to accomplish great things and they did. The monetary and fiscal induced expansions led to significant gains in average living standards. The failure, however, in the mid-1960s to slow the economy when it reached full employment caused accelerating inflation, and when the traditional Phillips curve seemingly disappeared in the 1970 recession, Keynesian economics was placed in a bad light. Economists searched for an alternative economic model, and the remarkable relationship between money growth and nominal GNP growth since the late 1950s, an ironic fact during the high point of Keynesian economics, suggested that the monetarists might have the answers.

ECONOMIC INSTABILITY AND INFLATION, 1971–1979

The U.S. economy during the 1970s was characterized by rapid inflation, unstable exchange rates, wage and price controls, erratic monetary growth rates, the appearance of two major supply shocks in the form of higher food and petroleum prices, and one deep recession. Much of this instability resulted from economic policy mistakes that certainly raised the inflation rate and probably made the 1974–1975 recession deeper than it otherwise would have been. In short, macroeconomic policymaking reached a low point during the period, surpassed only by the policy mistakes during the depression.

Expansion with Wage and Price Controls, 1970–1973

The decade began with the economy in the recession that started in 1969. In June 1970 there was a big bang: Penn Central, the largest railroad in the nation, collapsed and defaulted on $82 million of commercial paper. Since commercial paper was (and is) considered very low risk, the default shook financial markets. Some holders of existing paper tried to sell and move their funds into safer securities. The commercial paper-selling panic placed the economy on the brink of a liquidity crisis, and the Federal Reserve jumped in to help by informing banks that they were prepared to discount liberally. Over the next three months bank reserves grew at an annual rate of 25 percent and a crisis was averted. This upturn in monetary growth apparently played a major role in ending the mild 1969–1970 recession.

The recession ended in November 1970 and, as noted, passed without any sizable reduction in the inflation rate. This occurrence suggests, as is confirmed by natural rate data, that the recession was, in large part, a downward movement toward the natural rate of output. According to modern estimates, the recession moved output from $46 billion above full employment to $34 billion below full employment (1982$), and the expansion that followed took the economy back to full employment by 1971.I. However, in 1971 many economists believed the economy possessed excess capacity and argued in favor of further stimulus. The Nixon administration responded by initiating policies to raise economic growth and reduce unemployment. With the economy already at full employment, additional demand stimulus quickly caused a buildup of inflationary pressures.

The Nixon administration's stimulus plan was unveiled on August 15, 1971, when President Nixon went on national television to announce his "new economic policy" that had the following important features: wage and price controls, suspending the conversion of dollars into gold or other reserve assets, and imposition of a 10 percent import surcharge.[2] The wage and price controls would occur in four "phases" beginning with an immediate ninety-day complete freeze on wages and prices to be followed by gradual exemption of items covered until April 30, 1974, when all controls would be eliminated. The intent was for wage and price controls to reduce the inflation rate while monetary growth was gradually reduced to slow aggregate demand growth. Then, according to the plan, the controls would be lifted, and the U.S. would enjoy lower inflation without ever experiencing a rise in the unemployment rate. Economists' warnings that price controls would cause market distortions fell largely on deaf ears.

The suspension of dollar convertibility, which effectively ended the Bretton-Woods fixed exchange rate agreement, was in response to an overvalued dollar and outflow of gold reserves from the United States. Rapid U.S. monetary growth during the 1960s had placed the United States in a balance of payments deficit position, indicative of an overvalued dollar. Some countries, particularly France, insisted on exchanging excess dollars for U.S. gold reserves at the official rate which was allowed under the Bretton-Woods arrangement. This action caused a serious gold outflow from the United States which accelerated in early 1971 due to widespread foreign fear that the United States would devalue. This fear prompted a capital outflow from the United States and placed the United States in a dilemma—we could devalue by raising the official price of gold in terms of dollars, but this would not change the value of the dollar relative to other currencies since exchange rates were fixed in terms of the dollar. The United States had to devalue in terms of both gold and other currencies which was done by suspending dollar conversion and allowing the dollar to float. This action effectively caused all other currencies to float as well and unofficially ended the Bretton-Woods system. The resulting dollar depreciation along with the proposed import surcharge were designed to reduce existing U.S. trade and balance of payments deficits.

The wage and price controls might have achieved their intended purpose of reducing inflation without raising unemployment if aggregate demand growth had declined substantially. Quite the opposite occurred, however, as aggregate demand growth, largely driven by monetary growth, was rapid in an economy already at full employment. The Federal Reserve allowed M2 to grow 6.6 percent in 1970, 13.5 percent in 1971, and 13 percent in 1972. During those same three years nominal GNP rose 5.4 percent, 8.6 percent, and 10 percent, respectively. It is not completely clear why the Federal Reserve allowed such rapid monetary growth. Ironically this period was the high point of monetarist rhetoric from the central bank. Federal Reserve officials claimed they were attempting to moderate monetary growth but were unsuccessful because institutional factors had taken away their ability to control the money supply. This explanation was attacked by many as a lame excuse designed to defer blame (e.g., Poole 1975). Others argue that the Federal Reserve was attempting to use their power over the economy to ensure Nixon's reelection.

Whatever the reason, the fact is that monetary policy was highly expansionary, and, as so often happens during such an event, the increases in nominal GNP growth largely showed up first in output and then later in prices. During the period when price controls were in effect, output growth was probably greater and inflation less, than if the controls had not existed, although the actual amounts are not clear. Several researchers have investigated this issue and came up with varying estimates suggesting a 2 or 3 percent lower CPI inflation rate due to the controls (see Brittan and Lilley 1977, pp. 146–150). Darby (1976) estimates that when quality adjustments are made, the price controls had no influence on the inflation rate.

By 1972 the economy already had substantial inflationary pressures partially hidden by price controls when an unusual series of exogenous weather-related events added fuel to the fire: reduced crop yields in the Soviet Union, Southeast Asia, and the Midwestern United States such that world grain output was 3 percent below the previous year's output. The Soviet Union responded by buying large quantities of grains from the United States which, in combination with reduced yields, significantly drove up world food prices. Also, anchovies, an input into livestock feed, left their usual grounds off the coast of Peru which reduced the supply of feed and increased the cost of raising livestock. The resulting rise in food costs combined with price controls caused shortages of some types of foods in the United States by late 1972. At about the same time, distortions in other markets that economists had warned of began to appear, and the controls quickly lost popular support.

Despite the adverse effects of the rise in food prices, the economy continued to boom in 1972 and 1973, real GNP rising 5 percent in 1972 and 5.3 percent in 1973. Economic activity in 1973 included unprecedented levels of motor vehicle production: domestic manufacturers produced more than 13 million vehicles, an amount that would not be surpassed for several years. Among the reasons for the enormous vehicle demand were rising household income and the fact that Americans were aware that 1974 and 1975 car models would be fitted with federally mandated safety and pollution devices that would add several hundred dollars to the prices of new cars.[3] The 1973 output gains were associated with increased evidence of capacity pressures. The Federal Reserve's capacity utilization rate measure for total manufacturing hit 87 percent, the highest rate since the late 1960s; and the unemployment rate for 1973 was 4.9 percent, about 1 percentage point below the natural rate. GNP deflator inflation rose to 5.9 percent, 1.8 points higher than the previous year's, and the CPI rose 6.2 percent.

By the early months of 1973 the Federal Reserve realized that inflationary pressures existed and initiated a slowdown in monetary growth. From 1972 to 1973, M1 growth went from 9.2 percent to 5.5 percent, and M2 growth from 13 percent to 6.9 percent. The combination of reduced monetary growth and rising inflationary expectations put sharp upward pressure on short-term interest rates which caused a crisis in the housing industry by the spring of 1973. Federal regulations set ceilings on rates that both banks and savings and loans could pay depositors, and regulators were reluctant to change these rates. As inflation became increasingly serious, the inflation premium on nominal interest rates rose and pushed market rates above regulated deposit rates. Depositors withdrew funds from banks and savings and loans—a process called financial disinter-mediation—and used them to buy Treasury Bills and shares in the newly forming money market mutual funds. Savings and loans were especially hard hit. Since they were required to hold a majority of their assets in long-term fixed rate home mortgages, this disintermediation caused a severe reduction in funds available for new home loans. Residential construction plummeted; the annual rate of new private housing starts fell from 2.4 million units in 1973.I to 1.6 million by 1973.IV.

That same spring the fixed exchange rate system officially ended. After the United States had allowed the dollar to float in 1971, the Bretton-Woods agreement was patched back together later that year but did not survive, in part because continued rapid U.S. monetary growth and resulting inflation kept the United States in a balance of payments deficit. Finally, in March 1973, all major nations agreed to allow their currencies to float. The dollar depreciated again, putting further upward pressure on the U.S. price level.

Perhaps the most damaging blow to the U.S. economy in 1973 was the rise in petroleum prices that began in October. In protest of U.S. support of Israel during the Arab-Israeli war, the Middle Eastern members of OPEC (Organization of Petroleum Exporting Countries) decided to withhold oil supplies from the world market and stop selling oil to the United States. The embargo against the United States mattered little because America could buy oil from non-OPEC countries or acquire OPEC oil through Europe. The supply reduction, however, mattered much. Starting in October and lasting until late spring 1974, world oil prices quadrupled from $3 per barrel to $12 per barrel. The OPEC supply reduction also raised prices of oil substitutes such as coal.

The oil price increase had a negative impact on the U.S. economy for three reasons. First, since the short-run price elasticity of demand for energy products was quite low, households were suddenly faced with higher total expenditures on gasoline and home utilities. Thus, households allocated a larger proportion of their incomes to the purchase of energy products leaving less to spend on other goods and services. Second, since energy is an input into the production of virtually all goods and services, the marginal cost schedules of individual firms and, therefore, the aggregate supply schedule shifted to the left. Finally, since energy costs in the United States had been relatively low for years, much of the U.S. capital stock was not particularly energy efficient. The rise in oil prices made portions of our capital stock economically obsolete and reduced the U.S. natural rate of output growth.

Recession with Inflation, 1973–1975

By autumn 1973 the negative factors—declining monetary growth, rising interest rates, falling residential construction, poor sales of the 1974 car models, and the rise in energy prices—began to have serious effects on the economy. During 1973.IV real residential construction continued to decline, and, even more important, total real consumption spending fell—enough to precipitate a recession beginning in November.

Much of the fourth quarter decline in consumption spending was due to falling sales of domestically produced automobiles, but the downturn in the auto industry was just beginning. Part of the problem may have been that 1973 auto output was so extraordinary that it might have declined regardless. More important, the domestic auto industry was hit from two sides in 1974. First, the recession reduced household disposable income which reduced the demand for new autos.[4] Second, the OPEC-induced rise in gasoline prices reduced the demand for U.S.-produced autos both absolutely as well as relative to more fuel-efficient foreign-produced cars. The resulting decline in demand for U.S.-produced cars left domestic auto producers with huge unwanted inventories. Detroit automakers laid off workers by the thousands as 1974 domestic vehicle production fell to less than 9 million units for the year.

The recession lasted until March 1975. In terms of declining output, it was the worst downturn since 1937–1938. This was a recession of falling residential construction and consumption spending; in real terms the declines in those components of aggregate demand exceeded the decline in real GNP. Residential construction was devastated by high interest rates and the resulting financial disintermediation. Consumption spending substantially declined for a number of reasons including falling real wealth and disposable income. Real wealth fell 33 percent between 1973 and 1974, in part because rising interest rates and falling corporate profits lowered equity values. Disposable income fell as rising inflation rates cut real wages. Furthermore, the progressive income tax acted as an automatic destabilizer because prices rose faster than real income fell. Thus, nominal income rose and pushed households into higher average income tax brackets. Gains in nominal income also pushed workers into higher social security tax burdens (Okun 1975).

This recession dealt the death blow to the traditional Phillips curve. The unemployment rate went from 4.8 percent in 1973.IV to a peak of 8.9 percent in 1975.II while GNP deflator inflation rose from a 7 percent annual rate in 1973.III (before the oil price rise) to a peak of 12.1 percent in 1974.IV. Certainly this extraordinary increase in inflation during the recession was partly due to the elimination of price controls since the GNP deflator jumped 2.8 percentage points during the quarter the controls were eliminated. But prices rose for other reasons as well: rising energy prices, dollar depreciation, and remaining inflationary pressures from the stimulative policies of prior years.

The recession deepened during the second half of 1974 as the monetary contraction continued and firms realized that the recession was going to last a while longer. M1 grew a total of 1.5 percent during the second half of 1974 compared to 3 percent during the first half. According to Poole (1975), the Federal Reserve was unwilling to substantially lower the Federal Funds rate target band far enough to bring about monetary stimulus (i.e., as loan demand declined with output, interest rates did as well), and the Federal Reserve did not have to raise base growth to keep interest rates within their target range. The deceleration of monetary growth and rising inflation caused the real money supply to decline even further.

Firms' realization that the downturn would continue caused the recession to deepen and unemployment to rise. Through the first half of 1974, firms behaved as if they expected the turndown to be short and mild by retaining workers and allowing inventories to pile up. Indeed, by mid-1974 the unemployment rate was only 0.4 points higher than at the economic peak. During the second half, firms apparently woke up to the fact that output decline would persist and they severely cut production, laid off workers, and began to run down inventories. The unemployment rate rose 3 percentage points from 1974.II to 1975.I.

Expansion with Inflation, 1975–1979

The recession finally ended in the spring of 1975. The increases in oil and food prices were over, inventories were down, and monetary growth turned expansionary enough in early 1975 to raise real money balances by the second quarter. Interest rates declined rapidly, and an expansion began with consumption spending leading the way. Ironically, this expansion ranks as one of the longest in U.S. history (fifty-eight months), yet public dissatisfaction with the economy was high as the economy was afflicted with inflation, relatively high unemployment rates, and slow productivity and real wage growth.

In some ways the expansion from 1975 to 1979 resembles the expansion from 1970 to 1973 because in both cases government policies were enacted to stimulate an economy already at or near full employment. It is easy to identify the economic policy mistakes because hindsight is 20/20. Once again the problem was an overly optimistic estimate of full employment output. Thus, the story of the late 1970s is one of the central bank, goaded on by the administration, generating increased inflation by stimulating an economy that did not need it.

Contemporary estimates place the natural rate of unemployment at around 6 percent during the mid to late 1970s, compared to around 5.5 percent during the 1960s. The natural rate of unemployment was rising for a number of reasons including rapid entry of women and young baby-boomers into the labor force, and the fact that higher oil prices had reduced the productivity of existing U.S. capital. Given the unemployment rates attained during the 1950s and 1960s, however, actual rates of around 6 percent during the 1970s were unacceptably high to many. Policymakers were under considerable public pressure to get unemployment down, and economic policies during the period reflect this fact.

Monetary growth was the major tool in attempts to reduce the unemployment rate. Both M1 and M2 growth turned up mildly in 1974.IV, and then rapidly in 1975 as M2 growth averaged over 11 percent in 1975, and double digit growth of M2 continued through 1976. M1 grew less rapidly than M2 but was significantly up from its growth rate in 1974. Congress approved a tax rebate in 1975 to further economic expansion, but this discretionary change had virtually no impact on aggregate demand. Since the rebate was temporary and did not influence permanent income, households largely saved the rebate.

During the expansion's early stages, real GNP growth was rapid but unemployment remained high. Output rose at a 4.2 percent rate during the last three quarters of 1975, 4.9 percent in 1976, 4.7 percent in 1977, and 5.3 percent in 1978, yet the unemployment rate, which peaked at 8.9 percent in 1975.II, stood at 7.8 percent by the end of 1976. At least two factors were working to keep unemployment high: firms were reluctant to rehire idle workers, and the U.S. had developed a significant structural unemployment problem in industries that were based on previously cheap energy including domestic automobile and steel production. The structural unemployment problem was illustrated by geographic pockets of high unemployment. Eastern Ohio and western Pennsylvania were decimated by the shutdown of integrated steel mills, and many cities in Michigan by the downturn in domestic auto production. These regions incurred unemployment problems that persisted for years.

Another disturbing fact during the expansion was that inflation, while declining relative to 1974 levels, remained high. GNP deflator growth bottomed out for the year 1976 at 6.4 percent and then began the upward creep again, to 6.7 percent in 1977 and 7.3 percent in 1978. Some of this inflation resulted from negative supply factors such as legislation that raised the minimum wage in a series of steps from $2 per hour to $2.65 per hour in 1978 and finally $3.35 per hour in 1981, along with rising food prices in 1978. Also, negative demographic influences on the labor force continued. Furthermore, during this period the economy was in the early stages of the productivity slowdown, the decline in the growth rate of the average product of labor dating to 1973.[5]

The economy reached full employment in 1978 with unemployment at around 6 percent of the labor force. Thereafter, demand stimulus showed up mostly in the inflation rate; in 1979 the GNP deflator rose 8.9 percent while output growth fell to 2.5 percent. The inflation acceleration led the Carter administration to establish voluntary wage and price guideposts that were monitored by the Council on Wage and Price Stability. The guideposts were largely ineffective, however, because they were voluntary. Inflation was reflected in interest rates; short-term Treasury Bill rates which had bottomed out at 4.6 percent in 1977.I stood at 9.4 percent by the start of 1979. The inflation situation was similar to that of 1973, with the major difference being that this time price controls did not exist to hold down measured inflation rates.

In 1979 the public witnessed a déjà vu of events in 1973–1974: another large exogenous increase in oil prices. The cause this time was the Iranian revolution. Mass demonstrations in Iran had brought a declaration of martial law in September 1978, but the situation continued to deteriorate. By spring 1979 the Iranian economy was disrupted to the extent that Iranian oil production almost ceased. World oil prices went from around $14 per barrel to almost $29 per barrel by the end of the year, and since price controls were in effect on gasoline and certain types of domestically produced crude oil, long lines formed at gas pumps. The rise in oil prices and accelerating inflation closely resembled events of 1973, so there was widespread public concern that a recession would occur in 1979, certainly by 1980.

To the surprise of many, a recession did not develop in 1979, largely because consumption spending continued to grow. The generally accepted explanation contends that rapid adjustment of price expectations was the major reason. Here was a rare time when household inflationary expectations rose as quickly as the actual inflation rate. Therefore, consumption spending jumped because the public expected inflation to accelerate so they purchased consumer goods in an attempt to acquire them before the expected price increases actually occurred. The rising inflationary expectations raised nominal interest rates which reduced the return on money balances. Velocity rose almost 4 percent that year to feed the spending surge. Despite continued expansion in 1979, the consensus forecast was for a recession in 1980.

Comments on the 1970s

If asked to identify two episodes that have had the most profound influence on macroeconomic thought, most economists would probably mention the 1929–1933 Great Contraction and the sequence of events in 1973–1974 that led to the 1974–1975 recession. The Great Contraction led Keynes to write *The General Theory* that placed aggregate demand on a pedestal as the major source of economic fluctuations. The events leading to the 1974–1975 recession moved the emphasis away from aggregate demand and toward aggregate supply. As a direct result of this recession, supply influences were incorporated into the new-Keynesian model, and the real business cycle model was developed.

Inflation was a major economic problem during the 1970s. It was caused not only by the supply shocks but by excessive monetary induced aggregate demand growth as well. By the end of the decade, the American public demanded relief and elected a new President, Ronald Reagan, who promised to reduce inflation. He carried out his promise in the early 1980s, but the cost proved high—the deepest recession since 1937–1938.

INSTABILITY FOLLOWED BY A LONG EXPANSION, 1980–1989

The period from 1980 to 1989 is notable for unstable behavior of several economic aggregates and two recessions during the first few years, followed by the longest peacetime economic expansion in U.S. history. The first recession, in 1980, lasted only six months, making it the shortest on record. It was followed by a twelve-month expansion, also among the shortest ever. The second recession, from 1981 to 1982, was the deepest since the end of World War II and caused high unemployment that seriously disrupted several sectors of the U.S. economy. That recession was followed by an expansion which, at this writing, is in its seventh year and associated with the largest gains in average living standards since the 1938–1945 expansion.

Public policy discussions during the 1980s were dominated by the Reagan administration, in office from January 1981 to January 1989. Reagan and his supporters arrived in Washington with a plan: pursue moderate monetary growth rates to reduce aggregate demand growth, reduce income tax rates to stimulate aggregate supply growth, raise government purchases for defense, and reduce government purchases for nondefense. The net effect on government purchases was supposed to be a reduction (i.e., purchases for nondefense were supposed to fall by more than expenditures on defense would rise), which when combined with reduced monetary growth rates would reduce aggregate demand growth. This administration contended that the positive supply-side effects of reduced tax rates would offset the negative demand-side effects of reduced monetary growth, thus resulting in higher economic growth, lower unemployment, and reduced inflation. This predicted outcome was very controversial, and the economy's path during the administration's first few years did not go according to the plan. Economic instability, inflation, and unemployment were all serious problems. The remainder of the decade, however, was a period of substantial gains in living standards with low inflation rates relative to those of the 1970s.

A Very Short Cycle, 1980–1981

The widely expected recession finally occurred after the economy peaked in January 1980. Both consumption expenditures and residential construction declined to help bring on the shortest recession in recorded U.S. history—a six-month decline that lasted until July. Over the recession real GNP fell 2.3 percent, the unemployment rate rose from 6 percent to 7.8 percent, and the inflation rate increased from an annual rate of 7.3 percent in 1979.IV to 8.5 percent in 1980.II. The simultaneous output decline and inflation acceleration suggests that negative supply shocks, including the 1979 rise in oil prices, contributed to this economic downturn.

Rising energy prices were not the only factor; monetary policy was apparently responsible as well. During 1979 and 1980 monetary growth was designed more to extinguish inflation than to accommodate the rise in oil prices. The real money supply declined after peaking in 1978.I, and the combination of falling real money balances and rising inflationary expectations raised nominal interest rates to levels not previously witnessed during this century. During March, yields on ninety-day Treasury Bills averaged 15.53 percent, and yields on long-term treasuries averaged 11.87 percent.

The spending decline was not severe until March when interest rates peaked and President Carter authorized the Federal Reserve to impose selective credit controls. The credit controls were a series of measures designed to reduce the amount of credit banks could extend for new loans and credit card purchases. These credit controls, in combination with high interest rates, caused a significant decline in aggregate demand during 1980.II. During that quarter, real GNP experienced the fastest one quarter decline since the end of World War II with falling purchases of new autos and residential construction accounting for about two-thirds of the decline in final sales.[6]

By June, falling income had helped reduce short-term interest rates an incredible 850 basis points from their March peaks, and long-term rates were down over 200 basis points. The credit controls were lifted that same month, and the economy began to expand. This expansion lasted only twelve months and was disappointing in that inflation, while down slightly from rates in 1980.II, remained high. By the end of 1980 the GNP deflator was rising at about a 10 percent annual rate and the CPI was growing even faster. Another source of disappointment was the fact that the unemployment rate fell by only 0.2 percentage points during the entire expansion. The economy eventually peaked in July 1981 with inflation still running at close to a 10 percent annual rate. The 1980 recession had been much too short to significantly alleviate existing inflationary pressures.

The 1981–1982 Recession

By the end of 1980 it was apparent that the recession during the first half had done virtually nothing to reduce the inflation that was so worrysome to the public. Another, much deeper, recession was necessary to get inflation down, and this is precisely what happened from mid-1981 to the end of 1982: the deepest U.S. recession during the post–World War II period. This recession was the medicine needed to bring down inflation, but the cost was high. From the peak to the trough, inflation fell from 9.9 percent to 3.6 percent, while unemployment went from 7.2 percent to 10.8 percent. Of special interest here is the Federal Reserve's role in the recession. At the time, it was the subject of a lively debate between monetarists claiming that the central bank was primarily responsible and nonmonetarists arguing that the Federal Reserve was the innocent victim of exogenous changes in the financial system.

Our discussion of monetary events leading up to this recession begins with the October 1979 announcement by the Board of Governors that they intended to target monetary aggregates—in other words, to conduct a "monetarist experiment" to bring monetary growth rates under control. This announcement caused tremendous excitement among economists. Is the Federal Reserve actually going to adhere to the monetarist policy prescription of a fixed monetary rule? Will this be the closest thing the monetarists ever get to a controlled laboratory experiment?

Another important event occurred in March 1980 during the early stages of the "monetarist experiment." Congress passed, and President Carter signed, the Depository Institutions Deregulation and Monetary Control Act. As the name suggests, this important piece of legislation was designed both to deregulate the banking system and to provide the Federal Reserve with increased monetary control. The act initiated the deregulation of the banking system by phasing out over a six-year period ceiling deposit rates that banks could pay, and allowing banks to issue, starting in 1981, interest-bearing checking accounts called Negotiable Order of Withdrawal (NOW) accounts.[7] The act was also designed to enhance the Federal Reserve's ability to control monetary growth by giving the Board of Governors authority to set required reserve ratios for all banks, not just member banks as before, and allowing nonmember banks to utilize Federal Reserve services.

Time passed before economists could judge the monetary experiment, but fairly early on the monetarists were disappointed. Despite the Federal Reserve's claim of targeting monetary aggregates while possessing enhanced tools of monetary control to assist their effort, monetary instability increased after October 1979. The standard deviation of quarterly M1 monetary growth was about three and one-half times higher during the monetarist experiment than before (Friedman 1983, 1984). Monetarists viewed the so-called experiment with contempt—yet another divergence of Federal Reserve rhetoric from actions. The Federal Reserve countered by pointing out that despite the instability of quarterly growth rates, year-to-year annual monetary growth rates were quite stable from the late 1970s to early 1980s. Monetarists responded by stating that in an attempt to get from point A to point B the Federal Reserve was wandering all over the map rather than simply walking in a straight line.

This debate is illustrated by considering monetary growth data from 1979 to 1982. Attempts to discern if monetary forces precipitated the recession came to different conclusions when looking at annual versus quarterly data. Annual data suggested that the Federal Reserve was not responsible for the recession—from 1979. IV through 1981.II M2 growth averaged around 8 percent annually and M1 averaged 6 percent. These amounts are roughly comparable to growth rates in the preceding years. However, quarterly growth figures present a different story—that is, the recession did, in fact, have a monetary aspect to it. Specifically, during the last two quarters of 1980, M1 and M2 growth averaged 15 percent and 12 percent, respectively, and then grew 4 percent and 8 percent during the next two quarters. The fact that inflation remained at double digit rates in late 1980 and early 1981, combined with the sharp reduction in M1 growth in 1981.I, probably contributed to the rise in short-term nominal interest rates. Also, some argue the high interest rates were due to rising precautionary demand for money—the result of a high degree of uncertainty given the extreme instability of many macroeconomic aggregates (Friedman 1984). Rates reached during 1980 were surpassed when rates on ninety-day Treasury Bills exceeded 16 percent in May 1981. Since inflationary expectations were not rising as quickly as nominal interest rates, both before- and after-tax real interest rates were at levels not seen in decades (Holland 1984).

As in 1980, the high levels of interest rates caused a reduction in interest-sensitive new residential construction and spending on consumer durables, enough so to start the recession in August 1981. The major difference between the 1980 recession and the 1981–1982 version was that the latter was ten months longer and considerably deeper because nominal GNP growth stayed low for five quarters. After growing at an annual rate of 12.6 percent from 1980.III to 1981.III, nominal GNP rose at only a 3.3 percent annual rate from 1981.IV to 1982.IV. Nominal GNP growth stayed low because beginning in 1981.IV the income velocities of both M1 and M2 began following an unusual behavior pattern: declining significantly. In the case of M1 velocity, it fell at an annual rate of 12.6 percent in 1982.IV and declined 5.4 percent during all of 1982. M2 velocity fell 4.5 percent from 1981.IV to 1982.III. At the time, the causes of the velocity decline were not completely clear although many (e.g., Volcker 1983) considered banking deregulation a major suspect. They argued that the advent of interest-bearing checking accounts raised money's own rate of return. Therefore, since money became relatively more attractive to hold compared to other assets, the demand for money rose and velocity declined. (This velocity decline is discussed at length in chapter 12.)

As indicators of recession's severity, the unemployment rate averaged 10.6 percent during the trough quarter of 1982.IV when the output gap was just over $330 billion (1982$). Furthermore, high real interest rates were responsible for a dollar appreciation on the foreign exchange market that caused a shift in the composition of manufacturing away from U.S. tradeable goods and toward non-tradeables. The net export component of aggregate demand declined over 40 percent during the recession, and industries producing tradeable goods such as autos, farm machinery, construction equipment, and integrated steel encountered severe sales declines which contributed further to U.S. structural unemployment problems.

This recession was associated with very large federal budget deficits. While the federal budget virtually always moves toward deficit during recessions, this time it moved very rapidly with the real deficit changing from $67 billion in 1981 to $145 billion in 1982 (1982$). Much of this increase resulted from fiscal changes enlarging the full employment deficit, specifically the Reagan administration's defense buildup and the first stage of income tax reductions in 1982. The combination of the two moved the real full employment deficit to over $100 billion by the end of 1982, and in 1982.IV the actual deficit was running at a $200 billion annual rate. Many argue that these large deficits were partly responsible for existing high real interest rates.[8]

The legacy of the 1981–1982 recession is that it was both long and deep enough to reduce inflation to its lowest rate in years. The GNP deflator rose 3.9 percent in 1983, the lowest annual rate of price increase since 1967. Of course the cost was huge in terms of lost output and high unemployment, but the recession did lay the groundwork for the very long expansion that followed.

Economic Expansion, 1983–1989

Both monetary and fiscal policies became stimulative during the second half of 1982, and the economy moved into expansion by the end of the year. In the monetary arena, the Federal Reserve decided to abandon their monetarist experiment during the summer of 1982, the stated reason being that unstable velocity had weakened the link between the growth of the monetary aggregates and nominal GNP. Compared to rates during the first half of the year, during the second half M1 growth went from 4.5 percent to 12.3 percent and M2 growth went from 7.6 percent to 9.8 percent. The combination of falling inflationary expectations, declining output, and rising monetary growth lowered short-term interest rates from just over 12 percent in June to 8 percent by the end of the year. Fiscal policy also changed significantly. Real government purchases went from a 0.8 percent annual decline during the first half of 1982 to 9.9 percent annual gain during the second half. Furthermore, the first stage of the reduction in income tax rates took effect that year. Both consumer durables and new residential construction growth turned positive, and economic expansion was underway by December.

During the expansion's first two calendar years, output gains were rapid as the economy moved back toward its natural rate of output. In 1983 real GNP rose 3.6 percent, the unemployment rate fell almost three points, industrial production rose about 15 percent, and the inflation rate continued falling (to 3.9 percent) because considerable excess capacity still existed. In 1984 the economy followed a similar pattern with output rising 6.8 percent, and both unemployment and inflation continued to decline. During the next three years output grew at rates more consistent with trend growth: 3.4 percent in 1985, and 2.8 percent in 1986, and 3.4 percent in 1987. The unemployment rate continued declining as did inflation until 1986 when GNP deflator growth bottomed out at 3 percent. Thereafter, inflation began to rise while the unemployment rate fell, suggesting that the economy reached full employment around 1986 or 1987.

Two notable events occurred during the mid-1980s: the 1986 decline in oil prices and the 1987 stock market crash. In the case of oil prices, the OPEC cartel finally fell apart in 1986 when some oil producing countries, most notably Saudi Arabia, raised production. Another factor in the price decline was the fact that increased energy conservation by oil consuming nations was dampening demand, indicated by the fact that the U.S. ratio of energy consumption to GNP had declined about 26 percent since the first oil price shock in 1973.[9] The combination of rising supply and falling demand reduced oil prices from around $27 per barrel in 1985 to about $14 per barrel by 1986.

The oil price decline did not have as large a positive impact on the U.S. economy it might have had in earlier years because energy conservation had significantly improved since 1973. The big winners were U.S. consumers who paid lower energy costs. There were losers too. Since the United States is a high-cost producer of oil, the price decline rendered many U.S. oil and gas wells unable to compete with low-cost Middle Eastern producers. During just the first half of 1986 investment spending in the oil and gas industry fell by $10 billion and employment declined by almost 150,000 people (Council of Economic Advisors 1987, p. 25). While the benefits to consumers were spread across America, the bulk of the negative impact fell on the energy producing regions of the country, and the oil price decline was associated with a 0.6 percentage point decline in 1986 U.S. economic growth relative to 1985. Some contend a recession was averted because the Federal Reserve raised M1 growth to 17 percent in 1986.

With respect to the stock market, Wall Street was an exciting place in 1987. From January to August, the Dow Jones Industrial Average (DJIA) went from around 1,900 to over 2,700, and some expressed concern that speculative fever had taken over the market. Then, on October 19, 1987, the DJIA dropped 508 points, by far the single largest daily price drop both in absolute and percentage terms which "wiped out almost $1 trillion of financial wealth in the U.S." (Brimmer 1989, p. 11). Investors were very concerned and the leading indicator characteristics of stock prices were duly noted. The Federal Reserve behaved admirably immediately following the crash and perhaps averted a recession with their actions. Immediately following the crash, the central bank flooded the economy with liquidity by buying bonds and discounting liberally—that is, the Federal Reserve did everything in their power to prevent the crash from spreading to the real sector and apparently were successful. Soon afterward they removed the increased liquidity from the system, and economists and the financial community publicly applauded the Federal Reserve for a job well done. The crash's only noticeable effect on the real sector was a decline in real consumption expenditures during 1987.IV, which was households' response to increased uncertainty (Romer 1988). By the start of 1988 when it was apparent that a downturn was not on the horizon, spending returned to normal patterns and the economy rolled along.

The stock market crash is especially interesting for two reasons. First, it is as close as one ever gets to a ceteris paribus event in macroeconomics because no major identifiable event triggered the largest stock market crash in history. Investors must have been exceptionally nervous about inflated equity prices.[10] Second, almost two years after the crash a recession has yet to occur, and when one eventually does, economists will be hard pressed to tie any causality between it and the crash. In fact, the economy managed to shrug off the crash without any serious adverse effects, placing stock prices' accuracy as a leading indicator in serious doubt.[11]

The 1983–1989 expansion has exhibited some interesting characteristics. One is the strength of investment spending and consumer durables. From 1982.IV to 1988.III, real spending on consumer durables and total investment have both averaged 8.4 percent annual growth. In the case of investment spending, the pattern of the different components is striking. During the expansion's first few years all components were growing rapidly with residential structures up 62 percent over the first two years. The Tax Reform Act of 1986, however, raised effective tax rates on business structures. That component started declining in 1986, but investment spending kept on rising because the growth of the other components offset the decline in business structures.

Another notable feature is the growth of real government purchases which averaged 3.2 percent annually over the expansion. Almost half of the total growth resulted from rising federal purchases for defense. In fact, the pattern of federal defense purchases during the 1980s is quite similar to that of the 1960s; military spending in 1969 was about 31 percent higher in real terms than it had been in 1961. During 1988.III it was running at an annual rate 33 percent higher than during 1982. Therefore, the wartime/peacetime dichotomy sometimes drawn between the expansions of the 1960s and 1980s is rather weak.[12]

By late 1988 concern developed that the expansion was running out of steam, and forecasts for recession in late 1989 or sometime in 1990 became consensus opinion. Whether these forecasts are correct or not is impossible to say at this writing, but there are some warning signs. Unemployment has fallen for over six years, reaching 4.9 percent in March 1989 which is the lowest since late 1973. Inflation rates have risen since 1986, partly the result of dollar depreciation since 1985, rapid monetary growth in 1985 and 1986, and wage inflation.

The Federal Reserve began voicing concern about inflationary pressures in 1987 and, starting in July 1988, engineered a significant monetary contraction. From June 1988 to July 1989 both M1 and M2 growth rates were down significantly; in fact, M1 growth was negative during the first six months of 1989. Short-term interest rates rose sharply, and 1989 auto sales were below 1988 levels. We have no crystal balls, but the situation in the summer of 1989 resembles several other periods we have covered: an overheating economy and a central bank trying to reduce inflationary pressures. It remains to be seen whether a recession results in the near future.

Comments on the 1980s

The early years of the decade were a continuation of the economic instability that plagued the U.S. economy during the 1970s. The situation, however, reversed itself and the period from 1983 to 1989 was a welcome change that featured a very long, prosperous economic expansion generated by positive supply shocks in the form of falling oil prices, aging baby-boom workers, and the rapid proliferation of computers. On the demand side, important factors include rapid monetary growth during the mid-1980s and the federal defense buildup.

The decade's impact on economic thought remains to be seen. Since ideas lag events in macroeconomics, economists during the 1980s have been busy investigating the impact of supply phenomena that were so important during the 1970s and have turned out to be important in the 1980s as well. If the monetary contraction during 1988–1989 is followed by a growth recession or decline in the level of real GNP, then economists will probably go back and take yet another look at the importance of monetary growth. If a growth recession or a decline in the level of real GNP does not occur, then monetarism may be seriously questioned.

NOTES

1. An important piece of information for Keynesian economic policymakers was the result of Samuelson and Solow (1960) who examined the Phillips curve in the United States. They concluded that, given the position of the curve in 1960, price stability would be consistent with an unemployment rate of 5.5 percent while full employment (considered 3 percent unemployment) would require an inflation rate of 4.5 percent. These estimates implied that policymakers could choose where to place the economy on the curve. The authors suggested that this trade-off would exist "in the years immediately ahead."

2. Other features were tax changes involving repeal of excise taxes on autos, more investment tax credits, and reduced personal income tax rates.

3. "Detroit Bucks a Buyer Rebellion," *Time*, Dec. 2, 1974.

4. Okun (1975) contends that the decline in auto sales was largely the result of the decline in household disposable income.

5. Several studies attempt to explain the causes of this slowdown but a general consensus does not exist. See the comments by Nordhaus at the end of Griliches (1989). Some argue that the productivity slowdown may be the figment of faulty data. In this context, see Baily and Gordon (1988).

6. See Council of Economic Advisors (1981, p. 160) for a detailed discussion of the credit controls imposed during 1980.

7. The savings and loan industry was deregulated in 1982 by the Garn–St. Germain Act that allowed savings and loans to offer interest-bearing checking accounts. For a complete discussion of the Depository Institutions Deregulation and Monetary Control Act and the Garn–St. Germain Act, see Degen (1987).

8. This comment assumes that government budget deficits associated with an income tax reduction raise real interest rates. This is a controversial statement to say the least since many believe government deficits "don't matter." Interested readers will find the argument that "deficits don't matter" in terms of affecting aggregate demand or interest rates in Barro (1974). The opposing view that deficits do affect aggregate demand and interest rates is presented by B. M. Friedman (1978) and Feldstein (1982).

9. "U.S. Progress in Energy Efficiency is Halting," *New York Times*, Feb. 27, 1989.

10. The author is indebted to George Von Furstenburg for this point.

11. The leading indicator properties of stock prices are critically evaluated by Higgins (1988). He shows that, contrary to common belief, stock prices are a poor forecaster of future economic activity.

12. The author is indebted to Michael Ulan for this point.

12 | Some Macroeconomic Puzzles

Here we discuss some interesting issues in macroeconomics, each important to the study of business cycles. The coverage is fairly brief, but interested readers can pursue the topics further by studying the references.

REAL WAGES: COUNTERCYCLICAL, PROCYCLICAL, OR ACYCLICAL?

Following changes in aggregate demand, the monetarist, rational expectations, and new-Keynesian models discussed in chapters 5, 6, and 7 predict that real wages are countercyclical over the business cycle. According to those models, during economic expansions prices rise faster than nominal wages and so the real wage falls which induces firms to employ more labor with which to produce more output. Conversely, during recessions rising real wages induce firms to employ less labor and produce less output. The implication is that over the business cycle firms move along a relatively fixed labor demand schedule in response to changing real wage rates.[1] Over the longer run, the secular pattern of real wages reflects changing labor productivity.

This prediction of countercyclical real wages dates back at least to the classical economists who argued that aggregate demand-induced deviations of output from the full employment level move real wages in a countercyclical direction. This notion was embraced by John Maynard Keynes who states in *The General Theory* (Keynes 1936, p. 17) " [An] increase in employment can only occur to the accompaniment of a decline in the rate of real wages. Thus I am not disputing this vital fact which the classical economists have (rightly) asserted as indefeasable. In a given state of organisation, equipment and technique, the real wage earned by a unit of labor has a unique (inverse) correlation with the volume of employment."

This predicted result has been a thorn in the side of demand-side macroeconomic models for years. In the late 1930s economists published a number of empirical studies of the cyclical behavior of real wages and discovered that the countercyclical pattern was not at all obvious; in fact, several report procyclical real wages. One such attempt by Dunlop (1938) investigates real wages in the United Kingdom and reports that during the seven expansions from 1860 to 1913 real wages rose in all cases, and during the seven recessions over the same period real wages declined during three of them and rose during the other four. In other words, Dunlop finds no convincing evidence that real wages were countercyclical—instead, they were more likely to be procyclical. Dunlop's study prompted Tarshis (1939) to investigate U.S. cyclical real wage behavior, and he reports similar results: from 1932 to 1938 U.S. real wages were not countercyclical, they tended to be procyclical.[2] Yet another study by Richardson (1939) notes that while available data suggest procyclical real wages, the quality of available data is questionable because it tends to come from highly unionized or regulated industries. Furthermore, the data do not take part-time work and piece work into account. Richardson suggests that the issue may be unresolved until better data are made available.

Economists were relatively quiet on the issue for about thirty years until Bodkin (1969) attempted to take a "fresh look" with a greater quantity of data than was available when the earlier studies were published. He used both ante- and post–World War II U.S. and Canadian data and estimated the relationship between real wages (both actual and detrended) and the unemployment rate by regressing the real wage as a function of the unemployment rate. He obtained inconclusive results with Canadian data but reported strong evidence that U.S. real wages tend to be procyclical, particularly when the real wage is deflated by the CPI. He reported that periods of rising unemployment were associated with falling real wages, and periods of falling unemployment were associated with rising real wages. Bodkin noted that when the U.S. real wage is deflated by the Wholesale Price Index, he found some evidence that real wages were countercyclical. Taken as a whole, however, his results suggest that U.S. real wages were procyclical.

The issue quieted down again until Neftci (1978) published a study that utilizes Granger causality tests that had recently become available. Neftci estimated the causal relationship between employment and real wages using U.S. post–World War II data and presented evidence suggesting that real wages cause employment while only weak evidence exists that employment causes real wages. Furthermore the relationship between real wages and employment is negative (i.e., when lagged relationships are taken into consideration, real wages are countercyclical). Shortly after Neftci's study was published, his results were confirmed by Sargent (1978).

The Neftci/Sargent results reopened the can of worms and within a few years several more studies were published. This set of studies tends to show that, net of productivity trend, real wages are acyclical—rising during both expansions and contractions except during the 1970s when real wages were procyclical. Among these studies is that of Altonji and Ashenfelter (1980) who investigated the time series properties of post–World War II real wages for both the United States and the United Kingdom. They estimated a model that attempts to link the unemployment rate to the difference between the expected and actual real wage rates and found little evidence that they are, in fact, linked. They went on to test a random walk model for the real wage rate and concluded that they were unable to reject the hypothesis that real wages follow a random walk with drift (i.e., the real wage is acyclical because it moves randomly around a trend).

Geary and Kennan (1982) published yet another study that reports acyclical real wages. They considered real wage behavior in twelve Organization for Economic Cooperation and Development (OECD) countries where they measured the real wage as the nominal wage deflated by the Wholesale Price Index as opposed to the Consumer Price Index used by Neftci and Sargent. Geary and Kennan argue that their measure is preferable because it represents firms' product real wage. They find that real wages are statistically independent from employment (i.e., acyclical) and claim their results contrast to Neftci and Sargent's because of the different sample periods and different deflators used to calculate the real wage. Geary and Kennan suggest that real wages may be acyclical because both labor demand and supply could be shifting over the business cycle.

Bils (1985) argues that existing real wage studies may be flawed because they investigate the properties of average aggregate real wages. He notes that aggregate data cloak the fact that the composition of the work force changes over the business cycle. During economic expansions the increased employment of workers at the low end of the wage scale may bias the aggregate real wage downward, and during recessions the increased unemployment of those same low wage earners may bias the average real wage upward. Hence, the aggregate measure may appear countercyclical when in fact it is procyclical. Bils used disaggregated data and controlled for worker characteristics such as age and education and tested the cyclical characteristics of disaggregated real wages. He found strong evidence of procyclical real wages, reporting that a 1 percentage point increase in the unemployment rate corresponds to a 1.5 to 2 percent decline in real wages and noted that his results hold up for both disaggregate and aggregate data. He also reports that real wages of job changers are highly procyclical while those of people who stay at the same job are less procyclical.

In a recent article Kniesner and Goldsmith (1987) summarize the empirical literature by noting (p. 1257) that ''the real wage is acyclical during the postwar period, except for the 1970s when it is procyclical.'' This claim is illustrated in Figure 12.1 which shows the real wage deflated by the CPI from 1954.I to 1987.IV. From the start of the sample until 1973 the real wage shows very little movement around trend growth (which roughly corresponds the average labor productivity growth), thus real wages appear acyclical. From 1973 to the early 1980s procyclical behavior is indicated as real wages clearly fell during the supply shock recessions of 1973–1975 and 1980. During the mid-1980s the

Figure 12.1
Real Wages, 1954.I to 1987.IV

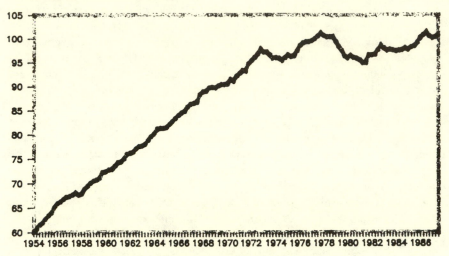

Index of Real Average Hourly Compensation, All Employees
Nonfarm Business Sector (1977=100)
Source: U.S. Commerce Dept., Business Conditions Digest

acyclical nature returns as real wages grew erratically during the 1983–1989 expansion. Also note the productivity slowdown shows up clearly with the definite kink in the real wage trend starting in 1973.

The growing evidence that real wages may be procyclical or acyclical instead of countercyclical threw demand-side macroeconomists for a loop. The results suggested that firms may not be moving along the labor demand schedule in response to changing real wage rates. Keynesian economists attempted to rescue demand-side macromodels by constructing the new-Keynesian model (see chapter 8) that argues that the cyclical behavior of real wages completely depends on where the initial shock comes from: aggregate demand or aggregate supply. In the case of demand shocks, real wages are countercyclical or acyclical depending on the relative speeds of nominal wage and price adjustment. In the case of supply shocks, they may be procyclical. Yet another macromodel, the real business cycle model (see chapter 9), was developed partly in response to real wage studies. This model focuses on the role of supply shocks and predicts procyclical real wages which is certainly more in line with empirical studies of real wages than the demand-side models.

The result that real wages are dominated by labor productivity growth with little apparent cyclical behavior except during the 1970s raises two questions: (1) Why are real wages acyclical during most of the post–WWII period? and (2) What was different about the 1970s that would make real wages procyclical?

With respect to the acyclical behavior, many economists contend that real wages are inflexible and cite several reasons why firms may be reluctant to force real wage cuts on their workers. Among the arguments cited include the existence of labor unions which may make real wage cuts difficult, firms' desire to maintain good will with their work force, the belief that labor productivity and worker morale depend on real wages, transaction costs of changing real wages, and the existence of implicit real wage contracts.[3]

The second issue, the real wage behavior during the 1970s, reflects the fact that recessions during that period were partly induced by negative supply shocks that shifted the demand for labor to the left, thus reflecting reduced labor productivity growth. In other words, procyclical real wages during 1970s-type supply shock recessions is exactly what economic theory predicts. To summarize then, the issue of cyclical real wage behavior is unsettled. The empirical evidence on the cyclical nature of wage behavior is mixed, although it appears real wages are typically acyclical and dominated by longer term trends in productivity growth. Furthermore, the fact that macroeconomic models cannot agree on a cyclical real wage prediction suggests that more work may be needed in this area.

THE 1980S M1 VELOCITY PUZZLE

From 1959 to 1981 the income velocity of M1 behaved in a stable manner, growing around 3.2 percent per year with little deviation around that rate. M2 velocity growth was also stable, growing about 0.3 percent per year. This stability of both velocity growth rates resulted in the close link between monetary growth and nominal GNP growth which is an important result of monetarism.

Starting in 1981.IV, however, the income velocities of both measures of money, especially M1, started to behave in an unusual manner—falling rapidly. From 1981.IV to 1988.IV, M1 velocity fell at an annual rate of 1.6 percent while M2 velocity declined 1.2 percent annually. Figure 12.2 shows the behavior of both M1 and M2 velocities from 1959 to 1988 and makes it apparent that M1 velocity has been much more erratic than M2 velocity which is why much of the economic research, and therefore our discussion, focuses on M1 velocity. The relationship between unstable velocity and nominal GNP growth during the 1980s is illustrated in Table 12.1 which shows growth rates of money, velocity, and nominal GNP from 1981 to 1988. What is striking is that during the first few years erratic velocity growth is associated with a high degree of nominal GNP growth variability, while during the second half unstable velocity growth is associated with stable nominal GNP growth.

Recent velocity behavior presents macroeconomists with an important puzzle. Not only does erratic velocity growth cause Federal Reserve policymakers to be uncertain about what rate of monetary growth will be consistent with a certain rate of nominal GNP growth, but it has also caused many economists to dismiss monetarism as an empirical relationship. Economists have worked very hard on

Figure 12.2
Income Velocity of M1 and M2, 1959.I to 1988.II

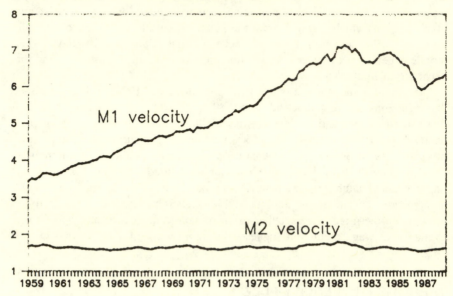

this velocity puzzle for several years now and turned out a number of research papers that attempt to resolve the issue. This research has resulted in a general consensus that a variety of factors were causes, although no one knows their relative importance.

One explanation considers the velocity decline unusual in the sense that it involves a change in the form of the money demand function. In other words, the amount of money people wish to hold in relation to their income changed for given values of the variables that enter the money demand function. A leading proponent of this view is Paul Volcker (1983), chairman of the Federal Reserve Board of Governors from August 1979 to August 1987. He argues that the velocity decline resulted from the introduction of Negotiable Order of Withdrawal accounts (NOW accounts) which pay interest on checking accounts with no check-writing restrictions.[4] Since NOW accounts are a component of M1, their introduction in 1981 changed the nature of M1 from essentially paying no interest to including a component that bears interest. Therefore, the return on money balances rose, causing the public to hold more money relative to their income. Hence, M1 velocity declined.

This explanation helps explain the decline in velocity shortly after NOW accounts were introduced but cannot explain later declines. The introduction of interest payments on money would cause a one-shot decline in M1 velocity, not the declines several years later because it seems unlikely that households would

Table 12.1
Sources of Nominal Aggregate Demand Growth, 1981 to 1988

Equation of Exchange: MV= Nominal GNP

GROWTH RATES

YEAR	M1	M1 VELOCITY	M2	M2 VELOCITY	NOMINAL GNP
1981	6.5%	4.9%	8.0%	3.5%	11.7%
1982	8.5%	-4.4%	8.8%	-4.7%	3.7%
1983	9.6%	-1.8%	11.8%	-3.8%	7.6%
1984	5.7%	4.8%	8.2%	2.4%	10.8%
1985	12.4%	-5.3%	8.4%	-1.8%	6.4%
1986	16.9%	-9.7%	9.6%	-3.6%	5.6%
1987	3.5%	3.1%	3.3%	3.3%	6.7%
1988	5.0%	2.4%	5.6%	1.8%	7.4%

take six years to adjust their money holdings to the advent of interest-bearing checking.

Other explanations contend that the M1 velocity decline is not unusual in the sense that the demand for money was simply responding to changes in the variables that enter the money demand function. Several economists—for example, Volcker (1983), Stone and Thornton (1987), and Poole (1988)—mention falling inflation and nominal interest rates from 1981 until 1986 as factors which raised the relative return on money balances and, therefore, reduced velocity.

Economists also suggest that M1 velocity was simply following the traditional pattern predicted by monetarists where velocity falls during periods of accelerating monetary growth and rises when monetary growth declines because the public takes time to adjust their actual money balances to desired levels. The data in Table 12.1 tend to support this view. Years when M1 growth accelerated relative to the prior year are associated with falling velocity, and monetary decelerations are associated with rising velocity.

Friedman (1984) argues that economic uncertainty, a variable in the money demand function, helped cause the fall in velocity.[5] He argues that increased economic uncertainty about the economic future led households to increase their precautionary money holdings for given levels of income. Friedman's proxy for uncertainty is the variability of money growth—the idea being that more variability of money growth leads to increased uncertainty about the future values of economic aggregates. This hypothesis has been tested by Hall and Noble

(1987) who report that increased monetary variability explains part of M1 velocity's behavior through 1984.II.

Finally, an increasing number of economists argue that velocity has been acting unusual because the interest rate sensitivity of money demand increased following the introduction of interest-bearing checking accounts.[6] These studies note that banks asymmetrically adjust rates on the interest-bearing component of M1 to changes in short-term market rates. The interest-bearing component of M1, called Other Checkable Deposits (OCDs), consists of NOW accounts, automatic transfer from savings accounts (ATS accounts), credit union share draft balances, and demand deposits at thrift institutions. During periods of falling interest rates, banks lower the rates on OCDs in step with market rates, but during periods of rising market rates, banks are slow to raise rates on OCDs. As a result, during periods of falling short-term interest rates—the case from mid-1981 through 1982 and again from 1984 until early 1987—banks lower rates on OCDs in step with market rates, and the rate differential becomes small which lowers the opportunity cost of holding M1. The OCD component of M1 rises, which reflects the increased demand for M1, and velocity declines.

When short-term market rates rise, banks, raise deposit rates slowly such that the spread between the two widens. Thus, the opportunity cost of holding the OCDs component of M1 rises, the demand for M1 declines, and M1 velocity increases. This analysis explains the slow growth of other checkable deposits during 1987 and 1988 when short-term rates were rising. These studies note a much higher correlation between short-term interest rates and M1 velocity during the 1980s than during earlier periods.

This discussion raises the following question: Why do banks asymmetrically adjust deposit rates to changing market rates? The answer is that the banking industry is less than perfectly competitive. Banks possess some degree of market power which is reflected in their adjustment of deposit rates to market rates (see Neumark and Sharpe 1989).[7] Banking has become increasingly concentrated under deregulation as banks have attempted to take advantage of economies of scale by absorbing other banks within regions of the country. This increased merger activity is indicated by the enormous growth of the "super-regionals" during the 1980s such as Banc One, North Carolina National Bank (NCNB), and National Bank of Detroit (NBD). Future easing of interstate banking restrictions will probably accelerate the trend of industry concentration. If increased interest rate sensitivity of M1 is the correct explanation for the erratic behavior of M1 velocity, then we can expect M1 velocity to continue the erratic pattern as short-term market interest rates rise and fall. This is why the Federal Reserve no longer announces M1 targets and is instead focusing attention on the M2 measure of money.

WHY HAS THE GNP PRICE DEFLATOR BEEN RISING SINCE 1949?

The U.S. implicit GNP price deflator has been rising steadily since 1949—the last year it declined over a calendar year.[8] There are a number of facts to consider about this secular price rise. First, we are not talking about hyperinflation; from 1950 to 1988 the average annual rate of GNP deflator inflation was 4.3 percent, and the inflation rate rarely reached double digit rates during four quarters over that period.

Second, this forty years of inflation is neither unique to the United States nor unusual in a historical sense. Post–World War II inflation has plagued most nations of the world. Inflation has been the rule, not the exception. Also, there are several historical examples where prices have risen over several decades. To cite just a few examples, France experienced fifty years of rising prices during the 1300s, prices in England rose from the mid- to late 1700s, and historically the United States has experienced a number of secular price increases (Schwartz 1973).

Third, the recent inflation here and abroad has been both rapid and prolonged enough to severely erode the purchasing power of nominal money balances relative to many previous inflations. Consider this: price levels in Britain, Germany, and the United States were about the same in 1913 as they were in the late 1700s. Granted, in each country they rose and then fell during that period, but the actual increases were relatively modest compared to rates over the past forty years. For example, the Wholesale Price Index in Britain was 101 in 1776, rose to 186 by 1800, and then cycled down to 100 by 1913. Ignoring Germany who experienced hyperinflation after both world wars, price rises in Britain and the United States have been such that the current U.S. CPI is about 450 percent higher than in 1950, and in the United Kingdom the CPI has risen over 1000 percent over the same period. Yet neither country has experienced hyperinflation!

Finally, it is important to understand that the U.S. postwar inflation has been continuous. Prior to World War II, periods of secular price increases included price declines during economic downturns. The inflation pattern since 1950 is different in that during the last forty years the U.S. GNP deflator has not fallen for more than one quarter during any of the seven recessions that occurred between 1950 and 1989. In other words, the inflation pattern over the U.S. business cycle has changed. Again considering the U.S. GNP deflator, from 1875 to 1949 the price level tended to be procyclical; whereas from 1950 to 1989 the inflation rate has been procyclical and never turned negative for two consecutive quarters.

The basic question, then, is twofold: Why have prices been rising for forty years? and Why have they risen continuously during that period despite the appearance of seven recessions?

The answer to the first part of the question, why have prices been rising for forty years, is quite simple: the Federal Reserve has been printing money at rates that have allowed nominal aggregate demand growth to exceed the economic growth rate. Taking 1950 as our starting point and 1988 as our end point, the U.S. economic growth rate has averaged 3.1 percent per year while nominal aggregate demand growth has averaged 7.5 percent. The excess nominal GNP growth over real growth is the inflation rate. The bulk of that 7.5 percent average annual nominal aggregate demand growth is accounted for by monetary growth.

Since 1950, M1 growth has averaged 5.1 percent per year while M2 has averaged 7 percent per year. Also, most of this monetary growth did not emanate from money multiplier growth but from the base which grew 5.4 percent per year over the period.

The amount that nominal GNP growth exceeds each monetary growth rate is the corresponding velocity growth rate: 2.4 percent per year for M1 velocity and 0.5 percent per year for M2 velocity. Since both of these velocity growth rates are less than the economic growth rate, we reach the inescapable conclusion that excessive monetary growth has resulted in nominal GNP growth in excess of the economic growth rate and, therefore, inflation. The obvious question, why has monetary growth been rapid, is addressed in the next section of this chapter.

We now know why prices have been rising since 1950, but why have they been continuously rising—that is, why has the inflation rate remained positive during recent recessions? A number of explanations have been offered. One is that recent institutional changes, including the postwar growth of labor unions, government involvement in the economy, and increased industrial concentration, have reduced the degree of wage and price flexibility. With respect to wages, DeLong and Summers (1986, p. 702) note that "long-term labor contracts were virtually nonexistent before passage of the Wagner Act" and that union power in the post–World War II period has been much higher than before. With respect to the government's role in the economy, DeLong and Summers argue that an increasing proportion of GNP is accounted for by government purchases, and, as noted by Mitchell (1941), prices in the government sector tend to be less flexible than in the private sector. Finally, with respect to industrial concentration, during this century the proportion of income accruing to sole proprietorships has been steadily declining while the proportion of total manufacturing assets held by the largest manufacturing corporations has been rising. Brock (1989) reports less competitive industries were far more likely than more competitive industries to raise prices during the 1981–1982 recession.

Another explanation recognizes inertia in the inflation process. If inflation has existed for several years, people begin to expect it to continue. Expected wage and price increases get built into contracts so that even during a period of declining demand, cost increases continue to get passed on in the form of higher prices. Also, during periods of secular price increases, the expected return on money balances is expected to continue declining so velocity grows more rapidly than it otherwise would.[9] This expected inflation effect on velocity may help explain why velocity (and nominal GNP) has not declined as rapidly during post–World War II recessions as it did during ante–World War II recessions.

Finally, DeLong and Summers (1986) and Zarnowitz and Moore (1986), among others, note that the business cycles after World War II have a much lower degree of amplitude than those prior to World War II. The last several recessions have been relatively mild compared with previous ones. Stated reasons include the existence of automatic stabilizers, the increasing share of services relative to goods, policymakers' adherence to the Employment Act of 1946 which states that it is a federal goal to promote employment, and the fact that nominal GNP growth has not declined as much during recent recessions, perhaps because velocity has been less variable during much of the post–World War II period than it was before. Hence, it has been several decades since the United States experienced a recession severe enough to actually reduce the price level.

We conclude with two final points. First, the U.S. experience of the past forty years does not imply that prices will never fall again. In fact, deflation (while no more desirable than inflation) would result in the event of a very severe recession or a huge positive supply shock. Second, secular price increases do not have to exist in the United States. Considerable postwar inflation has also occurred in Germany and Japan, yet both countries managed to achieve a degree of price stability during the 1980s without a recession by gradually reducing monetary growth to rates consistent with stable prices. There appears to be no reason why the United States cannot achieve similar results—after all, they were achieved during the 1920s.[10]

WHAT IS THE FEDERAL RESERVE DOING?

As I look at today's monetary policy debates, it seems to me very clear that the main issue is essentially the same as the one that has been around for many, many years. That issue is the weight to be assigned to controlling the money stock, given all the uncertainties, relative to the weight to be assigned to controlling or cushioning interest rate changes. That monetary policy issue is as central today as it has been over the last several decades.

William Poole (1984)

Few people would disagree with the stated goals of the Federal Open Market Committee: sustainable economic growth, full employment, and stable prices.[11] These goals, however, have not been achieved. Since World War II the U.S. economy has experienced secular price increases along with numerous business cycles, some severe. The discussion in chapters 10 and 11 mentions several policy mistakes committed by the Federal Reserve that economists believe increased the amplitude of certain business cycles, and the discussion in an earlier section of this chapter argues that the Federal Reserve is largely responsible for the post–World War II secular price increase. This divergence of Federal Reserve goals from economic outcomes raises a basic question: What is the Federal Reserve doing? Why have they allowed the money supply to grow over the past several decades at rates consistent with continuous inflation? Why have they allowed repeated monetary accelerations and decelerations that have certainly amplified certain business cycles, if not caused some?

The issue is not the goals of economic policy, but how to achieve them. The Federal Reserve contends that the proper way to conduct monetary policy is to monitor interest rates and use discretion as setting policy. They monitor interest rates with an eye toward keeping the path of interest rates smooth over time. They claim that if they did not conduct their policy in this manner, money demand instability would cause interest rate instability which would lead to uncertainty among economic transactors, disrupt financial markets, and cause general economic instability. They justify policy discretion on the belief that there are many sources of instability in an economy including external supply shocks, changing velocity caused by innovations in payment patterns and the introduction of new financial instruments, and changing fiscal policies. Federal Reserve officials argue that their ability to respond to these shocks in a proper manner helps promote economic stability.

Federal Reserve critics dismiss the Federal Reserve's arguments and contend that policy discretion and interest rate targeting are the source of much of our economic instability and inflation.[12] They contend that the Federal Reserve's method of interest rate targeting is incompatible with monetary control which is why the Federal Reserve rarely hits their stated monetary targets. According to the critics, the problem is the Federal Reserve's unwillingness to change interest rate targets often enough. For example, as an economic expansion gathers steam, the transactions demand for money rises which puts upward pressure on short-term interest rates. If the Federal Reserve keeps a low interest rate target, they end up injecting reserves into the banking system at a rapid rate, fully accommodating the rising demand for money which results in strongly procyclical monetary growth. If this policy is continued over a period of time, the errors tend to compound in what is called "base drift" where the Federal Reserve sets new monetary growth targets for the next year starting with the current level of the money stock. In other words, if money growth exceeded the target for the previous year, the targets aren't adjusted downward to correct the mistake; instead, the new targets start with the current level money supply which compounds the mistake. This, according to the critics, is a major source of the U.S. secular price rise.

The monetarists' complaint with discretionary policymaking (otherwise known as fine tuning) is familiar given our discussion of the monetarist model in chapter 5: the lag from money to nominal GNP is long and variable. Fine tuning is doomed to fail, the critics argue, because our knowledge about the timing from changes in money until it has its effect on macroeconomic variables is poor; thus, policymakers end up fine tuning the economy from crisis to crisis. According to the critics, a fixed monetary growth rule is preferable to policy discretion and interest rate targeting even though they admit interest rates would end up being more variable than they have been with the Federal Reserve's current operating procedure.[13] The critics consider increased interest rate variability a minor cost relative to the gains in economic welfare that they believe their rule would bring about.

For years, Federal Reserve officials have rejected calls for a fixed monetary growth rule. Here's a sample of two such comments by former chairmen of the Board of Governors. First, Arthur Burns (1975):

There is a school of thought that holds that the Federal Reserve need pay no attention to interest rates, that the only thing that matters is how this or that monetary aggregate is behaving. We at the Federal Reserve cannot afford the luxury of any such mechanical rule. As the nation's central bank, we have a vital role to play as the lender of last resort. It is our duty to protect the integrity of both the domestic value of the dollar and its foreign-exchange value. In discharging these functions, we at times need to set aside temporarily our objectives with regard to the monetary aggregates. . . . In particular, we pay close attention to interest rates because of their profound effect on the workings of the economy.

Second, an exchange between Congressman Stephen Neal (D-N.C.) and Paul Volcker:[14]

Mr. Neal: It has been suggested over the years that we might be able to devise some kind of formula for the conduct of monetary policy to assure noninflationary growth. . . . What is your feeling about that?

Mr. Volcker: If I were in an academic setting, I would have some sympathy for that view because I don't feel very comfortable with a situation that has had to rely on as much personal judgement as has been the case . . . in the past few years when we felt the relationships between money and nominal GNP and inflation and real growth were breaking down. A lot of weight had to be put on what could be denigrated, anyway, as ad hoc judgement. . . . The problem is: do you have a rule that's reliable enough so you want to put that kind of weight on it?

In an attempt to sort out the debate, let us first consider the problem of inflation. The vast majority of economists blame the Federal Reserve for the U.S. secular price increase because they accept Milton Friedman's famous statement that "every inflation has a monetary connection." Since the Federal Reserve ultimately controls the quantity of money with some degree of precision, they must accept responsibility for U.S. long-term inflation. Explanations for why they print too much money, besides the already mentioned interest rate targeting and fine tuning gone awry, include underestimating the natural rate of unemployment as was apparently the case during much of the 1960s and 1970s, printing money to finance the expansion of the Federal Reserve as an institution, and responding to public demand for inflation.[15]

The issue of whether or not a monetary rule would bring about price stability and reduced business cycle amplitude is an empirical question that cannot really be answered because the Federal Reserve has never targeted monetary aggregates for any length of time. Thus, we do not know what a monetary growth rule would do to the pattern of nominal GNP and inflation, although empirical evidence (e.g., McCallum 1988) has recently come to light that suggests that a variety of monetary growth rules would essentially eliminate inflation without inducing additional nominal GNP variability. This result comes from studies that simulate the U.S. economy under the assumption that the Federal Reserve is following a monetary growth rule. The rule has not been tested in the "real world'' for the United States at least, although evidence reported by Hall (1989) suggests that Germany and Japan have been conducting monetary policies in line with a rule for several years now with fine results. But the fact of the matter is that for the United States we cannot determine whether the Federal Reserve's policies are preferable to a monetary growth rule because a rule has never been a Federal Reserve policy for any significant length of time. Therefore, until the Federal Reserve institutes a growth rule for a monetary aggregate and we study the results, the debate over rules versus discretion may remain unresolved.

WHY ARE GROWTH CYCLES CORRELATED ACROSS COUNTRIES?

While it is true that levels of output move in similar directions in most industrialized countries during severe changes in economic activity (e.g., the Great Depression), it is more common that growth cycles are related across countries (Moore 1983). The top third of Table 12.2 shows the simple correlations between real GNP growth in several major countries from 1961 to 1987. This correlation of growth cycles emanates from similar growth patterns of both aggregate supply and aggregate demand among the different countries. In the case of aggregate supply, growth rates are related across countries because aggregate supply shocks can be, and often are, worldwide events. Rising world oil prices, weather-related changes in crop yields that alter world food prices, and major technological changes affect many countries in varying degrees and help cause worldwide movements in economic growth rates.

With respect to similar movements in aggregate demand growth, the story is more complicated. During the Bretton-Woods fixed exchange rate period, it was no surprise that aggregate demand growth rates moved in similar directions because the fixed exchange rates system allowed significant changes in one major country's monetary growth to influence monetary growth rates in other countries. This relationship existed because if one country, say the United States, stimulated monetary growth, then the United States would move into a balance of payments deficit indicating an overvalued dollar on the foreign exchange market. The flip side of the U.S. balance of payments deficit would be surpluses in other countries, indicating that their currencies were undervalued. Foreign countries would attempt to keep the exchange rate at the prearranged level by buying up dollars on the foreign exchange market which would be accomplished by selling their own currencies, thus increasing foreign monetary growth rates. Hence, a U.S. monetary stimulus would raise aggregate demand growth in other countries, and, not surprisingly, growth cycles were correlated across countries.

Monetarists complained about the fixed exchange rate system for years because it did not allow countries to independently pursue their own domestic monetary policies and choose their own inflation rate. Instead, they advocated a system of flexible exchange rates which, monetarists argued, would allow countries to pursue independent monetary policies. If one country, again the United States,

Table 12.2
Simple Correlations of Annual Economic Growth Rates (Fourth Quarter over Fourth Quarter)

Sample Period: 1961-1987

Country	U.S.	U.K.	Canada	Japan	Germany
U.S.	1.00				
U.K.	.42	1.00			
Canada	.73	.31	1.00		
Japan	.43	.36	.31	1.00	
Germany	.52	.43	.46	.57	1.00

Fixed Exchange Rates Period: 1961-1972

Country	U.S.	U.K.	Canada	Japan	Germany
U.S.	1.00				
U.K.	-.01	1.00			
Canada	.66	.002	1.00		
Japan	.30	.26	.05	1.00	
Germany	.06	.15	.12	.30	1.00

Flexible Exchange Rates Period: 1973-1987

Country	U.S.	U.K.	Canada	Japan	Germany
U.S.	1.00				
U.K.	.53	1.00			
Canada	.75	.39	1.00		
Japan	.59	.58	.36	1.00	
Germany	.77	.58	.62	.59	1.00

Data from Data Resources Incorporated. Output measure for all countries is real GNP, except for Canada where output is measured as real GDP.

raised monetary growth, the U.S. dollar would depreciate while foreign currencies appreciated. Foreign monetary authorities would no longer have to respond by buying and selling currencies on the foreign exchange market and could keep their monetary growth rates independent of other countries' monetary growth rates. Therefore, monetary induced aggregate demand shocks in one country would not spread to other countries, and the correlation of aggregate demand-induced growth cycles would be reduced. When the Bretton-Woods system collapsed, monetarists' arguments were partly responsible for the move to the current system of flexible exchange rates. The bottom two-thirds of Table 12.2 shows that lower correlation of growth cycles among countries did not occur after Bretton-Woods collapsed. Simple correlations of annual real GNP growth among several major industrialized countries have, in general, been higher instead of lower during the period of flexible exchange rates. Economists have spent considerable time and energy determining why the expected result did not occur.

To some extent, the higher correlations since 1973 reflect the fact that the more recent period has included several major worldwide supply shocks, including the 1973–1974 and 1980 oil price increases, the food price increase in 1973 and again in 1988, the oil price decline in 1986, and significant advancements in technology. Regardless of the exchange rate system, these supply shocks would affect the countries listed in Table 12.2 in a similar manner which certainly accounts for some proportion of the higher correlations of economic growth.

Some international economists (e.g., Krugman and Obstfeld 1988) contend that aggregate supply shocks are only part of the story and that aggregate demand changes are still carried across countries despite the existence of flexible exchange rates. While there is greater independence of monetary and aggregate demand growth rates since 1973, economists note a number of reasons why they are not completely independent. One reason is that most nations do not allow their currencies to freely float on foreign exchange markets. Instead, they follow what is called a "dirty" or "managed" float where they intervene in foreign exchange markets to influence movements in exchange rates. Among the more famous examples of intervention is the 1985 Plaza Agreement when the G–5 countries (U.S., Germany, Japan, U.K., and France) came up with secret target zones for their exchange rates (involving a depreciation of the U.S. dollar) which required a great deal of exchange rate intervention by central banks. The Plaza Agreement is just one of several examples in recent years of international attempts to coordinate economic policies to influence exchange rates. As long as nations do not allow exchange rates to freely float, monetary growth rates will be related among countries.

Even if countries did not intervene in foreign exchange markets and allowed exchange rates to freely float, there is still another reason why monetary shocks may influence aggregate demand in other countries. The flexible exchange rate result of monetary independence requires that both output prices and exchange rates adjust very quickly to monetary shocks. To see this, suppose that the United

States and all its major trading partners were in a steady state with inflation rates of zero and output growing in each country at the respective trend rates. Now consider the effects of a 10 percent rise in the U.S. money supply in excess of the amount compatible with stable prices. The long-run effect will be a 10 percent rise in the U.S. price level and a 10 percent depreciation in the value of the U.S. dollar on the foreign exchange market. Because prices of U.S. exports rise 10 percent while the dollar depreciates by the same 10 percent, there is no change in the real exchange rate and, therefore, no change in U.S. or foreign real net export positions. In this way the U.S. monetary expansion has no effect on aggregate demand in other countries.

However, before the economy gets to that long-run position, adjustments in the short run may cause changes in foreign levels of aggregate demand. The explanation involves the assumption of sticky prices, implying that time must pass before the U.S. price level adjusts fully.[16] Since foreign exchange rates are determined in a market that is akin to the stock market in terms of price flexibility, the U.S. monetary stimulus may cause the exchange rate to depreciate faster than the U.S. price level rises. During that time, the U.S. real exchange rate falls which causes a reduction in U.S. purchases of real imports from abroad, reducing both foreign real net exports and, therefore, foreign aggregate demand.

At the same time, two other channels work to stimulate foreign aggregate demand growth. One is the fact that the U.S. monetary expansion temporarily lowers U.S. interest rates which, given a high degree of world capital mobility, places downward pressure on interest rates abroad and stimulates foreign aggregate demand. Second, the U.S. dollar depreciation reduces the price of U.S. goods abroad and puts downward pressure on prices of foreign tradeable goods which reduces foreign price levels. For given foreign nominal money supplies, the lower foreign price levels raise real money supplies abroad and put further upward pressure on foreign aggregate demand. While it is not clear that the factors raising foreign aggregate demand offset the negative influence, it is certainly possible. Therefore, even with flexible exchange rates, a change in one major country's monetary growth may influence other countries' aggregate demand growth and cause growth cycles to be correlated.

Therefore, there are theoretical reasons why growth cycles are correlated across countries. The existence of flexible exchange rates has made it possible for countries to pursue their own monetary growth targets independently of each other but has not provided complete independence of aggregate demand from foreign monetary policies. Furthermore, the existence of worldwide supply shocks also makes growth cycles correlated across countries.[17]

NOTES

1. Under certain conditions, the new-Keynesian model does not predict counter-cyclical real wages following changes in aggregate demand. The cyclical behavior of real wages in this model depends on the relative speed of adjustment of nominal wages and

prices. If prices are more flexible than nominal wages, then real wages are countercyclical. If wages and prices are both fixed in the short run then real wages may be acyclical. Also, since the new-Keynesian model allows the labor market to move into disequilibrium, it does not necessarily suggest that changes in aggregate demand cause movements along a fixed labor demand schedule. See the discussion in R. J. Gordon (1987, chapter 8).

2. Also see Keynes' (1939) reply to Dunlop and Tarshis where he admits that something is amiss. Tarshis was not the first economist to study U.S. real wage behavior. See the article by Hansen (1925) and the accompanying references. Hansen reports that U.S. real wages tend to be procyclical.

3. Kahn (1984) reports evidence that U.S. real wages are "sticky" over the business cycle and dominated by trend productivity growth. Similar results are reported by Shaw (1989).

4. NOW accounts differ from money market deposit accounts and money market mutual funds, both part of M2, in that NOW accounts have no restrictions on the minimum balance, number of checks written, or on the values of the checks written. The M2 interest-bearing checking accounts have restrictions on minimum balances, number of checks written per month, or, in the case of money market mutual fund accounts, restrictions on the value of individual checks written.

5. The effect of uncertainty is formally modeled in the money demand function by Mascaro and Meltzer (1983).

6. See Stone and Thornton (1987), Moore, Porter, and Small (1988), and Carlson and McElravey (1989). Poole (1988) found a strong correlation between M1 velocity and the long-term Baa rate.

7. Roth (1987) offers additional explanations for the higher interest sensitivity of money demand.

8. On an annual basis, the Consumer Price Index last declined in 1955.

9. The conclusion that the postwar rise in the income velocities on money is the result of inflation is reached by Friedman and Schwartz (1963a) and Dewald (1988).

10. There are several proposals for monetary growth rules that may help stabilize prices. See, for example, McCallum (1988).

11. See "Record of Policy Actions of the Federal Open Market Committee," *Federal Reserve Bulletin*, January 1989, pp. 20–24. Similar statements can be found in almost any issue of the *Federal Reserve Bulletin* over the past several decades.

12. Milton Friedman has been the leading critic of the Federal Reserve for years. See Friedman (1982) for his complaints with the institution and its policies.

13. See Axilrod, et al. (1982) which is the transcript of an excellent debate between two leading monetarists and two high-ranking Federal Reserve economists.

14. *Conduct of Monetary Policy*, Hearing before the Subcommittee on Domestic Monetary Policy of the Committee on Banking, Finance and Urban Affairs, U.S. House of Representatives, July 21, 1987.

15. The argument that part of the inflationary monetary growth can be tied to bureaucratic expansion of the Federal Reserve is advanced by Toma (1982) and Shugart and Tollison (1983). The argument that the Federal Reserve provides inflation because the public demands it is advanced by Grieder (1987). For a criticism of this argument, see the review of Grieder's book by Sheffrin (1989).

16. This short-run model of exchange rate adjustment is suggested by Dornbusch (1976).

17. In a detailed empirical paper, Baxter and Stockman (1988) report little difference between the behavior of several macroeconomic aggregates under fixed versus flexible exchange rates. Also, Gerlach (1988) finds higher output correlations under flexible exchange rates than fixed rates.

13 | Economic Forecasting

Virtually all economic institutions are interested in future economic trends. Firms are interested in the path of general economic activity because it influences their future sales, borrowing costs, and prices charged by suppliers, and helps them plan for the future. Households are interested in the future because when they consider whether or not to buy a new car, build a new home, send a child to college, take an expensive vacation, or change jobs, their perceptions of the economic future are important. Future household income, interest rates, and prices of these goods and services are all important variables in their decisions. Governments preparing annual budgets are interested in future economic events. These budgets are composed of expected revenue and expected costs. Since many governments generate revenue from income and sales taxes, their revenue depends on income and sales during the upcoming year. Costs depend on the future prices governments pay to provide goods and services to their constituents.

An undeniable fact is that the economic future is uncertain. This uncertainty comes in varying degrees. Some events such as labor force growth we are relatively sure of one year into the future because we know the age composition of the population. We are highly uncertain about many other events, such as monetary growth rates over the next year, or the future path of energy prices. Because we do not know what the economic future holds, we make forecasts, or educated guesses, about future economic values. In many cases we base our current behavior on these forecasts, and for this reason economic forecasting serves a useful social purpose.

Unfortunately, it is very difficult to accurately forecast future economic events for two reasons. First, economic knowledge about the aggregate economy is poor. Economists don't really know the precise quantitative relationships and time paths of causes and effects among economic variables, especially in the short run. For example, in the context of the quantity theory of money, we know that a change in monetary growth influences nominal GNP growth, but we do not know the precise lag time nor do we know how the change in nominal GNP growth will separately influence output and prices in the short run.

The second reason why forecasting is difficult is that not only do current values of variables affect future economic activity, but future values of variables affect future economic activity. If we are trying to predict output and prices over the next one or two years, we need to know not only current values of factors such as monetary growth, government purchases, and tax rates, but also future values. Forecasters must make guesses of the future values of factors influencing economic activity which adds further uncertainty to the forecast.

Economic forecasting methods basically consist of two types. One method is to use leading indicators which involves identifying variables whose movements tend to predict future economic trends. This method is computationally inexpensive but has disadvantages including variable lead times and the fact that leading indicators are designed more to forecast turning points in the economy as opposed to actual magnitudes of future economic activity. The second method is econometric forecasting which estimates parameters of equations specifying relationships among economic variables. These estimated parameter values measure the quantitative relationships among the independent and dependent variables. Forecasts are derived by taking the estimated equations and plugging in actual current and past values of the independent variables as well as educated guesses of future values. This computation results in predicted values of the dependent variables which constitute the forecast. This method is relatively expensive computationally, although advances in computers have drastically reduced the cost in recent decades. The disadvantage of this method is that it is fairly inaccurate, often forecasting turning points after they have taken place.

A very wide array of variables are forecasted, running the gamut from aggregate variables such as GNP and inflation, to disaggregated variables such as demand for specific products that concern individual firms or entire industries. Our focus here is on forecasting aggregate economic activity, and the coverage is designed to provide readers with a general overview of forecasting. The same basic tools as those discussed here are used to forecast the host of other economic variables. Interested individuals seeking more detail can find several books on economic forecasting (e.g., Granger 1989). We begin by describing two major forecasting methods and then briefly summarize forecasting performance.

FORECASTING METHODS

Leading Indicators

Forecasting with leading indicators was developed early this century. It was popularized during the 1920s by the Harvard ABC curves where a measure of speculation was found to lead business conditions (R. A. Gordon 1961). The ABC curves did not predict the extreme severity of the Great Contraction, so they lost favor during the 1930s. The method was resurrected a few years later by National Bureau of Economic Research economists Wesley Mitchell and Arthur Burns (1938) who identified several economic indicators whose movements tended to foreshadow major changes in economic activity. This method has been quite successful, and for several years now the U.S. Department of Commerce has published a monthly index of leading indicators that is closely watched by a large segment of society.

When constructing an index of leading indicators, several criteria are used to determine which variables should be included. First, a series should be published frequently enough so that it can be used to forecast economic activity a few months ahead. Second, the series should not be subject to large revisions after initial publication (i.e., an indicator should be accurate and up-to-date). Third, the series should exhibit a consistent relationship with the variable being forecast. Obviously, we are not interested in an indicator that gives many false signals by moving in all directions before a general economic trend or major turning point. Finally, and this characteristic is perhaps the most difficult to satisfy, a good indicator should have a relatively constant lead time before economic turning points. If an indicator falls prior to recessions and rises prior to expansions, it would help our forecasting ability considerably if the time from the indicator's turning points to economic turning points is relatively stable across business cycles.

The U.S. Commerce Department identifies a set of indicators that fit these criteria reasonably well. The current index of leading indicators is composed of the following series:[1]

1. Average weekly hours of production or nonsupervisory workers, manufacturing.

2. Average weekly initial claims for state unemployment insurance (inverted).

3. Manufacturers' new orders, consumer goods and materials industries (1982$).

4. Contracts and orders for plant and equipment (1982$).

5. Index of new private housing units authorized by local building permits.

6. Index of 500 common stock prices.

7. Money stock M2 (1982$).

8. Vendor performance, percentage of companies reporting slower deliveries.

9. Change in sensitive materials prices, smoothed.

10. Change in manufacturers' unfilled orders, durable goods industries, smoothed (1982$).

11. Index of consumer expectations.

This set of variables is an eclectic hodgepodge consisting of factors stressed by monetarists (real M2) and Keynesians (stock prices, consumer expectations), measured commitments to future economic activity (manufacturers' new orders, plant and equipment orders, building permits, change in manufacturers' new

Figure 13.1
Index of Leading Indicators (monthly observations, 1982 = 100)

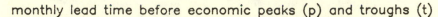

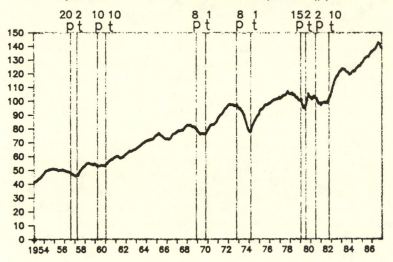

orders), and measures of capacity pressures (hours, unemployment insurance claims, vendor performance, sensitive materials prices). The index is formed by weighting the eleven series equally and detrending (see Hertzberg and Beckman 1989).

The index is plotted in Figure 13.1 along with peaks and troughs in aggregate economic activity, and the number of months the index led specific economic turning points. For example, the economic peak in August 1957 was preceded by a peak in the index twenty months prior (thus the 20 above that peak in Figure 13.1). Inspection of Figure 13.1 indicates why the leading indicator method is popular; it is a very successful predictor of economic turning points. Every recession in the sample period has been preceded by a decline in the index, and every expansion preceded by an increase in the index. The index's popularity also results from the fact that it is easy to obtain—simply a matter of checking the latest issue of *Business Conditions Digest* which is available at most libraries.

While the index is very successful at predicting economic turning points, it does have some shortcomings which are apparent from Figure 13.1. One is the existence of false signals which occur when the index predicts an economic turning point that never occurs. False signals show up in 1966 and 1984 when the index fell and then rose without being followed by a recession, although the 1966 decline preceded the 1967 growth recession and economic growth fell below trend in 1986.

Another shortcoming is the variable lead times from turning points in the index to turning points in aggregate economic activity. Lead times before recessions vary from two months before the start of the 1981–1982 recession to twenty months before the start of the 1957–1958 recession. Lead times before expansions vary from one month before the start of the 1970–1973 and 1975–1979 expansions to ten months before the start of the 1961–1969 and 1983–1989 expansions.

Another difficulty is the interpretation of monthly movements. The question is: How many monthly movements in a given direction constitute a signal of an economic turning point? There is simply no hard and fast rule. During economic expansions the index rises over several months, sometimes years. Often during one of these periods the index dips for one month and then rises for several more months. Therefore, a one-month downward movement during economic expansions is not a good signal of an impending recession. Two consecutive monthly declines, which have also occurred several times during the sample period without a resulting recession, are poor indicators of economic downturns although two consecutive monthly declines immediately preceded the 1981–1982 recession. Three consecutive monthly declines in the index have predicted every recession in the sample except the 1981–1982 episode, but has also given false signals in 1962, 1966, and 1984. Perhaps the best rule of thumb to predict recessions is to look for periods when the index is moving both up and down for several months with no strong upward or downward trend. This behavior is often the case near the end of expansions; the index exhibits erratic behavior, rising for a couple of months, then falling for a month or two, then rising again, and so on. In other words, when the index does not exhibit a sustained trend during an economic expansion, a recession is often close at hand.

When the economy is in a recession, forecasting upcoming expansions is relatively straightforward. The index predicts recessions with a short lead time. One- or two-month upward movements in the index have predicted all of the expansions in the sample period, although the total lead time has varied considerably. In large part, this ease of predicting expansions is a function of the relatively short duration of post–World War II recessions.

Yet another shortcoming of the index is that it provides little indication of the amplitude of forecasted recessions. In other words, there is little relationship between the magnitude of the decline in the index before a recession begins and the severity of the eventual recession. For example, the largest declines in the leading indicators, over 5 percent, occurred before the relatively mild 1957–1958 recession, the 1967 growth recession, and the short (but severe) 1980 recession. Small declines occurred prior to the two worst recessions in the sample: 0.4 percent decline before the 1974–1975 recession and a 1.5 percent decline prior to the 1981–1982 recession.

The index can be used to forecast economic magnitudes. Moore (1983, pp. 420–424) estimated an equation where annual real GNP growth in a given calendar year depends on the percentage change in the index of leading indicators during the previous July-September period. He found that this method forecasts the 1952–1967 period about as well as an econometric model and the administration's forecasts reported in the *Economic Report of the President*. Using the index to forecast output magnitudes in this manner, however, has not become widespread as the index is really more designed to forecast economic turning points than economic magnitudes.

Economists are always looking for more leading indicators, and in recent years considerable attention has been paid to the slope of the yield curve—the relationship between yields on bonds of different maturity but equal risk. Normally, the yield curve slopes up (i.e., long-term bonds bear higher yields than short-term bonds). There are two reasons for this upward slope. First, most lenders prefer to tie up their funds for a relatively short time (they desire liquidity) while most borrowers wish to borrow long term to match the term to maturity of their liabilities with their long-term assets. Lenders have to be compensated for lending long term, and this compensation, called the liquidity premium, takes the form of a higher yield on long-term bonds. Second, long-term bond holders are subject to more risk than short-term bond holders. This risk takes two forms, a longer horizon for unexpected events (e.g., unexpected inflation or changes in the real productivity of capital) to take place that influence bond yields, and the fact that changes in market interest rates cause long-term bond prices to change more than short-term bond prices.[2] Therefore, long-term bonds are more risky, and holders of these bonds are compensated for this risk with a higher return.

Sometimes the yield curve takes a negative slope when short-term interest rates become greater than long-term rates. Interestingly, a negatively sloped yield curve has occurred seven times during the period 1956–1989. For five of those times, recessions followed shortly after, in 1960, 1970, 1974–1975, 1980, and 1981–1982. An inverted yield curve also preceded the 1967 growth recession. The seventh instance was an inverted yield curve in spring 1989.

An inverted yield curve is a leading indicator because it is usually associated with reduced monetary growth. The Federal Reserve reduces monetary growth by buying fewer bonds. They normally operate in the market for short-term bonds, so when the Federal Reserve is reducing monetary growth, the demand for short-term bonds grows more slowly. Thus, prices of short-term bonds fall relative to prices of long-term bonds, and short-term rates rise relative to long-term rates. Reduced monetary growth also reduces inflation, but with a lag. Reduced monetary growth lowers the expected inflation premium on bonds, but, since a lag exists, bond holders expect the inflation rate to fall over the longer term but not necessarily over the shorter term. A much larger decline occurs in longer term expected inflation than in shorter term expected inflation, and short-term rates may end up exceeding long-term rates.

Stock and Watson (1989) have constructed an index of leading indicators that includes the slope of the yield curve measured as the difference between the yield on ten-year Treasury bonds and the yield on one-year Treasury bonds. While this measure is found to be important, their index is dominated by another variable—the spread between asset yields of the same maturity but difference risk, measured by the difference between the yield on six-month commercial paper and the yield on six-month Treasury Bills. Since commercial paper bears some default risk while Treasury Bills have no default risk, changes in this spread largely result from changes in perceived default risk on commercial paper. From 1959–1988 the average spread between the two was about 60 basis points and tended to rise before recessions and fall prior to expansions.

In sum, forecasting with leading indicators has a fine track record of predicting economic turning points. The indicators, however, do give occasional false signals, are unable to predict the severity of recessions prior to the actual event, and, perhaps most important, have highly variable lead times. For these reasons, some forecasters prefer using econometric methods that estimate future magnitudes of economic variables, thus forecasting both dates of turning points as well as business cycle amplitudes.[3]

Econometric Methods

Econometric forecasting methods involve statistically estimating equations that specify relationships among economic variables. A dependent variable is written as a function of one or more predetermined variables, and the equation is estimated, usually by the method of least squares that fits a line through the observations so as to minimize the sum of the squared errors. The estimated equation is then used to forecast out-of-sample.

Least squares is illustrated in Figure 13.2 where a line is fitted through the actual value of the log of real GNP from 1954.I to 1979.IV. The equation to be estimated is

$$\ln Y_t = c + \beta \, TIME_t + u_t$$

where $\ln Y$ is the natural log of real GNP, c is a constant term (the fitted line's vertical intercept), β is a coefficient to be estimated (the slope of the fitted line), $TIME$ is a set of integers that takes a value of 1 in 1954.I, 2 in 1954.II, . . . ,u is the error term, and the subscripted t's indicate time periods.

Least squares estimates the values of c and β that correspond to a fitted line that minimizes the sum of the squared errors where the errors are the distance between the fitted line and the actual value at each quarterly observation. The estimated version is

$$\ln Y_t = 7.23 + .0083 \, TIME_t$$

The fitted values of $\ln Y$ are computed by substituting the values of the right-hand-side variable, in this case $TIME$, into the equation. These fitted values are plotted in Figure 13.2 as the solid straight line.

This estimated equation can be used to forecast future values of the log of real GNP by substituting in out-of-sample values of $TIME$. The value of $TIME$ at the end of the sample period (1979.IV) is 104, so the out-of-sample values

Figure 13.2
Actual and Forecasted Log of Real GNP

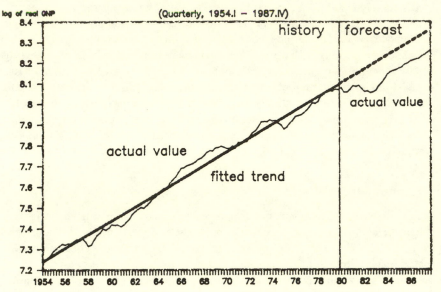

are 105 for 1980.I, 106 for 1980.II, and so on. These values are plugged into the estimated equation to obtain out-of-sample forecasts of the log of real GNP which are plotted as the dotted straight line in Figure 13.2. The out-of-sample actual path of $ln\ Y$ is also plotted, and the forecast error is the distance between the forecasted value and the actual value.

This method of forecasting with a fitted trend is often called the naive method because it simply assumes that the future trend will be the same as the past trend. In our example, out-of-sample forecasts of real GNP for the 1980s from this method are fairly poor, but in large part these errors result from the fact that the sample period was ended just before the onset of economic instability during the early 1980s. If a line had been fitted and extended into a more stable period, the out-of-sample forecasting accuracy would be considerably improved. Along these lines, McNees (1988) noted that naive methods forecasted quite well during the 1960s but their forecasting accuracy deteriorated significantly in the 1970s and 1980s.

Autoregressive models are another naive statistical forecasting method. The most simple autoregressive model is a first order version that specifies the log of real GNP to be a function of the previous period's value,

$$ln\ Y_t = c + \beta\ ln\ Y_{t-1} + u_t$$

Over the sample period 1954.I to 1979.IV estimation with least squares yields

$$\ln Y_t = .0103 + .9997 \ln Y_{t-1}$$

We can generate out-of-sample forecasts by simulating the equation starting in 1980.I. The predicted value of *In Y* in 1980.I depends on the actual value in 1979.IV; the predicted value in 1980.II depends on the forecasted value from 1980.I; the predicted value in 1980.III depends on the forecasted value from 1980.II, and so on. In actuality, this estimated model essentially provides the same forecast as the time trend model because the coefficient estimate of .9997 on the lagged GNP term is so close to 1 that the equation effectively models a constant growth rate for GNP. This result can be seen by recalling our discussion of the real business cycle model in chapter 8. If the coefficient on the right-hand-side lagged value equals 1, the model can be rewritten in terms of the first difference

$$\Delta \ln Y_t = c + u_t$$

where the change in the log of real GNP is the growth rate. Thus, in our example here the first order autoregressive model basically estimates a constant growth rate for real GNP (as does the time trend model) because the coefficient on the lagged value is very close to 1. In fact, similar results occur when estimating first order autoregressive models of many macroeconomic aggregates.

The naive time trend and autoregressive model generate forecasts that can be improved upon with more sophisticated models, but the naive models have one advantage that used to be very important: they are relatively easy to estimate. Since the estimated equations have only one right-hand-side variable, the computation costs are relatively small. Both equations were estimated with a personal computer and a standard statistical software package, and the actual computation time was somewhere between one and two seconds. If the equations had been estimated with a hand calculator, the total computation time would have been, perhaps, thirty minutes, and estimating them using only a pencil and paper would have required one or two hours.

When more independent variables are added to an equation, the number of individual calculations required to obtain estimated parameters increases rapidly, and if hand calculators or computers are not available, the estimation time becomes prohibitive. For this reason, before the advent of calculators and computers, equations with more than a few right-hand-side variables were rarely estimated because the computation time could easily have run into several weeks or even longer. The development of computers after World War II greatly reduced computation time which allowed much larger equations to be estimated. For this reason, econometric forecasting methods have made huge strides during the postwar era right along with advancements in computer power to the point where, today, a very sophisticated model that would have been effectively impossible to estimate before World War II can be estimated in a matter of seconds on a personal computer.

These more sophisticated econometric forecasting models generally fall into either of two categories. The first set are highly aggregated reduced form models that attempt to explain just a few economic variables such as output, prices, and interest rates. The second set consists of large numbers of equations explaining relatively disaggregated data. For example, separate equations may exist for each component of expenditures on consumption, investment, exports and imports, interest rates, industrial production by industry, and so on.

A version of the relatively small, highly aggregated models is an equation specified and tested by Andersen and Jordan (1968) of the Federal Bank of St. Louis. The equation is commonly referred to as the St. Louis equation and specifies the change in nominal GNP as a function of lagged changes in money and high employment government expenditures:

$$NGNP_t = c + \sum_{i=1}^{J} \beta_{1i} M_{t-i} + \sum_{i=1}^{J} \beta_{2i} E_{t-i} + u_t$$

where $NGNP$ is nominal GNP, M is the money stock, and E is high employment government expenditures which measures the level of government expenditures if the economy is at full employment. Andersen and Jordan estimated the equation with least squares and reported that the coefficients on lagged changes in money sum to over 5 while the coefficients on lagged high employment expenditures sum to just over zero. In other words, the St. Louis model finds that a $1 billion change in the money stock eventually causes more than a $5 billion change in nominal GNP, while changes in high employment expenditures cause virtually no change in nominal GNP. Not surprisingly these results became a focal point in the battle between the monetarists and Keynesians over the potency of monetary versus fiscal changes. Forecasting is carried out by making guesses of future values of M and E which, using the estimated equation, imply future values of $NGNP$.

The modern version of small aggregated models is the vector autoregression (VAR) system. Recalling our four-variable VAR model from chapter 8 that specifies a system with money (M), output (Y), prices (P), and interest rates (r),

$$Y_t = c1 + \sum_{i=1}^{J} \beta_{1i} Y_{t-i} + \sum_{i=1}^{J} \beta_{2i} M_{t-i} + \sum_{i=1}^{J} \beta_{3i} P_{t-i} + \sum_{i=1}^{J} \beta_{4i} r_{t-i} + u_{1t}$$

$$M_t = c2 + \sum_{i=1}^{J} \beta_{5i} Y_{t-i} + \sum_{i=1}^{J} \beta_{6i} M_{t-i} + \sum_{i=1}^{J} \beta_{7i} P_{t-i} + \sum_{i=1}^{J} \beta_{8i} r_{t-i} + u_{2t}$$

$$P_t = c3 + \sum_{i=1}^{J} \beta_{9i} Y_{t-i} + \sum_{i=1}^{J} \beta_{10i} M_{t-i} + \sum_{i=1}^{J} \beta_{11i} P_{t-i} + \sum_{i=1}^{J} \beta_{12i} r_{t-i} + u_{3t}$$

$$r_t = c4 + \sum_{i=1}^{J} \beta_{13i} Y_{t-i} + \sum_{i=1}^{J} \beta_{14i} M_{t-i} + \sum_{i=1}^{J} \beta_{15i} P_{t-i} + \sum_{i=1}^{J} \beta_{16i} r_{t-i} + u_{4t}$$

Each variable in the system depends on its own past history and the past history of the other variables in the system. The equations are estimated with least squares over the sample period to obtain parameter estimates.[4] Forecasts are generated in the same manner as with the autoregressive model—historical data generate the first forecast one quarter out and that value becomes a lagged value for the next forecast, and so on. In principle, forecasts could be generated for an infinite number of time periods into the future. The system can easily be expanded by adding more variables such as exchange rates and the unemployment rate. Forecasts from VAR models are relatively inexpensive to generate, the forecaster needs only a personal computer and a standard econometric software package to do so.

In contrast to relatively small VAR models, large-scale econometric models forecast hundreds of variables. The sheer size of the models, however, makes them relatively expensive to operate, and subscribers often pay several thousand dollars each year to receive these forecasts. Examples of large-scale models include the Wharton model, the MIT-PENN-SSRC (MPS) model, models developed by various government agencies (e.g., the Commerce Department Bureau of Economic Activity), and the Data Resources Incorporated (DRI) model. The DRI model, among the largest, forecasts about 1,200 different variables. These large models allow considerably more sectoral analysis than relatively small VAR models.

Large econometric models specify an equation for each dependent variable as a function of other dependent variables as well as many exogenous variables that are determined outside of the model. Exogenous variables may include government tax rates, the monetary base, output levels in the rest of the world, and population growth rates. These hundreds of equations are estimated with historical data to obtain parameter values, and forecasts are generated by assuming future values of the independent variables. Typically, these models do not generate a single set of forecasts. Instead, they are used to compute a set of forecasts based on separate assumptions for the values of the exogenous variables. For example, DRI may generate one set of forecasts that assumes a tight monetary policy, another based on more rapid monetary growth, one based on rising oil prices, another with stable oil prices, and so forth. One particular scenario considered most likely to occur is identified and the highest probability is assigned to the resulting forecast. Lower probabilities are assigned to forecasts assuming alternative scenarios. Thus, the forecasts incorporate considerable judgment on the part of the individuals generating the results, so it is not a purely statistical exercise (McNees 1988). Furthermore, if the forecasters consider the predicted outcomes, even given their input scenarios, unlikely, they often adjust the forecasted values up or down based on their own judgment.

An increasingly popular forecasting approach combines the forecasts of several individuals, most of whom rely on econometric models, to form a consensus survey. Several surveys exist; perhaps the two most popular are the Blue Chip consensus forecast published by Robert Eggert in Sedona, Arizona, and the consensus gathered by the American Statistical Association and National Bureau of Economic Research (ASA/NBER). The survey organizations ask several individuals their expectation of future values of output, unemployment, inflation, and the like, and the consensus forecast is formed as the median (or mean) value of the responses. Most of the individuals surveyed form their forecasts with econometric models, and considerable judgment is used as well.

FORECASTING PERFORMANCE

Stephen McNees of the Boston Federal Reserve Bank has performed a number of studies that compare the accuracy of alternative forecasting models. One measure McNees employs to compare forecasting performance is a statistical measure of variability called the root mean squared error (RMSE). The RMSE is computed by summing the forecast errors, dividing by the number of observations, and then taking the square root. This RMSE measure is distributed such that with roughly two-thirds confidence we can say that the true value lies within the forecasted value plus or minus the root mean squared error, with 95 percent confidence within the forecasted value plus or minus two times the root mean squared error, and with 99 percent confidence within the forecasted value plus or minus three times the root mean squared error.

One way to apply the RMSE to compare forecasting records is to compute separate RMSEs for several models' quarterly forecasts one quarter out, two quarters out, and so on. In other words, forecasting model X's one quarter ahead forecasts made in 1970.I, 1970.II, 1970.III, . . . are compared to what actually happened in the quarters for which the forecast was made to arrive at a mean squared error for that model's one quarter ahead forecast error. Similarly, mean squared errors are computed for a model's two quarter ahead forecasts, three quarter ahead forecasts, and so on. This procedure is applied to several models so that forecasting accuracy for different forecast horizons can be compared.

Applying this method, McNees (1986) compared the forecasting accuracy of several large econometric models and a VAR model. He reports that over the period 1980.II to 1985.I, RMSEs of forecasts of real GNP growth formed mid-quarter for the next quarter averaged around 3.5 percentage points at annualized growth rates, eventually declining to around 2 percentage points eight quarters out. In other words, McNees obtained the interesting result that econometric models do a better job of forecasting real GNP growth several quarters out than they do one quarter out, and in all cases the errors are fairly large. If we assume that the one quarter ahead average forecast of real GNP growth is in the neighborhood of 3 percent, the long-run average, then two-thirds of the time the actual value will lie between −0.5 percent to 6.5 percent (3 percentage points plus or minus the RMSE of 3.5 percentage points) which ranges from a recession to an absolute boom in economic activity. Yet McNees (1988) also reported that the median forecast error for one year ahead real GNP growth from 1971.II to 1985.I is only 0.3 percentage points. In other words, based on the median error, forecasts of real GNP growth are fairly accurate, but these forecasts have a very high degree of variability as measured by the root mean squared error.

How can forecasts be relatively accurate at the median but subject to a high degree of variability? The answer is there have been some huge errors, especially at major turning points in macroeconomic activity. For example, McNees (1985) reported some of the major quarterly errors of forecasting real GNP growth include overpredicting real GNP growth by as much as 6 percentage points during the 1974–1975 recession and by as much as 4.6 percentage points during the 1982 recession. During the expansion quarters of 1981, real GNP growth was underpredicted by almost 4 percentage points. Forecasts are relatively accurate when no major changes in economic activity take place, but the very large forecast errors at major turning points generate the high degree of uncertainty around the forecast.

McNees' discussion suggests that forecasters' inability to predict major turning points also explains why the forecast accuracy of near-term forecasts is poorer than forecasts of output several quarters away. In recent years, major GNP forecasting mistakes have occurred when a major unexpected shock influenced the economy: the oil price increases in 1973–1974, and the velocity decline in the early and mid-1980s. According to McNees, these shocks tend to reverse themselves—that is, the tendency is for forecast errors to be offset over time. If real GNP growth were overpredicted one quarter ahead because of a temporary shock that reduces GNP growth (e.g., drought), then the likelihood is that real GNP growth will rebound two quarters out and the two quarter ahead forecast may be more accurate than the one quarter ahead forecast. Consistent with this notion, McNees (1988, p. 23) noted that forecasts of real GNP over a six-month period (two quarters) are more accurate than individual forecasts of both quarters.[5]

With respect to the accuracy of different econometric forecasting methods, the evidence suggests that individual models specialize in forecasting particular variables. Some models are better forecasters of inflation, some do better forecasting output, and some are better at forecasting different components of aggregate demand. For this reason, one "best" forecasting model does not exist, although McNees does dismiss naive methods such as the random walk and a model where the forecast of output growth next quarter equals last quarter's or last year's actual rate as definitely inferior to more sophisticated econometric models, a VAR model, and the consensus forecast gathered by the American Statistical Society and the National Bureau of Economic Research. With respect to the different econometric methods, McNees reported that the VAR approach yields more accurate forecasts of real GNP growth but is an inferior forecaster of inflation relative to forecasts from large econometric models and surveys.

CONCLUSION

The fact that median forecast errors are relatively small suggests that economic institutions can base their behavior on forecasts that are actually quite accurate. However, these institutions should be aware that the forecasting industry has a history of occasionally making some serious errors.

Serious errors, however, are hardly confined to predicting business conditions. Meteorologists have difficulty predicting the weather, political scientists have difficulty predicting political changes in different countries, and geologists have a hard time predicting earthquakes. Predicting future events, no matter what the variable of interest, is difficult.

NOTES

1. These are the components of the index effective January 1989. See Hertzberg and Beckman (1989) for a detailed discussion of how the index is computed.

2. When market interest rates change, long-term bond prices change more than short-term bond prices because of the manner in which bond prices are determined. Assume for example that both short- and long-term bonds are discount bonds, had the same yield when issued, and have the same face value. The only difference between the two is the term to maturity. The price of each bond is the discounted present value of the face value at maturity. If market interest rates change, the present value of the face yield on the long-term bond changes more than for the short-term bond because the long-term bond is being discounted for a longer period of time.

3. Inflation is another variable that is often forecasted with leading indicators. For examples, see Roth (1986) and Furlong (1989).

4. Least squares can be applied when the lag lengths are the same in each equation in the system. If the lag lengths are not the same, more complicated methods should be used.

5. This "error offset" is peculiar to output forecasts. McNees (1988) reported that inflation forecasts have the opposite problem—the errors tend to compound, making near-term forecasts more accurate than long-term forecasts.

Bibliography

Adams, Walter, and James Brock. *The Bigness Complex*. New York: Pantheon, 1986.

Allen, Frederic Lewis. *Only Yesterday: An Informal History of the Nineteen-Twenties*. New York: Harper and Brothers, 1931.

————. *Since Yesterday: The Nineteen-Thirties in America*. New York: Harper & Row, 1940.

Altonji, Joseph, and Orley Ashenfelter. "Wage Movements and the Labour Equilibrium Hypothesis." *Economica* 47 (August 1980): 217–245.

Andersen, Leonall C., and Jerry L. Jordan. "Monetary and Fiscal Actions: A Test of Their Relative Importance in Economic Stabilization." The Federal Reserve Bank of St. Louis *Review* (November 1968): 11–24.

Axilrod, Stephen H., Peter D. Sternlight, Allan H. Meltzer, and Robert H. Rasche. "Is the Federal Reserve's Monetary Control Policy Misdirected?" *Journal of Money, Credit and Banking* 14 (February 1982): 119–147.

Baily, Martin Neil, and Robert J. Gordon. "The Productivity Slowdown, Measurement Issues, and the Explosion of Computer Power." *Brookings Papers on Economic Activity* 1988, no. 2: 347–420.

Balke, Nathan S., and Robert J. Gordon. "Appendix B: Historical Data." In *The American Business Cycle: Continuity and Change*, edited by Robert J. Gordon. Chicago: University of Chicago Press, 1986.

Ball, Laurence, N. Gregory Mankiw, and David Romer. "The New Keynesian Economics and the Output-Inflation Trade-Off." *Brookings Papers on Economic Activity* 1988, no. 1: 1–82.

Barro, Robert J. "Are Government Bonds Net Wealth?" *Journal of Political Economy* 82 (November/December 1974): 1095–1117.

Barro, Robert J., and Mark Rush. "Unanticipated Money and Economic Activity." In *Rational Expectations and Economic Activity*, edited by Stanley Fischer. Chicago: University of Chicago Press, 1980.

Baxter, Marianne, and Alan C. Stockman. "Business Cycles and the Exchange Rate Mechanism: Some International Evidence." National Bureau of Economic Research Working Paper no. 2689, August 1988.

Bernanke, Ben. "Nonmonetary Effects of the Financial Crisis in the Propagation of the Great Depression." *American Economic Review* 73 (June 1983): 257–276.

Bettmann, Otto L. *The Good Old Days—They Were Terrible!* New York: Random House, 1974.

Beveridge, Stephen, and Charles R. Nelson. "A New Approach to Decomposition of Economic Time Series into Permanent and Transitory Components with Particular Attention to Measurement of the Business Cycle." *Journal of Monetary Economics* 7 (March 1981): 151–174.

Bils, Mark J. "Real Wages over the Business Cycle: Evidence from Panel Data." *Journal of Political Economy* 93 (August 1985): 666–689.

Bodkin, Ronald G. "Real Wages and Cyclical Variations in Employment: A Re-examination of the Evidence." *Canadian Journal of Economics* 2 (August 1969): 353–374.

Bork, Robert H. *The Antitrust Paradox.* New York: Basic Books, 1978.

Brimmer, Andrew F. "Central Banking and Systemic Risks in Capital Markets." *Journal of Economic Perspectives* 3 (Spring 1989): 3–16.

Brittan, Samuel, and Peter Lilley. *The Delusion of Incomes Policy.* London: Temple Smith, 1977.

Brock, James W. "Industrial Concentration Ratios and Price Flexibility." Unpublished paper, Miami University, 1989.

Bryan, Michael F., and William T. Gavin. "Models of Inflation Expectations Formation: A Comparison of Household and Economists Forecasts." *Journal of Money, Credit and Banking* 18 (November 1986): 539–544.

Burns, Arthur F. Statement before the Subcommittee on Domestic Monetary Policy of the Committee on Banking, Currency, and Housing, House of Representatives, Feb. 6, 1975. Pp. 367–378 in Arthur F. Burns, *Reflections of an Economic Policy Maker, Speeches and Congressional Statements: 1969–1978.* Washington D.C.: American Enterprise Institute, 1978.

Burns, Arthur F., and Wesley C. Mitchell. *Measuring Business Cycles.* New York: National Bureau of Economic Research, 1946.

Cagan, Phillip. "The Monetary Dynamics of Hyperinflation." In *Studies in the Quantity Theory of Money,* edited by Milton Friedman. Chicago: University of Chicago Press, 1956.

Campbell, John Y., and N. Gregory Mankiw. "Are Output Fluctuations Transitory?" *Quarterly Journal of Economics* 102 (November 1987): 857–880.

Carlson, John B., and John N. McElravey. "Money and Velocity in the 1980s." The Federal Reserve Bank of Cleveland *Economic Commentary* (Jan. 15, 1989).

Cassel, G. *The Theory of Social Economy.* New York: Harcourt Brace, 1924.

Cecchetti, Stephen. "The Frequency of Price Adjustment: A Study of the Newsstand Prices of Magazines." *Journal of Econometrics* 31 (August 1986): 255–274.

Chenery, Hollis B. "Overcapacity and the Acceleration Principle." *Econometrica* 20 (January 1952): 1–28.

Clark, J. M. "Business Acceleration and the Law of Demand." *Journal of Political Economy* 25 (March 1917): 217–235.

Clark, Peter K. "The Cyclical Component of U.S. Economic Activity." *Quarterly Journal of Economics* 102 (November 1987): 797–814.

Cochrane, John H. "How Big Is the Random Walk in GNP?" *Journal of Political Economy* 96 (October 1988): 893–920.

Council of Economic Advisors. *Economic Report of the President*, 1981.
———. *Economic Report of the President*, 1987.
———. *Economic Report of the President*, 1988.
Darby, Michael R. "The Financial and Tax Effects of Monetary Policy on Interest Rates." *Economic Inquiry* (June 1975): 266–276.
———. "Price and Wage Controls: Further Evidence." In *The Economics of Wage and Price Controls*, edited by Karl Brunner and Allan H. Meltzer. Carnegie-Rochester Conference Series on Public Policy, 1976.
Degen, Robert A. *The American Monetary System: A Concise Survey of its Evolution Since 1896*. Lexington, Mass. Lexington Books, 1987.
DeLong, J. Bradford, and Lawrence H. Summers. "The Changing Cyclical Variability of Economic Activity in the United States." In *The American Business Cycle: Continuity and Change*, edited by Robert J. Gordon. Chicago: University of Chicago Press, 1986.
Dewald, William G. "Monetarism is Dead; Long Live the Quantity Theory." The Federal Reserve Bank of St. Louis *Review* 70 (July/August 1988): 3–18.
Dornbusch, Rudiger. "Expectations and Exchange Rate Dynamics." *Journal of Political Economy* 84 (December 1976): 1161–1176.
Dunlop, John T. "The Movement of Real and Money Wage Rates." *Economic Journal* 48 (September 1938): 413–434.
Eastburn, David P. *The Federal Reserve on Record*. Philadelphia: Federal Reserve Bank of Philadelphia, 1965.
Edgeworth F. Y. *Mathematical Psychics*. London: Kegan Paul, 1881.
Eisner, Robert, and M. I. Nadiri. "Investment Behavior and Neoclassical Theory." *Review of Economics and Statistics* 50 (August 1968): 369–382.
Ezekial, Mordecai. "The Cobweb Theorem." *Quarterly Journal of Economics* (February 1938): 255–280.
Feldstein, Martin S. "Government Deficits and Aggregate Demand." *Journal of Monetary Economics* 9 (January 1982): 1–20.
Figlewski, Stephen, and Paul Wachtel. "The Formation of Inflation Expectations." *The Review of Economics and Statistics* 63 (February 1981): 1–10.
Flamant, Maurice, and Jeanne Singer-Kerel. *Modern Economic Crises and Recessions*. New York: Harper & Row, 1970.
Friedman, Benjamin M. "Crowding Out of Crowding In? Economic Consequences of Financing Government Deficits." *Brookings Papers on Economic Activity* no. 3 (1978): 593–641.
Friedman, Milton. "The Methodology of Positive Economics." In *Essays in Positive Economics*, edited by Milton Friedman. Chicago: University of Chicago Press, 1935.
———. "The Quantity Theory of Money: A Restatement." In *Studies in the Quantity Theory of Money*, edited by Milton Friedman. Chicago: University of Chicago Press, 1956. Reprinted in Friedman (1969).
———. *A Theory of the Consumption Function*. Princeton N.J.: Princeton University Press, 1957.
———. *A Program for Monetary Stability*. New York: Fordham University Press, 1959.
———. "The Role of Monetary Policy." *American Economic Review* 58 (March 1968): 1–17. Reprinted in Friedman (1969).

———. *The Optimum Quantity of Money and Other Essays*. Chicago: Aldine Publishing Company, 1969.

———. "Monetary Policy: Theory and Practice." *Journal of Money, Credit and Banking* 14 (February 1982): 98–118.

———. "Monetary Variability: United States and Japan." *Journal of Money, Credit and Banking* (August 1983): 339–343.

———. "Lessons from the 1979–82 Monetary Policy Experiment." *American Economic Review Papers and Proceedings* 74 (May 1984): 397–400.

Friedman, Milton, and Anna J. Schwartz. *A Monetary History of the United States, 1867–1960*. Princeton, N.J.: Princeton University Press, 1963a.

———. "Money and Business Cycles." *Review of Economics and Statistics* 45 supplement (February 1963b): 32–64. Reprinted in Friedman (1969).

———. *Monetary Trends in the United States and the United Kingdom*. Chicago: University of Chicago Press, 1982.

Furlong, Frederick T. "Commodity Prices as a Guide for Monetary Policy." The Federal Reserve Bank of San Francisco *Economic Review* (Winter 1989): 21–38.

Galbraith, John Kenneth. *The Great Crash*. New York: Time Inc., 1961.

Geary, Patrick T., and John Kennan. "The Employment–Real Wage Relationship: An International Study." *Journal of Political Economy* 90 (August 1982): 854–871.

Gerlach, H. M. Stefan. "World Business Cycles under Fixed and Flexible Exchange Rates." *Journal of Money, Credit and Banking* 20 (November 1988): 621–632.

Gittings, Thomas A. "Capacity Utilization and Inflation." The Federal Reserve Bank of Chicago *Economic Perspectives* (May/June 1989): 2–9.

Gordon, Robert Aaron. *Business Fluctuations*, 2nd ed. New York: Harper & Row, 1961.

Gordon, Robert J., ed. *Milton Friedman's Monetary Framework: A Debate with His Critics*. Chicago: University of Chicago Press, 1974.

———. "Postwar Macroeconomics: The Evolution of Events and Ideas." In *The American Economy in Transition*, edited by Martin S. Feldstein. Chicago: University of Chicago Press, 1980.

———. "Output Fluctuations and Gradual Price Adjustment." *Journal of Economic Literature* 19 (June 1981): 493–530.

———. "Price Inertia and Policy Ineffectiveness in the United States, 1890–1980." *Journal of Political Economy* 90 (December 1982): 1087–1117.

———. *Macroeconomics*, 4th ed. Boston: Little, Brown, and Company, 1987.

Gordon, Robert J., and John M. Veitch, "Fixed Investment in the American Business Cycle, 1919–83." In *The American Business Cycle: Continuity and Change*, edited by Robert J. Gordon. Chicago: University of Chicago Press, 1986.

Granger, C. W. J. *Forecasting in Business and Economics*, 2nd ed. New York: Academic Press, 1989.

Grieder, William. *Secrets of the Temple*. New York: Simon and Schuster, 1987.

Griliches, Zvi. "Patents: Recent Trends and Puzzles." *Brookings Papers on Economic Activity*, Microeconomics (1989): 291–330.

Grossman, Richard S. "Bank Failures in Financial Crisis: Three Historical Perspectives." Harvard University Ph.D. Dissertation, 1988.

———. "The Macroeconomic Consequences of Bank Failures under the National Banking System." U.S. Department of State Bureau of Economics and Business Affairs Working Paper, January 1989.

Haberler, Gottfried. *Prosperity and Depression*, 4th ed. Cambridge, Mass.: Harvard
   University Press, 1958.
————. *The World Economy, Money, and the Great Depression 1919–1939*. Washington
   D.C.: American Enterprise Institute for Public Policy Research, 1976.
Hall, Thomas E. "McCallum's Base Growth Rule: Results for the United States, West
   Germany, Japan, and Canada." U.S. Department of State Bureau of Economics
   and Business Affairs Working Paper, February 1989.
Hall, Thomas E., M. Andrew Fields, and T. Windsor Fields. "On Allocating the Variance
   of Output to Permanent and Transitory Components." *Economic Letters* 30 (Oc-
   tober 1989): 323–326.
Hall, Thomas E., and T. Windsor Fields. "Anticipated Nominal Demand Shocks and
   the Speed of Aggregate Price Adjustment." *The Review of Economics and Sta-
   tistics* 69 (February 1987): 140–144.
Hall, Thomas E., and Nicholas R. Noble. "Velocity and the Variability of Money Growth:
   Evidence from Granger-Causality Tests." *Journal of Money, Credit and Banking*
   19 (February 1987): 112–116.
Hall, Robert E., and Dale W. Jorgenson. "Tax Policy and Investment Behavior." *The
   American Economic Review* 57 (June 1967): 391–414.
Hansen, Alvin H. "Factors Affecting the Trend of Real Wages." *American Economic
   Review* 15 (March 1925): 27–42.
————. *A Guide to Keynes*. New York: McGraw-Hill Book Co., 1954.
Hawtrey, R. G. *Good and Bad Trade*. London: Constable & Co., 1913.
Hayek, F. A. *Monetary Theory and the Trade Cycle*. New York: Harcourt Brace, 1933.
————. *Prices and Production*. London: Routledge, 1935a.
————. *Profits, Interest and Investment*. London: Routledge, 1935b.
Hertzberg, Marie P., and Barry A. Beckman. "Business Cycle Indicators: Revised Com-
   posite Indexes." U.S. Department of Commerce, Bureau of Economic Activity
   Business Conditions Digest. Washington D.C.: U.S. Government Printing Office,
   January 1989.
Hicks, J. R. "Mr. Keynes and the 'Classics'; A Suggested Interpretation." *Econometrica*
   5 (April 1937): 147–159.
Higgins, Byron. "Is a Recession Inevitable This Year?" The Federal Reserve Bank of
   Kansas City *Economic Review* 73 (January 1988): 3–16.
Hobson, J. A. *The Industrial System*. New York: Longmans Green & Co., 1909.
————. *The Economics of Unemployment*. London: G. Allen & Unwin Ltd., 1922.
Holland, A. Steven. "Real Interest Rates: What Accounts for Their Recent Rise?" The
   Federal Reserve Bank of St. Louis *Economic Review* 66 (December 1984): 18–
   29.
Hughes, Jonathan. *American Economic History*, 2nd ed. Glenview, Ill.: Scott Foresman
   and Co., 1987.
Jacobs, Rodney L., Edward E. Leamer, and Michael P. Ward. "Difficulties with Testing
   for Causation." *Economic Inquiry* 27 (July 1979): 401–413.
Jevons, W. S. *Investigations in Currency and Finance*. London: Macmillan, 1884.
Kahn, George A. "International Differences in Wage Behavior: Real, Nominal, or Ex-
   aggerated?" *American Economic Review Papers and Proceedings* 74 (May 1984):
   155–159.
Keynes, John Maynard. *The General Theory of Employment, Interest and Money*. London:
   Macmillan and Co., 1936.

———. "Relative Movements of Real Wages and Output." *Economic Journal* 49 (March 1939): 34–51.

Kindleberger, Charles P. *The World in Depression, 1929–39.* Berkeley: University of California Press, 1973.

Klein, Lawrence R. *The Keynesian Revolution.* New York: Macmillan, 1947.

Kniesner, Thomas J., and Arthur H. Goldsmith. "A Survey of Alternative Models of the Aggregate U.S. Labor Market." *Journal of Economic Literature* 25 (September 1987): 1241–1280.

Kondratieff, Nikolai D. "The Long Waves in Economic Life." *Review of Economics and Statistics* 27 (November 1935): 105–115.

Krugman, Paul R., and Maurice Obstfeld. *International Economics: Theory and Policy.* Glenview, Ill.: Scott, Foresman and Company, 1988.

Kydland, Finn E., and Edward C. Prescott. "Time to Build and Aggregate Fluctuations." *Econometrica* 50 (November 1982): 1345–1370.

Leijonhufvud, Axel. *On Keynesian Economics and the Economics of Keynes.* New York: Oxford University Press, 1968.

Level, Maurice, Harold G. Moulton, and Clark Warburton. *America's Capacity to Consume.* New York: Review of Reviews Corporation, 1934.

Litterman, Robert B., and Lawrence Weiss. "Money, Real Interest Rates, and Output: a Reinterpretation of Postwar U.S. Data." *Econometrica* 53 (January 1985): 129–156.

Long, John B., Jr., and Charles I. Plosser. "Real Business Cycles." *Journal of Political Economy* 91 (February 1983): 39–69.

Lucas, Robert E., Jr. "Expectations and the Neutrality of Money." *Journal of Economic Theory* 4 (April 1972): 103–124.

———. "Some International Evidence on Output-Inflation Tradeoffs." *American Economic Review* 63 (June 1973): 326–334.

Mankiw, N. G. "Small Menu Costs and Large Business Cycles." *Quarterly Journal of Economics* 100 (May 1985): 529–537.

Mascaro, Angelo, and Allan H. Meltzer. "Long and Short Term Interest Rates in a Risky World." *Journal of Monetary Economics* 12 (November 1983): 485–518.

McCallum, Bennett T. "On 'Real' and 'Sticky-Price' Theories of the Business Cycle." *Journal of Money, Credit and Banking* 18 (November 1986): 397–414.

———. "Robustness Properties of a Rule for Monetary Policy." *Carnegie-Rochester Conference Series on Public Policy* 29 (Autumn 1988).

McNees, Stephen K. "Which Forecast Should You Use?" *New England Economic Review* (July/August 1985): 36–42.

———. "The Accuracy of Two Forecasting Techniques: Some Evidence and an Interpretation." *New England Economic Review* (March/April 1986): 20–31.

———. "How Accurate Are Macroeconomic Forecasts?" *New England Economic Review* (July/August 1988): 15–36.

Mercer, L. J., and W. D. Morgan. "The American Automobile Industry: Investment Demand, Capacity, and Capacity Utilization, 1921–1940." *Journal of Political Economy* 80 (November/December 1972): 1214–1231.

Meyer, T. "Plant and Equipment Lead Times." *Journal of Business* 33 (April 1960): 127–132.

Mishkin, Frederic S. *A Rational Expectations Approach to Macroeconometrics: Testing*

Policy Ineffectiveness and Efficient-Markets Models. Chicago: University of Chicago Press, 1983.

Mitchell, Wesley Clair. *Business Cycles and Their Causes*. Berkeley: University of California Press, 1941.

Mitchell, Wesley C., and Arthur F. Burns. "Statistical Indicators of Cyclical Revivals." National Bureau of Economic Research Occasional Paper no. 69, 1938.

Modigliani, Franco, and R. E. Brumberg. "Utility Analysis and the Consumption Function." In *Post-Keynesian Economics*, edited by K. K. Kurihara. New Brunswick, N.J.: Rutgers University Press, 1954.

Moore, Geoffrey H. *Business Cycles, Inflation, and Forecasting*, 2nd ed. Cambridge, Mass.: Ballinger Publishing Company, 1983.

Moore, George R., Richard D. Porter, and David H. Small. "Modeling the Disaggregated Demands for M2 and M1 in the 1980's: The U.S. Experience." Paper presented at the Federal Reserve Board Conference on Monetary Aggregates and Financial Sector Behavior in Interdependent Economies, Washington D.C., May 1988.

Muth, John F. "Rational Expectations and the Theory of Price Movements." *Econometrica* 29 (July 1961): 315–335.

Neftci, Salih N. "A Time-Series Analysis of the Real Wages-Employment Relationship." *Journal of Political Economy* 86 (April 1978): 281–291.

Nelson, Charles R., and Charles I. Plosser. "Trends and Random Walks in Macroeconomic Time Series: Some Evidence and Implications." *Journal of Monetary Economics* 10 (September 1982): 139–162.

Neumark, David, and Steven A. Sharpe. "Market Structure and the Nature of Price Rigidity: Evidence from the Market for Consumer Deposits." Federal Reserve Board of Governors Division of Research and Statistics, Finance and Economics Discussion Series, January 1989.

Noble, Nicholas R., and T. Windsor Fields. "Testing the Rationality of Inflation Expectations Derived from Survey Data: A Structure Based Approach." *Southern Economic Journal* 49 (October 1982): 361–373.

Okun, Arthur M. "A Postmortem on the 1974 Recession." *Brookings Papers on Economic Activity* no. 1 (1975): 207–221.

———. *Prices and Quantities: A Macroeconomic Analysis*. Washington D.C.: The Brookings Institution, 1981.

Phelps, Edmund S., ed. *The New Micro-Economics Foundations of Employment and Inflation Theory*. New York: Norton, 1970.

Poole, William. "Monetary Policy During the Recession." *Brookings Papers on Economic Activity* no. 1 (1975): 123–139.

———. *On Key Economic Issues*. Washington D.C.: American Enterprise Institute, 1984.

———. "Monetary Policy Lessons of Recent Inflation and Disinflation." *Journal of Economic Perspectives* 2 (Summer 1988): 73–100.

Potter, Jim. *The American Economy Between the World Wars*. London: MacMillan Press Ltd, 1974.

Richardson, J. Henry. "Real Wage Movements." *Economic Journal* 9 (September 1939): 425–441.

Romer, Christina D. "The Great Crash and the Onset of the Great Depression." National Bureau of Economic Research Working Paper no. 2639, 1988.

Romer, Christina D., and David H. Romer. "Does Monetary Policy Matter? A New

Test in the Spirit of Friedman and Schwartz.'' Unpublished paper, University of California, Berkeley, February 1989.

Roose, K. D. *The Economics of Recession and Revival.* New Haven, Conn.: Yale University Press, 1954.

Roth, Howard L. "Leading Indicators of Inflation." The Federal Reserve Bank of Kansas City *Economic Review* 71 (November 1986): 3–20.

———. "Has Deregulation Ruined M1 as a Policy Guide?" The Federal Reserve Bank of Kansas City *Economic Review* 72 (June 1987): 24–37.

Rush, Mark. "Real Business Cycles." The Federal Reserve Bank of Kansas City *Economic Review* 72 (February 1987): 20–32.

Samuelson, Paul, and Robert Solow. "Problem of Achieving and Maintaining a Stable Price Level." *American Economic Review* 50 (May 1960): 177–194.

Sargent, Thomas J. "Estimation of Dynamic Labor Demand Schedules under Rational Expectations." *Journal of Political Economy* 86 (December 1978): 1009–1044.

———. *Rational Expectations and Inflation.* New York: Harper & Row, 1986.

Sargent, Thomas J., and Neil Wallace. "Rational Expectations, the Optimal Monetary Instrument, and the Optimal Money Supply Rule." *Journal of Political Economy* 83 (April 1975): 241–254.

Schumpeter, Joseph. *Business Cycles*, 2 vols. New York: McGraw Hill Book Co., 1939.

Schwartz, Anna J. "Secular Price Change in Historical Perspective." *Journal of Money, Credit and Banking* 5 (February 1973): 243–269.

Shaw, Kathryn L. "Wage Variability in the 1970s: Sectoral Shifts or Cyclical Sensitivity?" *Review of Economics and Statistics* 71 (February 1989): 26–35.

Sheffrin, Stephen M. *Rational Expectations.* New York: Cambridge University Press, 1983.

———. "Book Review: *Secrets of the Temple.*" *Journal of Money, Credit and Banking* 21 (February 1989): 128–130.

Shugart, William F., II, and Robert D. Tollison. "Preliminary Evidence on the Use of Inputs by the Federal Reserve System." *American Economic Review* 73 (1983): 291–304.

Sims, Christopher A. "Money, Income, and Causality." *American Economic Review* 62 (September 1972): 540–552.

———. "Macroeconomics and Reality." *Econometrica* 48 (January 1980a): 1–48.

———. "A Comparison of Interwar and Postwar Business Cycles: Monetarism Reconsidered." *American Economic Review* 70 (May 1980b): 250–257.

———. "Policy Analysis with Econometric Models." *Brookings Papers on Economic Activity* no. 1 (1982): 107–152.

Sinclair, Upton. *The Jungle.* New York: Doubleday, Page & Co., 1906.

Stock, James H., and Mark W. Watson. "New Indexes of Coincident and Leading Economic Indicators." Paper presented at the National Bureau of Economic Research Macroeconomics Conference, 1989.

Stone, Courtenay C., and Daniel L. Thornton. "Solving the 1980s Velocity Puzzle: A Progress Report." The Federal Reserve Bank of St. Louis *Review* 69 (August/September 1987): 5–23.

Strumpel, Burkhard, Charles Cowan, F. Thomas Juster, and Jay Schmiedeskamp. *Survey of Consumers, 1972–73.* Ann Arbor, Mich.: Institute for Social Research, 1975.

Tarshis, Lorie. "Changes in Real and Money Wages." *Economic Journal* 49 (March 1939): 150–154.

Temin, Peter. *Did Monetary Forces Cause the Great Depression*? New York: Norton & Co, 1976.

Tobin, James, and William C. Brainard. "Pitfalls in Financial Model Building." *American Economic Review Papers and Proceedings* 58 (May 1968): 99–122.

Toma, Mark. "Inflationary Bias of the Federal Reserve System." *Journal of Monetary Economics* 10 (1982): 163–190.

United States Department of Commerce. *Statistical Abstract of the United States*. Washington D.C., U.S. Government Printing Office, 1989.

———. *Handbook of Cyclical Indicators* Washington D.C., U.S. Government Printing Office, 1982.

———. *Business Conditions Digest*. Washington D.C.: U.S. Government Printing Office. Various Issues.

———. *Historical Statistics of the U.S.: Colonial Times to the Present*. Washington D.C.: U.S. Government Printing Office, 1976.

Volcker, Paul A. "Statement to Congress." *The Federal Reserve Bulletin* (March 1983): 167–174.

Waldo, Douglas G. "Bank Runs, the Deposit-Currency Ratio, and the Interest Rate." *Journal of Monetary Economics* 15 (May 1985): 269–277.

Walras, Leon. *Elements of Pure Economics*. Translated by W. Jaffe. London-Allen & Irwin, 1954.

Watson, Mark W. "Univariate Detrending Methods with Stochastic Trends." *Journal of Monetary Economics* 18 (July 1986): 49–75.

Wicksell, Knut. *Interest and Prices*. London: Macmillan, 1936.

Williams, Arlington W. "The Formation of Price Forecasts in Experimental Markets." *Journal of Money, Credit and Banking* 19 (February 1987): 1–18.

Williamson, Harold F., ed. *The Growth of the American Economy*, 2nd ed. Englewood Cliffs, N.J.: Prentice-Hall, 1951.

Zarnowitz, Victor, and Geoffrey H. Moore. "Major Changes in Cyclical Behavior." In *The American Business Cycle: Continuity and Change*, edited by Robert J. Gordon. Chicago: University of Chicago Press, 1986.

Index

About the Author

THOMAS E. HALL is Associate Professor of Economics at Miami University, Ohio. He served as Visiting Senior Economist at the U.S. State Department's Bureau of Economic and Business Affairs, 1989–90. He is the author of numerous articles which have appeared in such journals as the *Review of Economics and Statistics*, and the *Journal of Industrial Economics*.